# BABA'S DREAM

A PASHTUN WITH A MISSION FOR A LAND RAVAGED BY TALIBAN FIGHTERS AND DRONE STRIKES

JOHN TAMERUS

Title: Baba's Dream. A Pashtun with a mission for a land ravaged by Taliban fighters and drone strikes

Author: John Tamerus

ISBN 13: 9789492371584 (ebook)

ISBN 13: 9789492371577 (paperback)

Publisher: Amsterdam Publishers

Copyright © 2017 John Tamerus. All right reserved. No part of this book may be used or reproduced by any means, graphic, electronic or mechanical, including photocopying, recording, taping, or by any information storage retrieval system without the written permission of the publisher except in the case of brief quotations embodied in critical articles and reviews.

Photo cover: Aart Geesink, www.aartgeesink.nl

Translation: Alysa Tamerus

*To honor*

*My Father*

*Noor Mohammad Khan*

*An example for me and many others.*

*A man who strived to help others his entire life.*

*My dear mother's prayers,*

*&*

*Especially my wife and children*

*Dr. Mohammad Ashraf Khan*

# CONTENTS

| | |
|---|---|
| Foreword | vii |
| Introduction | xi |
| LalaJi Sharif Khoon | 1 |
| Small Pox Epidemic | 7 |
| Day house, Sarai-kair | 12 |
| The Donkey Ride | 19 |
| Cheegha | 26 |
| Working Towards Your Dream | 33 |
| Tribal Fight | 37 |
| Badal | 42 |
| Camels | 47 |
| Mullah Dindar | 56 |
| Namus | 61 |
| Anatkhun Lala | 64 |
| Balodai | 69 |
| The Damoon and Drums | 75 |
| Landaa & Michaghnaa | 80 |
| Half a Rupee | 86 |
| Haji Salehdin | 90 |
| Peshawar | 96 |
| Edwards College, Peshawar | 103 |
| The University | 111 |
| Conscription? | 117 |
| Maryam | 123 |
| Marriage | 131 |
| A New Job | 140 |
| The Conflict | 150 |
| Struggle for Power | 158 |
| The Dream is Back | 163 |
| Seriously Ill | 168 |
| Kidnapping in Miranshah - August 12, 2005 | 174 |
| Free? | 187 |

| | |
|---|---|
| Forget Your Dream | 196 |
| The Hospital Is Destroyed | 202 |
| Wadah | 207 |
| Against the Stream | 212 |
| Background information Pashtun ethnic group | 224 |
| Background information elements of Pashtun tradition | 226 |
| Background Information Operation Zarb-e-Azb | 231 |
| Background information list of drone strikes tribal areas | 233 |
| Selected Bibliography | 272 |
| Author's Profile | 274 |

# FOREWORD

Many ago I received a letter from someone in Peshawar, Pakistan, asking for advice for an Audiology clinic which he was about to build there. Pakistan and particularly the audiology situation was on our hearts and minds because at the time there were only 8 audiologists in all of Pakistan with its 200 million people.

And here was an ENT surgeon from Pakistan interested in audiology and Deaf education? It sounded almost like something too good to be true! As I did not know the writer we had no idea what to expect but were intrigued, and we invited him to come to Salt for a few days to see what we were doing.

It was the beginning of a long journey that our Holy Land Institute for Deaf and Deafblind Children shared with Dr. Ashraf Khan of the MAK institute (the Mohammed Ashraf Khan institute for medical services, rehabilitation and education.)

Slowly we came to know each other better and Dr. Ashraf came through as a highly motivated and almost driven man, focused and charming, erudite and a hard worker. A man of principles and a man of faith. His extended family of four generations with endless cousins that make you believe that all Pakistanis are related, are there to support him and his wonderful family of wife, son and two daughters, and 'Baba'. It did not take long for me to go and see his work in Peshawar, Pakistan, and to become an enthusiastic supporter while developing a precious friendship.

During his first visit to Jordan we discussed audiology and hearing aid fitting programmes as well as good amplification for hard-of-hearing children in mainstream schools. We talked about Deaf education with Sign language for profoundly deaf children and youngsters. We agreed that they are only parts of the package that should eventually culminate in better education and better jobs, economic freedom and independence. Ashraf absorbed it all. He spoke of his work as a medical practitioner in Saudi Arabia and as a surgeon in the UK. But more importantly, he shared his great desire to start an ENT hospital with a maternity ward and a trauma unit in one of the poorest districts just outside Peshawar. Meanwhile his hospital became a reality whilst a Sign language school for profoundly deaf children with poor speech is sure to happen soon.

When we meet people from different cultures we always ask: Who are they? How do they think, what are their dreams? Ashraf was keen to absorb the experiences of other people, perhaps not so much to avoid mistakes, but at least to make new ones that were his very own. This kind of courage and determination and an abiding faith in God's great mercies, makes dreams come true.

To answer all the people who have this burning question: "what's Ashraf up to?", here's the book - with a collection of anecdotes from his life; and what a life it is! But the drama and adventures are perhaps not the main features. It is the ordinariness of Pakistani village life that is both exotic, yet simple and ordinary. They are set against the day-to-day struggles of a lovely family, while the threat and cruelty of war are somehow balanced against the generosity, kindness and hospitality of a people.

This book takes us on a journey where we normally would not go, to discover life that is being lived to the fullest where perhaps we did not expect it. Yet it resonates with our own lives, hopes and desires. Indeed, in such living we meet our brothers and sisters and discover how similar we are in spite of everything that appears to be so very different.

In all its drama and tragedy, yet in all its ordinariness, this story builds bridges, brings people together, teaches us to understand, respect and love each other a little more. It invites us, together, to look further, behind, beyond the curtains.

I hope that this book gives you a life, a person, a family in Afghanistan / Pakistan to relate to. They are 'your' family in this strange and complicated, but beautiful part of the world, where the dream and wisdom of an elderly father became the mission of his son!

Brother Andrew A.L.de Carpentier

Executive Director

The Holy Land Institute for Deaf and Deafblind Children

Salt, Jordan

# INTRODUCTION

A forceful, deafening explosion sears the silence. Ashraf and his nephew grab their ears. The enormous pressure almost ruptures their eardrums and makes the mud houses quake. The two men wonder if they are still alive. Questioning and fearful, they look at each other in the dark. As if it was not enough. After all the hardships of kidnapping they had been through and survived. Will this be the place where they are going to die?

There are the sounds of screams and moans. "A missile impact. Another missile impact," says a harsh rough male voice in the Wazir dialect. A woman screams, and children cry. This one was very close. The thick walls seem to still be standing, even though you would expect there to be nothing left of the building after such an explosion. All the villages in Waziristan have endured rocket attacks. The tribal areas between Pakistan and Afghanistan are currently the hard and grim battlegrounds of a struggle between modern Western armies and ancient warriors who are known at this juncture of time as the Taliban, or Al-Qaeda. "Lie down, lie down!" screams Ashraf to his nephew. All around them they hear the sounds of gunfire, running footsteps, and shouting men. Then the sound of a hard, dull thud. Dust is everywhere. The village people that are around them shoot their Kalashnikovs wildly without aim, and their bullets, impacting the clay walls, add to the horrific sounds penetrating their ears.

A strange silence seems to gain the upper hand. Even Mother Nature holds her breath. Only in the distance, can the cry of a child be heard.

The rocket landed just next to the compound. Ashraf and his nephew remain lying flat on the ground. They cannot go anywhere. They are trapped. Captured and kidnapped by their own Pashtun people. Ashraf dares not to even think about it. If the thought just comes up, flames of fury surge through his body. Kidnapped by his own people. "Are you alive?" whispers Ashraf in the direction of his nephew. The grumbling and coughing on the other side of the dark room is proof that he is still alive. Again, there is gunfire and screaming. Both men scramble to their feet. Ashraf feels sick. Rage, fear, deprivation, and exhaustion have left their marks on the two men. The next hours are restless.

The next day, very early in the morning, the thick wooden door opens. They are grabbed roughly and moved to another location. Right next to the building, where they had been trapped, is an enormous crater. A big hole in the roof of the building next to the compound is a silent witness of a successful attack. This is the work of drones. The fear of every resident of the tribal areas. Unmanned aerial vehicles that are controlled by someone who is far away behind a computer screen. Like a computer game, young Western soldiers control the unmanned aircrafts and manage to flawlessly hit their targets, all without having to set their feet on the battlefield. No risk to their lives is involved in such an operation. They are cowards in the eyes of the Pashtun, who have grown up in a culture where man-to-man combat is a way of life. These are highly dangerous circumstances for the Pashtun people. How many innocent Pashtun civilians have been killed here? Ashraf has no time to think about this.

The captors dress their captives in shuttlecock burqas worn by the women in this area in order to keep them hidden. Resistance is futile and will only lead to disaster. Within a few minutes, the men, dressed in burqas, can only look at the outside world through the gauzy, narrow window in the dresses. They walk together with their captors through the village to another compound. They are pushed with force into a mud house. In the distance is a woman without a face covering holding a Kalashnikov. Her hard, vacant eyes watch Ashraf and his nephew, who are both veiled in women's clothing.

In the new compound, the men are forcibly pushed into a tunnel that had been dug deep into the ground. Hunched over, they stumble into the tunnel until they come to a very small area. It is humid, horribly dirty, and frighteningly stuffy. Ashraf and his nephew get almost no air. They quickly remove the women's clothing from their bodies. There is no ventilation. No oxygen. In this manner, they are nearly buried alive. The men realize that they will die if they do not manage to escape. They will suffocate. They shout, scream, and yell until they have no voice left. They will not survive this. The sounds of their voices slowly die off. One final time, Ashraf lets out a hoarse cry. It sounds like the creak of a door with old worn hinges. It seems to be a signal for his body. Before his last cry has died, severe cramps seize his body. A few seconds later he has a grueling case of diarrhea. His body holds nothing inside after his final shout, as if his body had postponed it until this moment. His body seems to want to dispose of anything left in it. In the corner of the dark room, he vomits the last bit of moisture he had in his body. Is this the end? Gasping for air in a stinking, dirty hole in the ground? Ashraf feels the last of his strength drain from his body. He had so many plans. So many dreams.

# LALAJI SHARIF KHOON

We go back to 1956. Mohammed Ashraf Khan is born in Darpa Khel village in North Waziristan near the main town Miranshah. This area will later be the playground of the Taliban and Al-Qaeda. For years, it has been ravaged by war, violence, and now a new enemy, drone attacks. It is a wild and uncontrolled, even mysterious, area between Pakistan and Afghanistan, inhabited by the tribal Pashtuns. They are the indigenous people, with Islam for their religion, and their age-old traditions, customs, and rules govern their society.

The father of Ashraf is Noor Mohammad Khan. He is a disciplined, hard-working, righteous man. A purebred Pashtun who lives faithfully to the traditions of his people and country. At one time it had been his dream to study medicine. He wanted to make health care accessible to everyone in the inhospitable and often dangerous land of the Pashtuns, where avenging vendettas are the way of life. Eye for an eye, tooth for a tooth, yet all in a community where hospitality has an unsurmountable value.

Noor Mohammad Khan's dream was shattered when, at the young age of fourteen, he lost his father. Because he was the eldest son, the responsibility fell on him to care for his mother, five sisters, and two other brothers. By working hard and by conducting wise and ethical business, he became a man of honor and wealth and was able to pass on his dream to his brothers and children.

In these circumstances, Ashraf grew up as the second son of Noor Mohammad Khan, and the dream of his father slowly, but surely, became his own dream and life mission.

"Here he comes," whispers the little six-year-old Ashraf. Despite the darkness of the night, the air is still scorching hot in the courtyard of Ashraf's family high-walled compound, which they call ket, just on the outskirts of the village of Darpa Khel. The incredible beauty of the bright and starry sky transforms this ancient scene into a magical spectacle. Darpa Khel is one of the large, untouched villages in the inaccessible area of North Waziristan, a remote region escaping the influence of modern time.

The little Ashraf is one of them. One of the Pashtuns. A centuries-old people with equally ancient traditions, customs, and rules. A nation that is connected and divided by its tribal structure, strong family ties, and Muslim faith.

"Look, here he comes," says the gentle but penetrating voice of Ashraf. A blend of tension and respect can be heard in his voice. The little Ashraf lies with his brothers and cousins in the courtyard. It is too hot to sleep inside. The simple, traditional wooden beds are positioned in rows in the courtyard. No bed is the same. The rough, round wooden legs and wooden frame are all different in every bed. Is it possible for there to be a bed that does not wobble and creak? Also among the rough wooden frames are ropes, stretched as to make a mesh, each having their own unique pattern and crunch with every movement that Ashraf makes. The boys look small and insignificant lying in such large, sturdy wooden beds.

From the darkness emerges the shadowy figure of an elderly man. "LalaJi," sounds from the bed next to Ashraf. All the boys look expectantly into the darkness. They hear the lingering sound of someone walking in slippers, and with each alternate step, a hard thud. Then LalaJi, as the boys respectfully call him, appears. In Pashtun culture, *lalaji* means older man or older relative.

The real name of LalaJi is Sharif Khoon, a cheerful Pashtun of about fifty years who has a short fuse and weathered face. Back in the day he was a respected muleteer. He cared for a large number of wayward donkeys which he had transformed into pack animals, transporting heavy-laden carts filled with tons of goods through the mountainous land of the Pashtuns. Sharif Khoon can proudly speak of this time, of his adventures, of the country far behind the mountains of North Waziristan where all sorts of strange things can be seen. Sharif Khoon is happy to talk about the great heroes of his Pashtun people. If Ashraf should believe all that he says, then Sharif Khoon himself is perhaps the greatest hero in the history of the Pashtuns. The light from the starry sky reveals a modest smile on the dark-tinted, boyish face of Ashraf.

But the heyday of Sharif Khoon is over. By some obscure manner, his left hand and left leg became paralyzed. This is the reason he always drags his left leg a bit oddly, while his right leg overcompensates by stomping at every step. His left arm hangs with a bit of an unnatural appearance and seems to stubbornly protest every move that Sharif Khoon makes.

All the boys are now upright in their beds. The heat and mosquitoes have been forgotten. Sharif Khoon shuffles silently toward the center of the rows of beds. Warily, he rubs his shaggy beard while his nearly black eyes wander past the boys on their beds. The white of his *salwar kameez* contrasts with the deep dark night that surrounds him. No one speaks a word. Even the usual nocturnal sounds of this part of Warzistan seem to join in the silence.

Sharif Khoon clears his throat with exaggeration and lowers himself onto an empty bed. His wrinkled face, weathered by both wind and weather, shows no emotion. His dark eyes transform into narrow, shimmering stripes. Again, he clears his throat and spits on the floor beside him. Without introduction he begins to explain.

"It happened nearby, boys. In our country. In North Waziristan." The deep, dark voice of Sharif Khoon creates tension on the faces of the boys even before the story started. Calmly, he continues. The almost monotonous humming sound of his voice, coupled with the mystical warm night and glistening starry sky, create a peculiar atmosphere. "It was incredibly hot, boys. Hotter than it had been in a hundred years in Wazristan. It was the middle of the day, and the sun shone down mercilessly from the sky. Humans and animals were hiding behind every shadow in sight.

"Suddenly, through the burning heat, one fighter called out for Mirza Ali Khan in a loud voice, 'Haji Sahib?' The name was called with audible respect. Once again, the loud and penetrating voice asked, 'Haji Sahib?' It seemed that there would be no reaction, boys. It was then that this one fighter thought that no one would respond. However, unknown to him, there were dozens of heavily armed tribal fighters behind rocks, trees, or horses. They were moving slowly, but surely, but for now lying hidden and motionless on the ground with a fixed gaze.

"It was the legendary Mirza Ali Khan who came from behind his horse. The man whose name sent shivers down every man's spin. It happened only a few years ago. He was the biggest, smartest, most dangerous and most feared Pashtun warrior we've ever known in North Waziristan."

Sharif Khoon let a long silence fall. The eyes of all the boys stared at him impatiently, for Sharif Khoon is a true storyteller, knowing how to keep his audience in suspense. At exactly the right moment, he continues.

"Yes, boys, this Mizra Ali Khan who came from behind his horse was not so young anymore. He was born in 1897 and was known as the Fakir of Ipi." Again, Sharif Khoon lets a silence fall. There was almost an ominous feeling to the silence.

"He was a genuine tribesman and loved Islam and pashtunwali like all of us. He was born and raised in North Waziristan. The Fakir of Ipi was the most determined, implacable, and invincible opponent who the British Raj in India had ever known. A purebred Pashtun. So unyielding and stubborn. Unbelievably brave in battle against his opponents.

"It happened at a time when nearly forty thousand British and Indian soldiers were being deployed to catch the Fakir of Ipi. But this story not make sense at all. The Fakir of Ipi laughed. Before this, he had never had more than a thousand brave Pashtun fighters, and now this time, according to him, this should be more than enough too. One tribesman for every forty British soldiers. Big, strong, brave, and invincible Pashtun warriors. Men like me with beards and armed with old rifles and a few machine guns. And the British? Yes, boys, believe it or not, they had modern artillery, tanks and aircraft, and forty times more soldiers.

"The Fakir of Ipi, looked at his fighters. With a loud roar he gave the signal for the attack. Hard and ruthless was his command. Without waiting for his men, he jumped on his horse and galloped at the front in the direction of the British. The silence was torn by the roar of cannons, the ripping of gunfire, and the shouts and cries of angry and wounded men. Hundreds of Britons, supported by thousands of British Indian soldiers with guns and cannons, tried to shoot the Fakir of Ipi on his horse. The mountains of Waziristan were colored red with blood."

Again, a deathly silence. The boys hold their breath as Sharif Khoon trails off, anger and tension on his face, looking off in to the darkness at an unknown enemy. Just as the boys think Sharif Khoon will speak no more, the ominous, grisly voice pierces through the darkness.

"Not a drop of Pashtun blood." He paused. "The Fakir of Ipi overcame. The British turned back. Waziristan belongs to the tribesmen. Waziristan is ours and will remain ours. Waziristan is yours. You are the new fighters. You are the new brave Pashtuns."

The last words are almost roaring out of the mouth of Sharif Khoon. Here and there he has exaggerated the story. According to his own story, he had known the Fakir of Ipi, and had even fought on his side against the British. In a few bloody anecdotes, Sharif Khoon raises his voice so hard that he is almost screaming in the middle of the boys. With great anxiety, glistening eyes peer at him through the moonlight. Suddenly, he is dead silent.

"The Fakir of Ipi is dead!" he says sadly and ominously. Everyone holds their breath. Sharif Khoon waits until he can no longer hold the suspense. Grievously, he continues but delivers the last few words of his story in a proud tone.

"He has only recently died. A few years ago in 1960. Even after his death, the British still speak with great respect about their greatest enemy, the Fakir of Ipi. A Pashtun like me. A Pashtun like you.

His last words die slowly in a quiet whisper. With a jerk, Sharif Khoon turns around. He sniffs hard, once through his nose, as if it is the last breath of fresh air he can get. After some muttered gasps, he crudely spits on the ground among the semicircle of beds. The story is over. As suddenly as he appeared, he disappears again. It takes only a short time until the strange, unique sound of one trailing leg and one stomping foot has faded into the pitch black night of Darpa Khel.

Little Ashraf allows himself to fall backwards on to his bed and stare at the immense sky above him. Would he grow up to be like the Fakir of Ipi? As brave as a Pashtun warrior, fighting for the freedom of his people? Or will he be a doctor like Baba, like his father says? A pondering, unyielding gaze surfaces in the eyes of Ashraf.

## SMALL POX EPIDEMIC

The house where the little Ashraf was born was built by his grandfather Malik Ahmed Khan and his brother, and stands in a large walled compound. This compound is called ket and is situated on a higher ground on the outskirts of the village Darpa Khel. Ashraf's ket lies higher than all the other houses and other kets in the village, looking out over the vast fields in the area. The main housing area in Ashraf's ket has two big houses, one for Baba's uncle and his family and the other for Baba, his brothers, and families. Inside the ket are two large houses with stables in the back. Close to the typical Pakistani houses stands a small, yet beautiful, mosque, accentuating the inseparable role of their faith in their lives. The simple clay-made servant houses and the shelters at the back of the houses for the buffalos, cows, goats, sheep and chickens make life in the ket very pure and natural. The sounds of nature are heard day and night throughout the beautiful orchard and are like the finishing touches a skilled painter puts on his painting. The large clay walls that enclose the ket are around sixteen feet high. Like big strong arms, these robust walls seem to protect this peaceful scene from the evil, unknown world outside. A big, strong, rough wooden gate gives everyone a chance to come in or go out. For Ashraf, Baba is the uncrowned Pashtun king within these walls.

Baba is the son of Malik Ahmed Khan, a grandfather that Ashraf has never known. He died when Baba was just a very young boy. Whenever Baba talks about this, Ashraf sees pain and bitterness in his dark eyes. Eyes that, at any other time, gaze strictly, seriously, and pensively at the world. Eyes that always look beyond the present. Eyes that are searching for an unknown happiness. More than anyone else, Baba relies on his ears. Yes, Baba listens a lot and says little. That is why many people love and respect him. When Baba speaks, it is always important.

Baba wants his sons to go to college and become doctors. Occasionally he will talk about it. Usually late in the evening after evening prayers, when the men sit around eating together and discussing the issues and problems from the village or region. Ashraf likes to move close behind Baba's back to find a place in the dark where he can quietly listen to what he tells the men. Baba usually does not say much; he just listens. But when Baba speaks, everyone is silent. Baba knows everything, and everybody knows that, and as such, they often ask Baba for counsel or advice.

It has been a long time since the last evening prayer, called Maskhethan Meenz, concluded, and it seems that everyone is sleeping in the courtyard. The story of the Fakir of Ipi grinds in Ashraf's mind. One man against an army. A true Pashtun hero. And Sharif Khoon? Ashraf once heard Baba say that Sharif Khoon used to be big and strong. That he was a respected tribesman and that he wandered through the whole Waziristan with his stubborn, heavy-laden donkeys. When Sharif Khoon still had two strong legs and two strong arms. Ashraf tormented his brain. What happened? Why are his one arm and one leg not good anymore? Even one side of his face sometimes seem to not quite laugh like the other side of his face. Yes, even when he talks, one side of his mouth is not good. There is always a little bit of spit and drool with his words. Could this be the reason why Baba wants his son to be a doctor? So they can make Sharif Khoon's arm and leg better?

With eyes wide open, Ashraf looks at the eternal and immense star-filled night sky. Deep in thought, Ashraf listens to the sounds of the night. Despite the heat, a chill runs down his spine. The silence of the night is shattered by the terrifying and heartbreaking cry of a woman. It is not long before the heart- and soul-wrenching sounds of weeping women can be heard again. The high walls of the ket that stop every enemy seem powerless against the intense grief. The dark wave of grief slips over the wall and even into the heart of Ashraf. It is the umpteenth time in recent weeks that Ashraf has heard this ominous howling. Ashraf presses his hands tightly over his ears. But, like the high walls, his hands cannot stand against the fearful, mournful crying that alternates with plaintive prayer.

Ashraf does not want to die. Baba has talked about it with the men of the village tonight. A smallpox epidemic has broken out in Darpa Khel and the surrounding villages in North Waziristan. Smallpox is unrelenting and deadly. In recent days, when Ashraf went to Miranshah, he saw a few people who had survived. Sharif Khoon told him and his brothers and cousins. These people have huge scars on their faces and sometimes on other parts of their bodies. Again, a cold shiver down the small narrow spine of Ashraf. He tucks his head between his arms to escape the shrill sounds of weeping and prayer.

A little while ago, Baba had allowed him to be vaccinated, along with his brothers. This happened at the school in Miranshah. Baba even included all of the other family members in the vaccinations. Baba looked seriously at the little Ashraf, "You have nothing to worry about. This is why we need doctors in our country." Then he looked directly into Ashraf's eyes until Ashraf averted his gaze. Those dark eyes of Baba sometimes look deep into your soul, leaving a lasting impression. Eyes that exude hope, and at the same time grief and obstinacy. Eyes that Ashraf has inherited from Baba. But this, he does not yet realize.

Slowly, the sound of the crying and praying fades. Ashraf knows what he will see tomorrow. In the morning, a few people will walk by their house on their way to the cemetery with yet another victim killed by smallpox. Baba is always right.

Deep in the young heart of Ashraf is a battle between the fear of smallpox and faith in Baba. Is Baba stronger than the smallpox virus or will Ashraf and his brothers also die like so many other people in their neighborhood? And the Fakir of Ipi? Did he die during one of his battles against the mighty British soldiers, or is he a victim of an even more dangerous enemy, smallpox!

Little Ashraf clambers quietly out of his bed and walks to the part of the house where the maids stay. In the corner sits Khachani Meir. She is the mother of one of the maids. He loves this woman, almost as much as his mother Aday. Khachani Meir is sitting on a rug on the floor in the corner of the courtyard. In the eyes of Ashraf, she is very old. Though blind, she hears everything. Ashraf does not understand how this is possible and has been thinking about it a lot. Khachani Meir can probably see with her ears because even though she is blind, she always seems to know what is happening and who is present. Khachani Meir has her head turned towards Ashraf and stretches her arms wide to the little boy. Ashraf quickly crawls against her. The soft arms encircle the little boy as a fragile treasure of unrivaled value. Khachani Meir always smells a bit strange. A strange sweet fragrance of sweat mixed with the typical smell of curry and burnt wood. Here, Ashraf feels safe. Without asking, Khachini Meir starts talking using a soft melodious voice. Or is it singing? Ashraf is not listening. She has no teeth anymore. He feels small splashes on his face as she softly speaks to him. He is pressed closely against the woman. Her soft voice and the gentle pressure of her arms around him make him peaceful. Again, Ashraf looks up into the sightless eyes of Khachani Meijr. Then the little Pashtun falls into a deep, carefree sleep.

When everything and everyone is in a deep rest, Khachani Meir shuffles to the courtyard. In her arms, she is carrying the little Ashraf. She turns her head and listens to the sounds of the night. Then she shuffles gently, but steadily, towards the beds in the courtyard. She seems to know, by some inexplicable means, where the bed of the young boy lies. Again she stands still and tilts her head. Her blind eyes stare briefly at the starry sky. Then she seems to know for sure. This time she turns her head gently towards the beds where the boys are sleeping. Her leg brushes against the rough wooden frame of the bed on which she carefully puts down Ashraf. She pulls her veil a little bit over her face. Her hand tenderly rustles the scruffy hair of Ashraf. A tender smile appears on her dark face. The bright moonlight and the countless twinkling stars seem to capture her smile forever. But then she turns and shuffles back to her corner.

# DAY HOUSE, SARAI-KAIR

The smallpox epidemic is over. Old men, young women, men and children have died. There is a lot of crying and a lot of praying. It is over. There are many fresh graves. Ashraf is secretly going to look. Little piles of dirt indicate there is someone laying below. Baba has said that it is over. Ashraf is alive, and so is Baba. Aday and all his brothers are too. Ashraf wants to forget it quickly.

A new event is there. Ashraf heard the story from his brother Usman. He was just back from a long trip to the missionary school in Murree. Murree is a place in the mountains close to what now is Islamabad, the capital city of Pakistan.

A week ago, Baba had decided to take Ashraf's brother Usman to a missionary school. Another man had convinced Baba that it would give the boy a good foundation for his future life and education. Usman was scared. The nuns were nice but strict. But their strange black clothes with their white caps and their mannerisms were so different. They did not go to the mosque, but they did pray. Not five time a day, at a cross that hangs on the wall. Most cloistered nuns followed the Rule of St. Benedict which requires prayer seven times a day, plus 'shortly after midnight.' Their faith is different. Everything was different. It was not fun, and Usman wanted only one thing. To go home.

Usman really didn't like it. He is so young, and he really wanted to be close to Aday, close to his family, close to Baba, close to everything at home. Every night while at the school, Usman went to sleep with a knot in his stomach. What was going to happen tomorrow? His face divulged his doubt and fear. In Usman's eyes, the beautiful hills of Murree had transformed into a hostile place of danger.

Then a miracle happened. Baba picked Usman up. Was he going home? Usman was sitting in the backseat of Baba's car. Was he really going home? After a long day's drive, they arrived back at Darpa Khel.

And now? Usman shares the whole story with Ashraf, recounting all the details of Murree and the nuns. When Usman stops, Ashraf hears the recognizable, stumbling footsteps of Sharif Khoon getting closer. Any doubt he had is swept away as he hears the stumbling sound interspersed with gasping that characterizes Sharif Khoon.

Usman and Ashraf lie close together in the courtyard. The other children are already sleeping. Sharif Khoon gently lets himself down among Usman and Ashraf. His face appears older than normal in the meager light of the moon and stars. "LalaJi," murmurs Ashraf softly. It is not a question, and there is no answer. It is a gentle invitation to the slowly aging Pashtun to say what he has to say.

The dark eyes of Sharif Khoon stare off in the direction of the boys. He runs his hands a few times through his beard. In the dark, you can still see that his other arm is still not cooperating and that one half of his face does not want to join the rest. Ashraf suppresses a feeling of pity. Is there no one who can make this man better? A glistening trail of drool drips down his slightly lopsided mouth through his grubby beard. Where did that heroic muleteer go? To where has his strength and courage fled? Suddenly, in this dark night, Sharif Khoon seems like a helpless old man.

One more time, he clears his throat. "Baba heard rumors that Usman and all the other boys in that school were breastfed by the nuns every day." These gentle, penetrating words hung in the courtyard as if they would never disappear. Usman and Ashraf did not say a word. Bewildered, they looked, wide-eyed at Sharif Khoon. The words ring a thousand times in the heads of the boys. "Baba has heard rumors that you and all the other boys are breastfed by the nuns every day."

It was not a question. Sharif Khoon was not waiting for an answer. Like a statue from another world, he looks intensely towards the hills around Darpa Khel. He slowly turns his head slightly up towards the sky. The only sound they can hear is the raspy breathing of Sharif Khoon. With a muffled groan, Sharif Khoon stands up, and without giving a glance to the boys, he gently stumbles into the darkness, disappearing from sight. Usman and Ashraf say nothing. Ashraf looks into the eyes of Usman. Then, a smile appears on Ashraf's face. His brother is home again!

Fortunately, it is not so hot in Waziristan anymore. The familiar sounds of the call for Saboo Meenz, the morning prayer, have given way to the mooing of the cows and the bleating of the goats. Baba and other men are back from their morning prayers in the mosque in the ket. It is the start of the daily routine for life in their small, peaceful ket on the outskirts of Darpa Khel. With his brother, cousins, and Sharif Khoon, Ashraf walks on a sandy path towards the river. On the other side, the contours of Miranshah can be seen. Everything there is bigger than in Darpa Khel. The roads, the bazaar, the mosque, the buildings. Everything is not only bigger, but also much busier. There are many more people. There are many more animals. Often there is a huge caravan of camels along the way. They are on their way to Bannu, Sharif Khoon says. There are gigantic trunks tied to the backs of camels. Many of the rugged men who must bring the large caravans to their destinations lean their backs up against their camels to sleep. They all wear the same, dusty, worn-out clothing. Their traditional clothes, the salwar kameez, are various colours. The dark brown shawls they wear around their necks and heads appear the same color as the big camels. Some with black beards and some shaven, only sporting mustaches of various shapes and sizes. Their dark eyes in weathered faces, look bored and with futility at the world. Many of the men wear wide belts of ammunition and have all kinds of guns at hand. Some sit in a small circle and drink tea or smoke the beautiful water pipes that they pass along without having to make a request.

Years ago, when his left leg and arm were paralyzed, Baba hired Sharif Khoon as an attendant. Now, every day he takes the boys from Darpa Khel to the day house in Miranshah. It is a house in the town where Baba has a sort of office where the boys can stay when they are not in school. The boys and girls have given the day house their own name: Sarai-kair or in the local dialect, Sarooi. They have also given Miranshah its own name: Sarai. In Waziristan, Sarai is the nickname for Miranshah.

Miranshah actually lies just a stone's throw from Darpa Khel. It is just over a mile of walking, and it is quite a nice walk. The green and sometimes dry landscape, quickly changes into a reddish brown sandy path full of boulders near the river. It is a peculiar and mysterious river that cannot be predicted. Sometimes they must wait until the river becomes calm before they can safely cross to the other side during monsoon season. Sometimes the water is so wild and rough that it almost seems impossible to ever get across. Today it is not too bad. The rushing water is low, and through it, the bottom of the riverbed can be seen. Like young acrobats, the young boys deftly leap from stone to stone, reaching the other side. Here and there someone slips, wetting their brown sandals. A mischievous Ashraf silently hopes that someone will stumble and get soaking wet from their fall. But it should not be today. Quickly running, the boys rush on their way to the day house to pick up their school bags stuffed with books. Sharif Khoon stammers and spits on the ground as he calls for them to get in order. The children listen obediently and walk the last bit in an organized manner. Sharif Khoon sometimes accompany them at every step. After he has delivered the girls to the girl's school and then the boys to the boy's school, he goes to the day house.

When the school day is over, around one o'clock, Sharif Khoon comes again to pick them up. Just about every afternoon, accompanied by the lame, bearded Pashtun, the boys walk the back streets to Sarai-kair where they eat and have a short nap. They remain there throughout the day because in the afternoon they receive additional lessons by one of the schoolteachers who has been provided accommodation by Baba on the first floor of the day house. They also get extra lessons about basic Islamic studies by Qari Sahib, the imam of the big mosque in Miranshah.

Sharif Khoon has strict orders from Baba not to take the young boys the short way, through the bazaar. Baba does not want his boys to come into contact with large groups of teenagers who do not want to go to school or with boys who ended up going down the wrong path. Many boys from Miranshah do not go to school. Ashraf looked pensively through the narrow streets. What is the actual reason these boys don't go to school? Some already carry large weapons with large ammunition belts. Are they possibly the Pashtun heroes of the future? Just as the Fakir of Ipi? But the Fakir of Ipi was not just a hero, he was also smart, Sharif Khoon always says. Did the Fakir of Ipi ever go to school? A bit further, Ashraf sees a few boys leaning against the wall. They're just hanging around, looking bored. Their clothes are dirty and worn.

When Baba talks about it, Ashraf watches his dark eyes. It is a determination, but somewhat melancholic look, that he does not loose. What is it? Ashraf has no reason to doubt Baba's words. Besides, even if there were reason to doubt Baba's words, it is unthinkable to break Baba's rules when it comes to school and studies. Actually, he would much rather be a doctor than a fighter like the Fakir of Ipi. Although...

Now it's summer vacation. It is warmer than the previous weeks. Baba, against the request of Sharif Khoon on behest of the children, says that the boys must go to the day house also during the vacation time. In the village, they will only get into mischief. Sharif Khoon has relayed the message to the boys. It does not really matter to Ashraf. He is accustomed to the tight rhythm. But tomorrow is a special day. The boys can stay home one day. Ashraf thinks about what he will do. Shall he secretly swim in the pool of the mosque or snatch some one else goat's milk along with the other boys of the village to make some tea in the orchard outside of the ket. Just thinking about it gives him a mischievous smile on his face. Not too long ago they had secretly milked the big goat that belonged to some one else and then made tea. The first time it completely failed. They had used green tea, so when they poured the milk, it was a strange, unknown color, and it tasted so foul that the boys had to spit it out. It looked very different from the brown color that they were used to. They couldn't understand it. Sharif Khoon had to laugh. "Green tea does not become brown, stupid boys," he roared, laughing and shaking his head as he walked away in his usual manner.

Secretly riding a donkey sounds even more fun. The longer Ashraf thinks about it, the more certain he becomes. Yes, he will secretly try to catch a donkey, jump on its back, then try to ride it around like a big Pashtun warrior. Ashraf's round face and dark eyes glow in anticipation. Outside their ket lies a large, green meadow where the people from Darpa Khel and surrounding area let their animals graze. Sharif Khoon has told a lot about his donkeys. According to him, there is no other animal that is so stupid yet so smart, so strong yet so stubborn, so brave and yet so headstrong. According to Sharif Khoon, a donkey is the most extraordinary animal in the world and has the same character as some tribesmen. They are both incredibly brave, stubborn, and headstrong, and the most special of their kind in the world.

# THE DONKEY RIDE

It's hot, even before the day has begun. Ashraf and the other boys are still fast asleep. The familiar sounds of the morning Saboo Meenz prayer echo throughout the village. Ashraf, with his sleepy eyes, looks at Baba and the other men walking to the mosque. The men wash themselves in accordance to the silent protocol, called *audaas*, that everyone, without exception, adheres to. These regular mandatory prayers are a a strict way of praying and reading the Quran. Ashraf knows it by heart. He has learned it from Baba as well as from Qari Sahib at the dayhouse. Every Pashtun knows what this means and how it should be done.

In the mosque pool, the men first wash their lower bodies. Then they wash their hands three times, then their mouths three times, and finally they rinse their noses three times. After that, they wash their faces three times, then their right arms up to their right elbows, and finally their left arms up to their left elbows. Then they rub their hands over their head and conclude by washing their feet, first the right foot up to their ankle, and then repeated on their left foot. Ashraf does not know any differently and assumes every person in the world knows and does this. Ashraf is not yet old enough to go to the mosque regularly for prayers.

Lazy and sleepy, he stretches and rubs the sleep from his eyes. His gaze wanders over the courtyard. The other boys are awake. Nimbly, he bounces off the wooden bed. For a moment he peeks at the long line of women and children who are already waiting at the gate. This, too, is part of the daily ritual at his house. The women, dressed in their traditional salwar kameez and headscarfs, are lined up waiting at the gate. Everyone, without exception, is carrying some sort of pot. Shabbily dressed children scurry around their mothers or hang on their legs. Beneath the dust, the beautiful colors of the salwar kameez can be seen. The beautiful colors of blue and pink contrast starkly with the much more sober colors of the skin of the mothers. Under the veils are weathered faces. Exhausted, wrinkled, and tanned by the hard life in North Waziristan. The tired yet brave look in the eyes of the women betray their daily battle against Nature.

Aday gives buttermilk to everyone. No one will be left out. Aday will regulate this together with the female family members and servants. Aday has lovely eyes. Her beautiful, partially hidden face always looks friendly to the world. Aday is for sure the most awe-inspiring, fascinating and incredible woman in Ashraf's life. Her day starts long before Ashraf is awake and stops long after he is asleep. Sometimes Ashraf wonders whether or not she ever sleeps. As she looks at the long row of women, her eyes seem to be sweeter and softer than ever. Together with the servants, she makes sure that everyone receives enough buttermilk that was prepared from the yogurt made over night from the milk of their own cows and buffalloes. Ashraf likes to be near his mother. He loves Aday. She is the sweetest and most wonderful mother of the entire world.

Baba is away. Many of the men are at work or in Miranshah for business or shopping. Ashraf climbs out of the water basin behind the mosque which, today, serves as a pool for the young boys to swim in. He lazily hangs against the edge of the water basin all wet, when he suddenly spots Aaj. His heart almost leaps with joy. His eyes glisten. It cannot be any better.

Aaj Mohammad is Ashraf's best friend. Aaj is three years older than Ashraf, however he is only in one grade higher than Ashraf at school.

It happened like this: Baba wanted Ashraf to be in the class with his older brother Usman who was two grades ahead of him. Baba decided to go and to talk to the school, and it was decided that Ashraf will move up two classes over time.

Aaj lives with his three brothers and mother in a small mud house behind Ashraf's ket. Baba had given them the land and the house after their father had passed away. Aaj does not like school and homework. He is a sportsman and is good in every sport. He is a very good striker on the soccer team in school. If Ashraf is lucky, he might watch Aaj play. Baba has forbidden his sons to play sports though. "It is detrimental to your school performance" is his simple, incontestable explanation.

Here comes Aaj. He's herding a few donkeys ahead. It's as if Aaj has known that Ashraf has been wanting to ride a donkey specifically on today. It takes only a few moments before the donkeys are standing in the center of the ket. Aaj draws a broad smile on his face as he lowers himself next to Ashraf. The boys talk incessantly and moments later they are gallivanting around on the donkeys in delight. Aaj has a thin stick in his hand with which he can drive the donkeys. Beads of sweat leave thin traces upon his face. Everything seems to be covered in a thin blanket of light brown dust.

Ashraf nimbly leaps on to one of the donkeys. He rides around the ket triumphantly. Skillfully, he dodges the flower beds. Aaj laughs and cheers him on. Ashraf tries to encourage the donkey. The narrow legs of the donkey go faster and faster across the ket. Now with advanced skill, Ashraf, with a straight back, passes all the obstacles. Then suddenly, the donkey seems to startle at something, and then goes on a wild rampage. First, his fore legs lift off the ground. It looks like the failure of a prancing thoroughbred. With a hard blow, his front hooves hit the ground. Almost simultaneously, his hind legs fly high in the sky. Ashraf feels his teeth mercilessly slam shut, but he has no time to think of the pain. The head of the donkey almost touches the ground, so much that he is looking back through his front legs to his hind quarters.

Aaj is petrified looking at the whole scene. He does not believe his eyes. The donkey is almost upside down in a handstand. Miraculously, Ashraf still hangs on to the donkey, half on the donkey's back and half on the donkey's side. His small but strong hands are like the claws of an eagle, clinched into the shaggy coat of the donkey. But it is an unfair fight. Just as the hind legs of the donkey touch the ground again, and Ashraf thinks that it is over, the donkey dives back again with his front feet to the ground. This time he even hits his head on the ground. The deafening and shrill braying of the donkey echoes around. Again, his hind legs fly up like a catapult.

Horrified, Aaj looks at the flying Ashraf. Like a rag doll, he flies through the air, spinning, and comes crashing down on the concrete edge of the small narrow water canal next to the mosque. For a moment, the world seems to stand still. Ashraf lies on his back and does not move. Aaj, with eyes as large as saucers, stares rigidly at the body. The donkey stands perfectly still and looks as if the whole rampage never happened. The dust in the ket drifts slowly back down. The dusty soil around Ashraf's leg slowly turns red with blood.

Aaj moans. Is Ashraf dead? Then the sound of a deep groan. Ashraf gently lifts his head up. Aaj rushes to him and supports him as he tries to come up. The boys look at the pool of blood spreading around the leg of Ashraf. The blood is seeping from a large gaping wound on Ashraf's shin onto the dusty ground. The boys bend over

Ashraf's leg. A piece of white bone can be seen through the blood. Ashraf moans again, while a couple of big tears roll down his cheeks. Again he looks at his leg. "Baba can't find out about this," he moans. Supported by Aaj, the two boys search for a place in the shade. The look of pain on Ashraf's face betrays the severity of the injury. Aaj tries to convince him that he needs to call Baba or Aday to care for his leg. Or Sharif Khoon, who knows all about donkeys and probably also about wounds caused by donkeys. Grimacing in pain, Ashraf shakes his head. "Baba cannot find out about this," he moans again. Baba can get very angry, usually with only words and curses, but, very rarely, he also gives the boys a firm spanking. It is all very painful. Though when Baba only expresses his anger through his words, the furious look in his eyes is just as painful as if he had spanked them with his hands.

The bleeding does not stop. The boys discuss frantically. A long time ago, Ashraf had once witnessed a doctor rub ointment on a wound to heal it. With wide eyes, he had watched the entire spectacle. It had been an elderly man who, in one way or another, had acquired a large open wound on his arm. The doctor had taken a sort of brown ointment from a jar and smeared it on the wound. Yes, Ashraf was sure. It was the color of wet mud and sand. Groaning in pain, he concludes that this is the solution. The boys immediately start to make this miracle medicine. Aaj helps by collecting mud from the canal. Aaj grabs a small metal pot that is lying in the courtyard and gets some water from the canal. After some stirring and kneading, the boys smear the beautiful, sticky mud over the large open, and still bleeding, wound. Aaj goes searching for cloths. A few minutes later he is back with a few grimy rags. Just like a seasoned doctor, Aaj binds the cloths to his shins. The bleeding has stopped. With a painful, yet happy, look on his face, he looks at his leg and is pleased with the result. The baggy pants of the salwar hide the entire event.

The two boys look at the donkey that has caused all of this. He looks ignorant, as if nothing has happened, and he is not aware of the harm that has been done. Ashraf thinks back to the words of Sharif Khoon, "There is no other animal that is so stupid yet so smart, so strong, obstinat, brave, and stubborn as a donkey." Pensively, he looks at the donkey and moans softly as he gently moves his leg. "This is a very dumb donkey," he moans softly, with a face distorted in pain. The wound hurts. It's throbbing. The bleeding has stopped, but that is the only good news. Ashraf does not dare to lift up the cloth off of his leg. There is a hard lump under the cloths. Also, around the mud on the wound, large brown spots are appearing. Walking also does not go well. Not only the wound, but the entire leg hurts. This morning, Aaj comes by to see how it was going. Carefully, Ashraf pulls his salwar up his leg. Aaj grimaces, "It stinks, man," he whispers. Ashraf is convinced that it is the ointment that smells. Aaj says that he's as stupid as the donkey if he does not ask Baba or Aday to look at his leg. Ashraf does not reply but rather gazes with a determined look, giving the impression that he holds a solution that only he seems to know.

Ashraf's younger brother, the little Asghar, sees the two boys looking at the leg. Curious, he comes closer, and Aaj tells him the whole story of the donkey ride. Every time Aaj tells the story, it gets even more exciting. "Listen Asghar," said Aaj, "when Ashraf was launched by the donkey, he soared over the mosque." Asghar listens with a gaping mouth, looking back and forth at Aaj and the wound on Ashraf's leg. In a beseeching tone, Aaj concludes his story with the message that everything must be kept secret and that Baba must not find out. Ashraf sighs. He knows his brother like no other. He doesn't have the nickname "Daky", or "postman," for nothing. Asghar always tells Baba everything. It is not a matter of if Baba will hear, but when.

A few hours later, the moment has arrived. Mashoom Meenz, the evening prayer, is over, and the women have put the food outside. Baba sits with the family around the steaming food. A few times he sniffs his nose in the air and looks around, as if he is searching for something. His eyes wander around, looking over at the boys. Then his gaze fixes on Asghar who is moving up and down while he is sitting on the ground. While looking at Asghar, Baba sniffs again with his nose up in the air. The little boy cannot contain it any longer. "Baba, Baba... Ashraf has fallen from the donkey and...he flew through the air higher than the mosque and...he has a big wound on his leg...and it stinks like a dead goat and..."

Ashraf sighs and looks at the ground. He does not need to look at Baba to know that he is very angry. Baba harshly removes the cloths from the leg. The hardened mud breaks and the wound begins to bleed excessively. Aghast, Baba looks at the dirty, stinking wound in amazement. He wants to say something and gasps for air. Then he purses his lips together so hard that they look like tiny white stripes. Baba is so angry that he walks away without saying a word. His eyes spit fire. Baba is coming back with some stuff and start to clean the stinking wound as best as he can. A huge wide border around the wound is red. The wound itself looks diseased. White, yellow, red, and brown pieces of meat and skin seem to compete for who looks the dirtiest. The blood from the wound drips on to the floor. There is such a horrible stench from the wound, the cloths, and the remaining mud. Ashraf does not utter a sound. A few fat tears roll silently down his cheeks. Baba looks silently at the wound. He shakes his head and turns away in silence. Ashraf does not dare look him in the eyes. He lays motionless on his back with the clean dressing on his wounded leg. Continuously he looks at the door through which Baba just left. Ashraf does not see Baba again until the next morning. Without exchanging a word, they go to the hospital in Miranshah. The doctor listens to Baba's brief explanation. Shaking his head, the doctor looks at the wound and then to Ashraf. Baba does not need to lecture Ashraf anymore.

A huge scar has branded him and has forever tied him to this donkey ride.

# CHEEGHA

The Pashtun population of which Ashraf is a part of, lives in a huge area stretching from the city of Herat in the west of Afghanistan to the banks of the Indus River all the way in the west of Pakistan. It is an area that stretches from the wide plains of South Afghanistan via beautiful valleys like the Kabul and Peshawar Valley until deep in the dry and barren plains of Pakistan. Different Pashtuns can be recognized by the way they are dressed. For example, North of Peshawar, tribesmen do not wear turbans. Whereas in the south, almost every man does. A majority of the Pashtun men can be recognized by the manner in which they take the cloth that hangs over their shoulders and wrap it around their heads as a turban. Nowadays the turban is gradually replaced by different types of caps. In Waziristan they mostly wear the cap which is known as Chitrali topi. It is made of hand-woven wool which originates from the Chitral region in the north of Khyber Pakhtunkhwa. The characteristic facial features and beards give them often an implacable, rough and powerful look. Almost everyone wears the traditional wide trousers called salwar and the long shirt called kameez. An often dark and longer sleeveless vest coat known as a waskaat and leather sandals known as chapli make the outfit complete. A relative large group of tribal women wear a burqa, a garment that completely covers their bodies and face.

Ashraf is part of the tribal Pashtun population that lives in the isolated areas between Afghanistan and Pakistan. They are a people group that never accepted the sovereignty of anybody else other than themselves. Many tried by force, but no outsider in history was able to control the tribes for long. It is one of the reasons that the tribesmen are always suspicious of outsiders. These tribesmen differentiate themselves by their long history of traditions and customs. These traditions and customs are centuries old, and the Pashtuns remain loyal to them to this very day. It is an incredible mix of Islam, ancient traditions, tribal structures and their love for weapons, drums, fights, dancing and good food. Especially in the area where Ashraf lives, the community is an authentic tribal society in which everyone is very aware of his position within the family, clan, sub-clan and confederation of tribes.

A real Pashtun speaks Pashto, an old Iranian language which is close to Persian. If he doesn't speak his mother tongue, he is not recognized as being a real Pashtun or is not accepted as such. Besides the Pashto as a language, the Islamic faith and deeply-rooted traditions are the characteristics of a real Pashtun. It is a combination of faith, traditions and a culture that rise above other norms, values and laws. These traditions are transferred from generation to generation.

The character of little Ashraf is also polished by these unwritten laws and rules that emphasize honor (*nang*) and the so-called code of honor (*pashtunwali*). This code of honor determines the daily life. Matters like hospitality (*melmastia*), asylum (*nanawatai*) and, not to forget, vendetta, or blood revenge (*badal*). Eye for eye, tooth for tooth. A comparable price must be paid for someone's death. The government, army nor police are not coming to these isolated areas between Pakistan and Afghanistan. Instead, these are matters that are dealt with within the community between families, clan or tribes. If there is need for mediation or jurisdiction this usually happens in a meeting of the tribes, called maraka or jirga. It depends on how large or how complicated an issue to be solved is.

Some people call the land where these real Pashtuns live 'Pashtunistan'. This nickname is burdensome, especially for the Pakistani government who considers this area part of Pakistan.

In this Pashtunistan, far away from the house of Ashraf, are two smudgy, lazy Pashtuns hanging against the wall of their small clay houses. They don't work and seem to spend half of every day sleeping. In between their naps, they sluggishly smoke their water pipes and drink tea. Once in a while an older lady brings them some food. The men have guns laying next to them and big bands of ammunition hang over their shoulders. Their salwar kameez haven't been washed in a long time, and their turbans are matte and grey from the dust. These are the kind of people that Baba wants his sons to stay away from. "They are deadbeats, bums," says Baba with a look in his eyes that is somewhere between compassion and frustration. They are men and boys that have a negative influence on everything and everyone around them. They are boys that are too lazy to study and work, and who eventually end up going down the wrong path.

Today the two men are actually a bit more active then the days before. They are acting tense and talking busily towards each other. They are constantly glancing around themselves, paranoid. They have already picked up their guns ten times to checked if they were still working correctly. It seems that the moment of truth has arrived. The men stand up and walk in a straight line to a house nearby. Then there is shouting. Shots are fired. Again shouts, this time of a woman fearing for her life. Then the shouting changes into crying. It is the crying of a woman and little children. Another shot is fired. Then only the sound of running footsteps and the painful crying of the woman and the children can be heard. Close by a dog is barking as if he is calling up the people around him to stand up against this cowardly attack.

Ashraf focuses his ears. The barking stops, and it doesn't take long before the sound of the drums begin. Or is it something else? The wind is in the wrong direction. He's not sure if he is hearing it correctly. Yes, now he's sure. It is the monotonic but threatening sound of the drummers from the village. Every village has its own drummers, called damoon. One such drummer is called a dum. He may be even the most important man in the tribal area. At the same time, he is the only man without a weapon. These men drum during official moments like weddings and births, and wakes the village people during Ramadan. But this is a different sound. It is the sound that signals an emergency. Ashraf gets on his feet and runs to the gate.

In these kind of emergencies, the damoon always stand on their own roof and hit their drums in a certain emergency rhythm. It is the beat of the Cheegha, the beat of the call. Like an invisible hand, the Cheegha direct men to a meeting point close to the drummer.

This time the drums are beating a very different rhythm then the one during a party. Ashraf looks through the gate. Is there a fire that needs to be put out somewhere? It doesn't look that way. There is no sign of smoke or anything. It could also mean that there's a flood, but it doesn't seem like that either. There must be some crime that has been committed in the neighborhood, or a murder or a robbery.

The men from the village run along the gate. Then an old toothless Pashtun with a beautiful white beard screams that there was a robbery. Within several minutes, the main part of the story is clear. Two men robbed a house in the neighborhood. No one is wounded or murdered, but they stole money and possessions. All the men grab their weapons. Guns, pistols and big bands of ammunition hang over the shoulders of the village people. It looks very dangerous and threatening. As guided by the same invisible hand of the Cheegha, they are directed and run in a certain direction. The inciting sound of the drums seem to stir the men forth in the direction of the robbers. The dark and deep sound of the drums sound alarming and is interchanged by gun and pistol shots.

In the meanwhile, Aaj has joined Ashraf. The boys creep out of the ket's gate as far as possible to the place where the robbery must have taken place and where the men started their pursuit. On a small hill, the boys have an excellent overview and wait tensely for the events that are about to happen. The sound of shouting and gun fire seem to move further away and even to die out. But then the sounds come closer and closer by again. The gunfire and shouting is now very close. Just as the boys decide to hide themselves behind the bushes, the gunfire stops. You hear curses, sounds of beating, hard shouts of crying and pain.

From behind the bushes the boys can see both of the robbers being tied up dragged over the road. Half walking, half stumbling, crying, moaning and crawling, the men are being cursed and triumphantly escorted by the men of the village. Out of the group, you hear hard commands. A young Pashtun with a thin black beard releases himself from the group and runs away. Just a bit later, he comes back with a hand full of cloth and a can of paint or something that looks like paint. The cloth is dipped deeply in the cans. With quite some force, the robbers are pushed to the ground, and within a few minutes their faces and upper bodes are painted black. They are then seated on two donkeys and given a round in the village streets.

The whole village ran out. The men are displayed as complete idiots and made fun of. From all sides, they are kicked and beaten. The whole village screams and curses along. Through the black paint, the pain on their faces can be seen. They lost their guns and ammunition. Their faces and clothes are stiff from the half-dried up black paint. For a few more minutes, with lowered heads, they are still standing in front of the crowd from the village. For one last time, the curses are flying around their ears. Then they are beaten with sticks, kicked and kicked out of the village.

Ashraf sighs deeply. Aaj looks satisfactory at his friend. They followed the whole scene from up close. Nothing new for the boys. The drums are silent. The tears of the woman who was robbed are dried. The children are playing again before her little house. Aaj put his arm on Ashrafs shoulder. The two boys walk home, hand in hand. In the courtyard, a skinny dark brown donkey makes some unexpected jumps and brays as if he is giving his own emergency signal. But then his head lowers to the ground again. Rest has been restored in Darpa Khel.

Later on, Ashraf hears that the robbers' houses were destroyed, leveled to the ground. All their possessions were burnt and destroyed. These Pashtun criminals are not worth being called a Pashtun. This is pashtunwali. This is honor revenge. Eye for eye, tooth for tooth.

Now, it is time to make some fun. Ashraf's younger brother Umar has an idea. Let's take one of the best sheep from Aday's collection, in the animal house to the annual sheep show in Miranshah. Aaj and Ashraf don't deliberate for a single second about this great idea. Together the boys try to find the most beautiful sheep in the courtyard. The boys have a very small dispute about which sheep is the most beautiful. Then the trip to Miranshah begins. It is not easy to guide the sheep from the ket to Miranshah without being seen by Baba. Then the exciting show and competition starts. The first show is about bulls and buffaloes. The judges are checking every animal. They closely look to their size, their health and many more details. The boys are excited. Now the sheep competition starts. Umar keep the rope around the neck of the sheep. It is one of the biggest in the show. As a last detail, the boys clean some dirt around the sheep's eyes. Their hearts are beating fast and hard inside their bodies. The judges seem to stay a little bit longer with their sheep. Then there is an announcement. Their sheep is declared the best one in the sheep category. The first prize comes with the handsome amount of five rupees. The boys jumped into the air, dancing around and shouting from happiness. Aaj receives the five ruppies. They have to share. Aaj and Ashraf look to each other. They are both the elder ones. They look to Umar. He is at least four or five years younger than they are. The decision is made. Umar gets a ruppie. Aaj and Ashraf divide the rest. Umar looks to the boys. There will be a time that he will get his fair share. He will not forget.

# WORKING TOWARDS YOUR DREAM

Baba is a strict, hard-working, and intelligent man from the tribal areas. Faithful, he lives closely to the traditions of his people and country. He is not only strict with his own children, but also with himself and others in his sphere. Within his family, tribe, and even beyond, he is a respected man. When he was fourteen, Baba lost his own father. This event has had an impact on the following years of his life. Baba has five sisters and two brothers. He is the oldest man in his own family. According to the traditions of the Pashtuns, when his father died, the responsibility of the family was transferred to Baba, even though he was so young. Baba rarely talks about his father and this period of his life. Baba's father was called Malik Ahmed Khan, and throughout his life, he was a hard-working contractor and business man. He had large and high-profile projects, such as building the airport in Miranshah were built by him.

After the death of his father, Baba soon dropped out of school in order to care for his mother, brothers, and sisters. It had been his dream to study medicine and become a doctor. Baba wished that everyone in his country could go to a doctor and receive medical care. This dream could not go on now. Baba could not go to college. He had to work hard, very hard. A very heavy responsibility pressed on his young shoulders. He could not accomplish his dream. And yet, that dream was not lost. Fortunately, Baba's brothers and children do not have to endure the same fate as him. Baba decided that everything would be done so that they could study at the university and become doctors.

Baba knew, more than anyone, that the price that they would have to pay to achieve this goal would be high. Not only in money, but also in terms of commitment and perseverance. Baba started doing business early in life. The family owned a fair amount of land, which was divided between Baba and his uncle Barkat Shah. In the first years, it was primarily a struggle to provide enough food for his mother, brothers, and sisters.

But Baba knew that his dream would cost him more. He worked even harder and eventually got the highly sought-after contract to supply food to the Tochi Scouts. Not so long ago, Ashraf learned in school about the history of the huge military complex of the Tochi Scouts near Miranshah.

Lord Curzon, the Viceroy of British India, founded the Frontier Corps in 1907 with the purpose of organizing seven militia and scout units in the tribal areas along the Afghan border. These seven units were known as the Khyber Rifles, the Zhob Militia, the Kurram Militia, the Tochi Scouts, the Chagai Militia, the South-Waziristan Scouts, and the Chitral Scouts. Just like the other units, the Tochi Scouts in North Waziristan were led by a commander, a British officer with the rank of Colonel.

Baba did not have enough money in the beginning to provide supplies for the Tochi Scouts and asked around for help. No help was available. Some people even went behind Baba's back and spoke to the commander, asking why he had given Baba the contract as Baba would not be able to honor the contract because of a lack of funds. Perhaps these people were jealous, or they wanted the contract for themselves.

The commander of the Tochi Scouts summoned Baba to his office. He looked at Baba with a firm military gaze, sizing him up. When he asked Baba if it was true that he did not have enough money, Baba honestly admitted it was so. The commander looked at him again and made a surprising decision. He shot him two hundred thousand rupees. At the time, it was a lot of money. With this, Baba was able to start the deliveries, and it developed into a good opportunity to make money through fair trade.

Later, the commander who had helped Baba, was replaced by another, and still later, this commander was replaced by another. The story of how Baba had originally acquired the contract was forgotten. But after a long time of doing good business, corruption crept into to the system of the Tochi Scouts. This became the reason that Baba later left the contract with the Tochi Scouts.

The little Ashraf knows Baba's dream and knows the history. Silent and breathless, he listened to the story when Baba told it to him and his brothers in the *hujra*, the community place close to the mosque. "These were life lessons," Baba said.

Pashtun hujras are used mainly to entertain male guests in a household, although sometimes community hujras are also maintained by tribal units. In individual houses, the size and adornment of a hujra are sometimes indicative of family status. A hujra is a community club normally situated in each village or ket. Though they are sometimes owned by a well-off family, they are shared by the whole community. Members of the hujra that is near Ashraf are mostly close relatives and other people from neighborhood. The elderly people spend their day to enjoy the hubble-bubble and chat over tea. The younger men, in their spare time, listen to the stories of the elders and bring up issues to resolve, while the children play about, waiting for a request from one of the elders to take a message or bring some fresh tea. Ashraf and his brothers love to serve tea or food to the older people.

At the same time, all sorts of Issues are put on the table. The men work on a solution and arrive at a consensus before they bring the issue to the wider community. Without any reservations, everyone brings his daily events and issues to the table. Though the hujra is considered to be a secular place, it is closely associated with the mosque in the neighborhood. The hujra is, for Ashraf, the first practical school for wisdom. Here the lessons about the unwritten traditions of the tribesmen, Islam and daily family issues are for free, and serving Baba and the older tribesmen give Ashraf a feeling of pride and respect.

In addition to being a hard worker, Baba is a smart and upright man and a strict father to his sons. It is told many times during the hujra, studying is not a matter of the will, it is a must. Yes, Ashraf and his brothers must study, and Baba makes it clear that he will do everything within his power to keep his boys on this track. It is clear for the young boys, working toward your big dream is hard work.

# TRIBAL FIGHT

Every honorable Pashtun is aware of his place within the family, clan, sub-tribe, tribe, and confederation of tribes. They are all descendants from the Pashtun ancestor, but also descendants of all of the different confederation of tribes. Ashraf also knows how important it is for one to know his place within the family and tribal structure.

If there are conflicts in the village or in the area, then the village elders or tribal leaders get together to discuss the matter. Such a gathering of elders is called a jirga or maraka.

At the hujra, Ashraf is listening to what the elder tribesmen are chatting about over their tea, and what issues they are raising with each other. Ashraf is waiting for a call from one of the elders to take a message or bring fresh tea. But Ashraf knows this is also the place to initiate a jirga.

The jirga is a meeting of a group of tribal men that have the authority to settle a dispute in a way that is acceptable to both sides. The origin of the word jirga is derived from the Turkish word 'jirg' which means 'circle'. This origin is plausible because the members of the jirga usually sit in a circle in order to ensure that there is no head position of the meeting and therefore no one shall be considered privileged or powerful. There is no chairman among the jirga members. All of them are equal. The jirga is held in an open public space, for example at a mosques or at the grave yard of a tribe's ancestors, and every male can attend. However, at times there is a secret jirga, whose place is not revealed to everyone.

A *tabar* (Pashtun tribe) is divided into many khels (a unit of kinship group). These khels are then divided into *plarinas* (units of the tribe which have a common ancestral father). These plarinas are further divided into different *kahols* (extended family). The maraka is a jirga at the plarina and kahol levels. The kahol institution deals with matters of small importance within or between families.

The *qawmi jirga* is a jirga at the level of the khels and tabars. This jirga deals with more important issues that are central to the social order of the tribe.

The highest level of jirga is the *loya jirga*. It is an important institution where tribal leaders gather in order to discuss crucial national issues and make collective decisions regarding sovereignty, national unity, selection of a ruler, adoption of a new constitution, and the declaration of war.

Pashtunwali and the jirga are major aspects of the Pashtun and, more widely, of the Afghan's identity. The jirga is always led by pashtunwali, the code of honor within the Pashtun culture. However, the family structure also plays a major role in every judgment that comes from the jirga. The decision of the maraka or jirga is binding and, in principle, every Pashtun abides by it.

In the 17th century, a Pashtun named Nimatullah described the different tribes and their origins for the first time. He divided the Pashtuns into four groups with four patriarchs from which all Pashtuns would have emerged. Three of these progenitors would have been sons of Abdul Rashid Qais, a Pashtun who, according to tradition, descended from the famous Israelite King Saul. The three sons of Qais Abdul Rashid were Sarban, Gharghash and Bet. They are seen as the ancestors of all Pashtuns in southern and eastern Afghanistan and of the Peshawar Valley.

In South Waziristan, there is the Wazir tribe and the Mahsud tribe. Where Ashraf was born, in North Waziristan, there are two major tribes, the Daur tribe and the Wazir tribe. Ashraf was born into the Daur tribe which is then divided into two sub-tribes, the Laar Daur (eastern) and the Baar Daur (western). Ashraf's family belongs to the Baar Daur. To further complicate things, this Baar Daur tribe is divided into many sub-tribes, one of which is Darpa Khel. Darpa Khel has three sub-tribes, the Manakhel, the Lamakhel, and the Akthikhel. Ashraf and his family belong to the Manakhel which was led by the father of Ashraf's mother, Malik Mirjan Khan.

Baba always says that the Wazir are very smart people. They are cunning and analyze a situation before acting. The Daur people, to which Ashraf belongs, are rather emotional people. The men often react by their instincts, especially in regards to conflicts.

Today there is talk about the Wazir. Ashraf stands behind Baba's back as he talks to the men in the courtyard. They sit on the floor upon rugs and with big pillows supporting their backs. Mosquitoes circle around their heads as the water pipe passes from hand to hand. An elderly gray-haired man with a beautiful white beard and turban tells the whole story. There is a major conflict between the Mada Khel Wazir tribe and the Bannuchi people of Bannu. Bannu is forty miles from Miranshah on the road to Peshawar. The argument is about Bakha Khel, a piece of land on the border of the tribal areas with settled area of Pakistan. The Wazir have come down from the mountains in search of more farmland. With a serious face, the elderly gray-haired man says that they are going to try to conquer land near Bannu. In the coming days, he expects that their fighters will move along the direction of Bannu. The men listen to the rest of the story but do not respond. After all, it's not their fight. Let the Wazir do what they like. Baba says nothing. He looks gravely at the old man. The men continue to talk about other things. Ashraf does not hear any more about it. He feels sleepy. In the background he hears the murmurs of voices. He is still trying to listen to what the men are saying, but soon his eyes grow heavy and moments later, he is deep asleep.

A few days later it is time. As they walk to school with Sharif Khoon from the village, they hear the drums. The sound is still far away. Sharif Khoon stops and reverses. He does not trust it and decides to take the boys back to Darpa Khel. All the men from the village are talking with each other. The sound of the drums is good to hear. It's the rhythm of the fight. A loud, fast, hallowed rhythm. Ashraf goes with his brothers and Aaj and secretly check the situation out. It is now certain. The Wazir are going to fight. They are now coming out of all of the villages in the hills and are on their way to Bannu, marching by foot. They walk, led by drummers, with weapons in their hands. Big long guns with impressive belts hang across their chests. Each one of these men are dangerous. Many men have black turbans wound around their heads with the ends of the cloth left fluttering over their shoulders.

Sharif Khoon is excited. He enjoys the tension. It seems that he would like himself to be in the battle. He stumbles around the village with his lame leg going from one group of men to another. Then, a small group of men from Miranshah come running. There is a lot of shouting. The men talk together and then run to their homes or huts to arm themselves with guns.

The Wazir have started looting Miranshah. What is going on? This is not in line with all the stories they have heard so far. Everybody thought the Wazir would go to Bannu and fight for farmland. It is unbelievable. They made a mistake. The Wazir had never seen Miranshah and thought they had already reached Bannu. Are these men so dumb? Shaking his head, Ashraf watches the Wazir fighters pass. They quickly move forward on foot with their weapons and drums. They are on the move again to their actual battle in Bannu.

The Bannuchi are no match for the Wazir. The Wazir are fighters from the tribal area, hard fighters who are formidable. The battle is short but intense. There are deaths in both camps. The Wazir overcome and plunder the area. The drums resound as the Wazir return to their own area. The drums sound differently now. Cheerful. The men drag along the spoils: pots, pans, blankets, cattle, chickens. Everyone goes back home.

There is a qawmi jirga some days after the fighting. A ceasefire is called. A ceasefire agreement is called *korain* which literally means 'stone.' After calling a ceasefire, the qawmi jirgra begins negotiations for the settlement of the conflict. Each side gives their claims and lists their immediate losses, which include several dead and wounded.

The proud Bannuchi tell that they have slain many of Wazir. They do not realize that this bragging is incredibly stupid. In this way, they will have to compensate the Wazir a lot. The Wazir are much smarter. They affirm the exaggerated story of Bannuchi. Many deaths and many wounded. The qawmi jirga does its job. The Bannuchi must pay a lot of money and give a lot of land to the Wazir as compensation for the many, supposedly, fallen victims.

# BADAL

The school day in Miranshah is over. There were the ordinary lessons of language, mathematics, and religion. Sharif Khoon is in his normal position, waiting faithfully at the entrance of the school. Indifferent, he leans against an old worn wall. When Ashraf and the other boys have gathered around him, they walk to the day house, Sarai-kair.

Ashraf hopes they will walk through the bazaar. The bazaar full with all of its shops, people, camels, and donkey carts. It looks like a beehive, where the constant swarm of colorful people go in and out. Ashraf loves the fuss. All those beautiful colors and scents. All the people. Like the guy who sits behind his large baskets with herbs, or the old man who seems to have a permanent battle with the flies that have swooped down on his butcher shop. Men and all rushing to and fro from the bazaar, carrying their goods on their heads, backs, donkeys, or camels. Old men, with their snow-white and red henna colored beards and shining flaxen hair and faces that look like old parchment paper.

Sharif Khoon follows Baba's instructions and walks in a large arc around the bazaar. Instead of through the sea of colors and scents, they walk along the boring high sand-colored walls that surround the houses. Here and there awaits a donkey, head bowed until someone climbs onto his cart and towards an unknown destination. Ashraf looks grumpily to the donkey and wall. He had hoped that this time they would go through the bazaar to get to the day house.

Before the boys arrive at the day house, they smell food. Ashraf's mouth begins to water. Baba's cook, Makan, makes food every day and lives at the day house. Makan has a wife and children in Darpa Khel village. Ashraf is convinced that Makan is the best curry cook in all of Waziristan. When he makes curry, Ashraf always wants to have the oily top part. Everyone finds this part the tastiest. Each time, it is like a game to get Makan to give this part to Ashraf. Makan mostly ignores Ashraf and usually says that everyone may have that portion.

With dark and sad eyes, Ashraf looks at him, and tries to make clear with an accusative tone in his voice that he is convinced that Makan puts his own children first and saves the best part for them. Ashraf knows that it's not true, but it's worth a try. For a moment, it seems to do the trick. Makan looks despairingly at the indignant face of Ashraf. Then he shrugs and without saying anything gives Ashraf the same as all the other boys. What a disappointing day. First, they did not walk through the bazaar, and now he did not get the oily part of the curry. Silently, though muttering to himself, Ashraf looks for a place to sit with his plate and starts eating.

Makan lives at the day house with the tutor, Hardal Ustad. After lunch, the boys go to sleep for a few hours, and after that they receive a few hours of tutoring. Baba has arranged this. He wants his boys to get the best results. For no reason may they fall behind. Baba also let new physicians or school principals live at the day house as his guests until they can find a home of their own.

Miranshah is a town where people come from the outside to go to work or to go shopping. In the evening, everyone goes back to their villages in the area apart from the government employees who have come from other parts of the country. In the evening and night Miranshah feels like a ghost town.

Ashraf and the other boys have slept for a few hours after their meal. The hottest part of the day is over, and the boys are doing their homework. Suddenly, there is a loud noise. Two heavily armed men storm the day house and walk straight to Baba's room.

Ashraf and the boys sit stiffly on the ground. They carefully shuffle back until they sit with their backs against the wall. Loud conversation is heard coming from the room. Then they hear Baba's voice. Loud and commanding. It becomes quieter. Ashraf shuffles cautiously towards the door. His curiosity overcomes his fear and terror. The other guys carefully shuffle behind him.

Panting and shaking, the men tell their story. It is possible to hear well through the narrow crack of the door. With tence heavy voices the men tell that they have just killed a boy of the Mamaday family. One remains silent. Then unclear, commanding sounds come from Baba. Ashraf cannot hear what he says, but the men continue their story. They are members of the Pir Saman family, who live fifteen miles west of Miranshah in a village called Mohmamad Khel. It is an muddled story. The door slides a little bit more open. Ashraf can look through the gap. Baba is sitting on the Persian carpet with his back against a big round pillow called a *takia*. The men seem to be as little boys, waiting in front of the court for a judgment. Large piles of papers are in front of Baba on the carpet. Far above his head on the cupboard is a Quran.

Baba looks long and silently to the men. It's a look that Ashraf does not recognize. Baba thinks deeply before he goes to say something or to ask a question. The silence is almost ominous. The men both have large old British 303 guns in their hands. Around their shoulders are the large recognizable ammunition belts. Dark turbans adorn their heads. Baba also has weapons. Every Pashtun has a weapon. But Baba has no gun in his hand. It is not needed, as the men look respectfully and expectantly to Baba. Baba turns half around and looks, preoccupied, up to the Quran, as if to find the answer there. The Pashtuns always place the Quran high above their heads as a sign of respect. Usually it is positioned on a nice wooden stand. Baba stands like a statue in the room, and the silence almost hurts. No one is moving.

Baba and the men and the victim are from the same Baar Daur tribe. Some time ago, a feud broke out between these families. Someone was slain and the clear result was badal, revenge! The killer, or someone from his family must be slain. sooner or later. Revenge must be taken in this manner. It is a time for badal. As a result, the men killed this boy. Baba breaks the silence and asks for the boy's name.

Ashraf is white. He feels sick. The boys around him are holding their breath. He is a boy from their school. They just saw him this morning. He was only fifteen years old. Ashraf's head begins to spin. He feels dizzy and nauseous. With his head bowed, he turns around. The other boys also have no need to continue listening. Dread is on their faces. Quietly they sneak back to their room at the day house. In the distance, they can still hear the voices of Baba and the two men. If only they had not heard. If only they had not seen anything.

The Pashtun-driven murder hangs like a dark, all-encompassing, depressive blanket in the room. Nobody says a word. No one looks in his books. They sit motionless with their heads bowed. Sharif Khoon comes for them to take them back to Darpa Khel. They stand up silently. Without a word, they walk home. The only noise that disturbs the oppressive silence is the regular snort and gasp of Sharif Khoon.

It does not let loose of Ashraf. For weeks, at night, he thinks of that boy from his school. The same day he was killed, he was buried. This happens in Waziristan. The pashtunwali ensures that the number of killings in Waziristan is the lowest number in all of

Pakistan. These are the words of Baba. If you kill someone, you, or someone very close to you, will be slain. Someone you love. Someone from your family or tribe. Imprisonment does not stop this badal. For as soon as someone is free from prison, he may be killed any time.

Pashtunwali and badal have no time and no hurry. Baba has explained it all. In settled areas of Pakistan, a person may come to court, and if they have money they take a lawyer or pay off the officials. In those cases, a person can escape punishment. This does not happen in Waziristan. Here, they apply pashtunwali. Here they apply badal. Here there is always punishment. Eye for an eye, tooth for a tooth. The murdered innocent school boy will not disappear from Ashraf's mind. Waziristan, the territory with the fewest murders as a result of hard, and often horrible, badal system. Is it good? Is it wrong? Ashraf does not know. It is long after midnight. Ashraf falls into a fitful sleep.

# CAMELS

Ashraf is already out of bed early this morning. The sun is still hidden behind the mountains. The other boys are still sleeping. Ashraf sits with his back against the wall and looks around. It was so hot last night that the boys slept in the courtyard. Each day, when the first light falls on the mountains and hills around Darpa Khel, a group of poor children and their mothers will gather with pots and pans by the main door of Ashraf's house gate. It is the daily recurring ritual. Aday is already awake and shares buttermilk and a few pieces of bread, called *naghan*, with a few other women.

Every night and every day the cows and buffaloes get milked. This too is a daily ritual. The servants make buttermilk from the milk that is fermented during the night.

With more interest than usual, Ashraf looks at the women and children. He is accustomed to the daily rhythm of recurring events. As by a strict military schedule, Baba has organized everything. On a day like today, it is wonderful to follow the entire daily ritual by starting with morning prayers in the mosque. Baba has said the mosque was built by his father Malik Ahmed Khan, along with his brother Malik Barkat Shah. Their names were written on the left and right sides of the outside of the mosque. Baba still tells this story with a smile. The right side is for Baba, the left side is for Uncle Barkat Shah. When Baba goes to pray in the mosque, he sits on the right side. His side.

The call for morning prayer sounds not only from the mosque in the ket but also from the other mosques nearby. Depending on which way the wind is blowing between Darpa Khel's mountains and hills, the call to prayer can sometimes be heard coming from different directions. It is a familiar and soothing sound. It brings inner peace to his troubles. This is his home. The ever-recurring call to prayer that belongs to Waziristan, like the sound of a bird in the sky. The call of the imam is heard everywhere, always around the same time and with the same message. In Ashraf's eyes, this is the noise that happens all over the world five times a day. But his world is Waziristan.

It is not long before the men wash themselves in water and run to the entrance of the mosque. The women stay at home with the children. They pray at home.

Ashraf does not yet go to the mosque in the morning. That is for when you are an adult. Girls are considered to be adults from the time they get their first menstruation. For boys, it is when they experience their first wet dream. Because a boy is ashamed to take a bath at home after he experiences his first wet dream, he jumps into the water basin of the mosque in the morning to cleanse himself. Of course, this draws attentions and others usually make jokes about it. In Waziristan, Pashtuns call this special moment "water over his head." Once this moment occurs, the boys are considered adults, and they join in the daily rhythm of prayer.

Ashraf is not yet an adult. He waits until Baba comes back to the house from the mosque. When Baba walks by, Ashraf leaps to his feet and runs after him towards their breakfast meal. Aday and the servants have had the *parata*, fried eggs and *malai* (fresh cream) long prepared. Parata is a circular peace of bread fried on a pan. Everything is ready and is waiting for them.

Ashraf is near Baba on the ground. In the middle of the room lies a big, beautiful dark-colored carpet. Around it are soft-colored cushions where everyone slowly finds their place. Baba looks around. Ashraf, his brothers, some cousins, and other family members sit around over the big carpet. When Baba takes the parata and fried eggs, it is a sign to everyone to take their food. It goes in this arranged way.

Baba loves order and cleanliness. Evaluating, his eyes wander over the boys and family. The parata, tea, and eggs disappear slowly from the large rug that is at the center of the family. Ashraf loves the freshly prepared breakfast cream made during during the night. He grabs one last bit of parata.

After washing and showering Ashraf sees that Aaj is already waiting at the gate. They have to go to school. Ashraf quickly grabs his stuff together. Sharif Khoon is again snorting and spitting like an old engine that has yet to warm up. Impatiently, he snaps his good leg to his lame leg. He looks annoyed at Ashraf, who finally comes running. Usman and the others are ready.

As they walk from Darpa Khel towards the River Khwar, Aaj shows Ashraf something in his back pockets. Under his salwar kameez is a beautiful slingshot. He proudly shows it to him. "It's new. Home-made," Aaj whispers in his ears. Fascinated and in anticipation, he looks at the new slingshot. He knows that his best friend Aaj is not only the best sportsman of the Darpa Khel area, but he is also the best slingshot shooter. "With this catapult, I shot the left leg off of a fly hundreds of yards away." Aaj is exaggerating his skills. Ashraf smiles. Meanwhile, they have crossed the river. Sharif Khoon looks suspiciously over his shoulder at the two boys. Ashraf looks innocently back. As if it doesn't interest him at all, Sharif Khoon takes another deep sniff. His left leg seems to be dragging behind him more aggressively than before, but it's probably just his imagination.

Almost every day, hundreds of camels line the roads. Midway between Miranshah and Darpa Khel is a sort of resting place for the camels and their owners. Everyone calls that place "Camel Sarai" or "Ishooney Srooi" in local Pushtu dialect. In the western part of North Waziristan, about fifty miles from Miranshah, lies Shawal. It is a big, old forest where timber for construction is cut. That wood is brought by camel caravans to Bannu. Twenty or thirty camels walk in succession with large, long rectangular cut beams on their backs. Next to each camel, runs his owner or a camel driver. Ashraf and the boys see it every day. They are used to it. Yet, every day, it is an impressive and magnificent spectacle.

Baba has said that this is the cheapest way to transport those huge beams. If you want to do with a truck, you must apply for a permit. It costs a lot of money. Those licenses are issued to the maliks, the village elders of Waziristan. It is issued by a bureaucrate who is of the rank of a deputy commissioner in the Pakistani government. This bureaucrate is responsible for governing Waziristan. These maliks in turn, sell these licenses for a lot of money to merchants and truck drivers. Ashraf does not know if this is according to Pakistani law or if it is corruption. It really makes no difference to him. These problems are for adult men.

Baba also explained to Ashraf something about the maliks and mashars. Both are respected, wise leaders in the tribal areas. Many people believe that a malik and a mashar are the same. Most people think that they are both older and respected tribesmen who are, more or less, the wise, intelligent and experienced leaders in the tribal areas. But there is a difference. The Arabic term malik was introduced by the British and came to be adopted as a term for a tribal chieftain in the tribal areas of Pakistan, especially among Pashtuns. In tribal Pashtun society, the maliks serve the government as de facto arbiters in local conflicts and interlocutors in state policy-making and tax-collection. The are the heads of village and town councils and delegates to provincial and national jirgas as well as to Parliament. And there is the *mashar*. The mashar is not selected by the government like a malik. Instead, he is the wise, intelligent, experienced and highly respected man in the family. He represents the family in all kind of official occasions and makes all the important decisions his the large family.

Going back to the cheapest way to transport the huge beams: Baba says it's simple. For camels, all those permits are not necessary. They transport the timber to Bannu, then walk back alongside or on the main Bannu-Miranshah-Data Khel road to the huge pine trees of Shawal. The trip to Bannu takes several days. Baba created a sort of resting place for the camels and their owners between Darpa Khel and Miranshah on his own land near the Khwar River.

This camel sarai (house) is the the first place a traveler encounters on his walk from Miranshah to Darpa Khel after crossing the Khwar River. Baba built this on about two acres of land at the bottom of a small mountain called Thair Warsaak. He enclosed this as a sort of compound with high mud walls and a tall two-piece gate made of thick heavy wood that is covered on each side by thick sheets of metal. The north side has a long veranda with a roof along the whole northern wall with the gate in the middle part. On both sides of the gate, the verandas were made into rooms for the live-in watchmen.

The room of the camel sarai on the west side is also used as a very basic convenience store for the camel drivers. People can get basic amenities there, things like matches, soap, or naswaar, a locally-made tobacco mixture. One can also get things like sweets, ghee, lentils, flour, tea leaves, sugar or *gurr*. This gurr is made from pure sugar cane juice which is thickened by gradual cooking in a large pan. When the water has evaporated, it is made into small round brown balls without any other additions. Gurr is the main sweetner for tea in these days as people can not afford sugar.

On top of this room there is another room which served as a watchtower. The room on the east side of the gate is for the family of the watchman. The rest of the ket is an open courtyard where different camel driver groups converge mainly in the spring and summer. There was a well dug up towards the southwest end of the ket where water can be collected by a bucket. This bucket was made from a worn out tire and can be lowered into the deep well by a thick, hand-made rope called a *paraai*.

In return for his hospitality, Baba collected the droppings that the animals left behind and used it to fertilize the land. This manure is collected on the northwest of the the ket. The gates of the camel sarai are locked everyday after the sunset and opened at dawn. It is arranged that way in order to keep the wooden logs and camels safe from miscreants. During the night, the camel drivers can rest in a secure place without worrying and would not have to stay awake to stand guard. This is the only secure ket built for the camel drivers along the entire route from Shawal to Bannu. If night falls while the camel drivers are along other parts of the route, they have to camp out in the open where they were vulnerable to criminals, snakes, wild animals, and poor weather conditions. Years later, when Ashraf was much older, it still fascinated him as to how Baba thought about this idea which had been a great social service and benefited so many people.

Sometimes, if there is not enough space inside, some caravans rest just outside of the camel sarai on the empty, rigid land on the east side of the ket.

Also now, as the boys are walking home to Miranshah, they see the hundreds of camels resting and grazing. Sharif Khoon has told a story a few times that these camels from Waziristan sometimes try to catch children. They love it when a child walks across their view, and when they see their chance, they chase the child and kill him with one bite. According to Sharif Khoon, camels have an enormously good memory, and they don't forget a face for their entire lives, especially the ones who have been cruel to them. When Sharif Khoon tells this story, he looks so mean that he sends shivers down the spines of the boys.

Ashraf and the boys know from experience that there are camels among the herd that can roar enormously loud. It is a very distinct sound that's between a burp and a cow's moo sounding hard and horrible. It's a strange, eerie sound that is sometimes joined by other camels until it becomes such a deafening noise. The saliva drool run from the mouths like big supply of froth, and sometimes something like a red balloon hangs out of their mouths. Whenever they pass the camels, the boys walk with a bit of fear and keep an extra eye on the beasts that lie or stand.

Today, the camel drivers are in groups, drinking tea and eating. A little further on, a camel driver is playing a flute. A few men around him sing songs and dance to the melody. Shabaz Khan Wazir is one of the camel drivers sitting there singing. He can sing beautifully. Sometimes, Sharif Khoon stays there just to listen. Much later, when Ashraf became older, Shabaz Khan Wazir was discovered by a radio station and became a famous singer in Pakistan and Afghanistan. For now, he just sings his song along with the other camel drivers, though he did sing much much better than all the others.

The camels are quiet. Ashraf and Aaj monitor them from the corners of their eyes. Just as they have almost passed the big group of camels, Aaj picks a pebble from off the ground. Sharif Khoon walks about ten feet in front of them. He has not noticed. Aaj chuckles. Ashraf gives him a larger stone. The excitement can be read on both of their faces. Aaj pulls the elastic of the catapult back far. The familiar sound of the elastic snapping sounds. The small stone released from the catapult hits one of the camels full-speed in the head.

The camel comes at a faster than normal speed and lets out long, strange sounding roar. The resulting events seem to be occurring in slow motion. Another camel and then another camel, and then even more camels begin to rise. Drivers begin to jump up, letting their tea cups and water pipes fall to the ground. The boys are in the middle of the road. The roar of that one camel seems to have been a signal for all the hundreds of other camels around him. A peaceful scene has turned into a jumble of camel drivers, dust, and camels. A few camels break loose and start running towards the boys, who are petrified and are standing as if they are nailed to the ground. Aaj still has the catapult in his hands. Sharif Khoon gives a harsh roar. A couple of camel drivers come at the boys with sticks in the hands, urging them to run.

As if their lives depended on it, the boys run towards Miranshah. The other boys have no idea what happened in the last half minute but they also start to run as they see the camels coming. Sharif Khoon is in the middle of the road holding up his arms, spread wide, as if to get the camel drivers and loose camels to stop. During the racing, Ashraf sees the lame Sharif Khoon stumble into the middle of the road. Images flash through his head. Is Sharif Khoon, the hero that fearlessly fought beside the Faqir of Ipi against the British? He has no time to think about this anymore. The pounding, roaring, and shouting is fast approaching.

Aaj, Ashraf, and the other boys need to focus all their attention to fleeing, to running and, especially, not falling in the path by the camels. Fleeing not to be bitten to death by one of those hundreds of camels.

The boys run without looking back once as if their lives depended on it. Without slowing down for a moment, they sprint to the outer boundary wall of Miranshah. Panting and trembling, they fall against the outside wall. Exhausted and drenched with sweat, they look at each other. No one is caught by the camels. No one is bitten. But where is Sharif Khoon? Would he be trampled by a horde of camels or be bitten to death? Would the camel drivers club him and kick him? In the distance, the roar of the camels dies slowly. The mystical. Like an invisible hand, these sounds direct men and women to their place of prayer. Moments later, this same invisible hand brings them to their knees for ritual prayer. The imam is the leader of prayer. 'Imam' is an Arabic word which originally designated a certain leadership role within Islam. There are different views about the role and significance of the imam, but inside the largest Sunni branch, the imam is a leader in prayer, called *salat*. It is often thought that the imam is a special profession, or that he should have special training. But the ability to lead prayer is traditionally the sole criteria for being an imam. This applies to the tribal area where Ashraf lives.

In addition to the imams, there is the mullah. He is an Islamic cleric who has intensively studied the Quran, Hadith, and Fiqh. The Hadith is a collection of recorded observations about the doings and sayings of the Prophet Muhammad (PBUH), while the Fiqh is a sort of jurisprudence of Sharia, the Islamic law.

Mullahs are considered to be experts in every field that touches the Islamic faith. That also makes them an influential voice in the worldly matters.

Mullah Dindar is such a person. Today, he is headed to Miranshah. Everyone is talking about it. He is a religious figure from the Daur tribe originating from Idak. This mullah is a colorful but forceful figure. He is a slender man with dark eyes and a long, black beard. Ashraf has seen him a few times Darpa Khel. When he comes he is always heavily armed and wears ammunition belts across his body. Even so, he has a large group of guards accompanying him.

This time, Mullah Dindar is leading a *lashkar,* a large group of men assembled to fight, from Idak westward along the Tochi river. His declared mission is to enforce Sharia law along the Tochi valley. Most villages don't have problems with it and go ahead and implement Sharia law, the original Islamic law. However, not every village, family, or tribe goes along without a fight. Some refuse, and as a result a difficult and unrelenting struggle occurs between

Mullah Dindar's lashkar and the opposing village. Today, it is Miranshah Village's turn, which is a village on the North Bank of the Tochi River, over a mile to the south of Miranshah Town.

Ashraf was with Aaj and some other boys in the meadows around Darpa Khel playing when he heard the first gunshots. The boys are both scared and excited. The battle with Mullah Dindar has begun and is close. It's the middle of the summer during monsoon season. The rainy season, with lots and lots of heavy rain.

This morning, the people of Darpa Khel are preparing for the arrival of Mullah Dindar. Ashraf overhears Baba. Darpa Khel will also reject Mullah Dindar's brand of Sharia. Not because they are against Sharia, but rather, they are against the way in which this happens. A real Pashtun won't stand by and let this happen. Everyone is ready to go to battle. From a hilltop, Ashraf and Aaj watch the fighting men near the village of Miranshah. The gunshots are violent. They really cannot see it well. Occasionally they see men running to and fro. Sometimes the shooting seems to fall silent, but moments later, all hell breaks loose again, with shots and explosions occurring in rapid succession like continuous machinegun fire. When the gunfire begins to come closer, the boys rush home and barricade themselves behind the thick, high walls of the ket built by Ashraf's grandfather and granduncle, at the eastern border of Darpa Khel village.

All the men of Darpa Khel are heavily armed and stay back to defend the village in case Mullah Dindar decides to invade it. There seems no end to the struggle. Ashraf is trying to get as close as possible to the men in the village so that he can hear stories and news. The battle lasts for almost two days. Sometimes he sees the wounded or even the dead. It is an eerie sight. The limp bodies and dead eyes that see nothing any more. Gruesome wounds, bloody clothes, and then often the sounds of screaming women and children. There are casualties on both sides. Names are spoken, but Ashraf does not recognize them.

The hard, unyielding faces reveal that the men of Miranshah and Darpa Khel villages will never give up. Fear, pride, and a host of other feelings fight for first place in Ashraf's soul. Baba and Sharif Khoon have joined the men who fight against Mullah Dindar. Ashraf wants a gun. Does Aaj already have one? Probably not. Otherwise Ashraf would have already known about it. Aaj is definitely a real Pashtun warrior. He's already good at fighting, shooting and playing sports.

After fighting for two days at Miranshah Village, with dead and injured, the result of the struggle is still unclear. Mullah Dindar moves on towards Darpa Khel. But he bypasses it and moves westward along the Tochi River. Passing through some small villages, he reaches the bridge over Tochi River at Boya, about ten miles west of Darpa Khel. This bridge is guarded by the Pakistani army offshoot called the Tochi Scouts. The battle that occurs here is nothing like the battle at Miranshah Village. It is more violent and bloodier. Mullah Dindar mistook the power of this army. This short, but intense, battle claims an enormous amount of lives. Beaten, badly battered, wounded, and many dead, the fighters of Mullah Dindar give up and turn towards the Tochi Pass back to Idak. Ashraf watches from a safe distance the long procession of wounded and slain men. The surviving fighters carry the dead with them as a sad symbol of this futile struggle and stubbornness of one individual.

Every once in a while, Mullah Dindar appears on the stage. Years later, when Ashraf is an adult, Mullah Dindar ran in the parliamentary elections. He won the seat for the national assembly for North Waziristan. Soon after, stories about corruption arose. Rumors also emerged that he was supported by corrupt elements within the government, and that long ago, when he wanted to introduce Sharia law to Waziristan, it would have had the same corruption.

As a young boy, Ashraf has no knowledge of all this yet. His world begins and ends each day in Waziristan. A world where Islam reigns hand in hand with pashtunwali. A beautiful country that seems in a permanent battle between the desire for beauty, faith, and culture on one hand and the reality of violence, death, and destruction on the other. With each coming day, a fight that encroaches more and more upon the thinking and doing of Ashraf's young life.

# NAMUS

Every day, young Talibs and Charain come to the houses in Waziristan asking for food. The poor people from the countryside send their children to a *madrasa*, a religious school. They are children from families who are so poor that they do not have enough money to support them. Here, at the madrasa, these children live, sleep, eat, and study for free. It is an ancient tradition, and actually a nice solution. Each madrasa is attached to a mosque, and in Darpa Khel, several mosques have madrasas.

Until they are ten years of age, students at the madrasa are called *charain*. After the age of ten, they are referred to as *talibs*, known in the western world as Taliban. When the talibs and charains come asking for food, they always bring a basket and small bucket with them. Ashraf has often sat watching this daily ritual. In front of the gate of each house, the boys call and make themselves known, always using these same words: "Bring out the food." Like an inaudible command, the women get busy and bring food and drink to the young talibs. The basket is filled with naghn and the pot with curry. In the end, their pot is full of a miraculous mixture of all the different types of curries from the various houses.

Baba has explained it all before. Talibs eventually become mullahs, or they will do other work as soon as they are old enough. A madrasa is different from the school that Ashraf attends. At a madrasa, students learn to read the Quran, but they do not learn to write. Talibs primarily associate only with each other. Ashraf actually never plays with them. Yet, one way or another, they are inter-related and make themselves a part of the community. They are good boys who, later in life, fulfill their roles as mullahs and will play an important role in the faith and Islamic traditions of the Pashtuns.

At times, the role of the talibs in daily life is quite prominent. For example, when someone dies, they recite the Quran. And, if you'd like, when opening up a new store, you can ask them for a *khatam*, where ten or fifteen of them will read the entire Quran at the same time. It is done in an hour or so. This is meant to bring luck and prosperity.

Aday has a lot of compassion for the young charain and talibs. Ashraf likes to watch how Aday ensures that all the bowls of the young boys are filled. Ashraf has thought a lot about it. It is good to help people.

Everyone in the area knows that Baba and Aday rescue people who are struggling or who are at risk. Sometimes it is women who are being abused at home by their husbands or families. But sometimes it is widows who have sons, and the lives of these sons are being threatened by other men in the family in order to claim the family's inheritance. Ashraf has heard the conversations between Baba and Aday.

Aday always wants to help everyone and take them into her family. Baba always asks important questions about the background of the situation, and then provides people a place for them to stay and has them help with the household chores.

Sometimes the arrival of new guests is kept a secret. Because it is well known that Aday rescues women, family members searching for their missing women know that they might find them with in Ashraf's family. In cases where family members come searching for their missing women, Aday and Baba will deny that the women are with them unless the women had given prior permission to talk to their families. Usually, there would be a first meeting with Baba, where he quietly, but confidently, asks for a guarantee that the abuse will stop. In that moment, the dark, unyielding eyes of Baba cause the men to look away. Only when Baba is convinced that promise is genuine, the woman is reunited with her husband. If Baba does not believe the promise, the women stay. Sometimes for a very long time.

One woman just arrived with children. Baba sees the questioning in Ashraf's eyes. Baba looks at Ashraf for a long time and then tells him what it means for a Pashtun:

"It is the duty of every true Pashtun that he defends a woman's honor at any cost against mental and physical violence. You are a Pashtun and *namus* means you protect the honor of a woman. At any price. A Pashtun must always strive for good in thought, word, and deed. Pashtuns must behave respectfully to people, to animals, and to the environment around them. It means righteousness."

*Khegaṛa. Shegaṛa.* These are the words for righteous in Pashtu.

The conversation is over. Ashraf looks into the dark, thoughtful eyes of Baba. Namus. This is another moment when Baba's words are engraved upon his soul. Non-negotiable. He will never forget it!

# ANATKHUN LALA

Ashraf loves his mother. He has deep respect for her. He also loves the blind Khachani Meir. How often, as a child, had he sat on her lap? He also loves his sisters. As a young boy, he has grown up with a deep respect for women. Someone on the outside might misunderstand this form of respect that only seems to be understood among the deep tribal areas.

Men play a dominant role in everyday life. A role that is often exaggerated. But there is a famous saying in Islam to which the Pashtun adhere: "Heaven lies under the feet of the mother." A Pashtun keeps his mother in a very high regard. For the most part, she has control over numerous family matters and over the daily running of her household. She controls the household finances and has an overwhelming influence on the upbringing of her sons and daughters. There is no doubt that tribal women work hard. Early in the morning they are there already caring for their husband and children and late in the evening they are the last going to bed. For the most part, the women see this as a normal division of labor between men and women. Although, to the outside world, the man plays a more visible, dominant role and the women a more subordinate role, this does not mean that women do not receive respect. It is precisely the opposite. As a daughter, she is loved unconditionally. As a woman, she is deeply respected. And as mother, she is most highly revered.

The moral standard around respecting women is particularly high in the Pashtun culture. It is so high that the appreciation of a woman's beauty by someone outside of the tribal areas is not tolerated. Admiration of their women by outsiders is seen, without exception, as a gross insult to their honor. Furthermore, immoral practices such as infidelity, adultery, or the seduction of a woman is punished harshly. Even death, in such cases, is a very normal and accepted punishment.

Women also try to avoid contact with outsiders. If they happen to encounter a man in a narrow lane or road, she covers her face and quickly turns her back to him until he has passed. It is the etiquette of the Pashtun to not make eye contact with a woman. He will automatically shift his eyes downward, looking towards the ground, and take a side-step if he encounters a woman.

Women are rarely involved in tribal violence. In principle, conflicts between tribe and families and also acts of blood revenge, do not involve them. The main point with the Pashtun is that women are exempted from retaliations and vendettas. The same applies to children under the age of twelve. They are also exempt from retaliation and revenge.

The role of the women generally focuses on housework and the raising of children. Within the culture, women will not burst out laughing in the presence of outsiders or with people to whom they are not closely related. Usually they will remain in the background and will not be visible to an outsider. For a long time, it was unusual for the Pashtuns to allow girls to go to school. It had less to do with the inferiority of women, and more to do with the fear that school would have a pernicious influence on the mind of young girls.

During the time that Ashraf has grown up, many of these prejudices have disappeared. One thing Ashraf has learned is that tribal women deserve respect, and it is a sacred duty to defend their honor. Every day he observes that the women around him are diligent and dedicated. Aday and Khachani Meir are his great examples.

Most Pashtun women wear simple clothing that resemble the clothing of the men. They wear wide pants, the *partoog*, and equally wide, long shirts called a kameez. All women cover their heads with a large scarf or cloth, called a *chaddar* or *dupatta*. They love a wide variety of jewelry such as pendants, bracelets, and necklaces. Nose rings and anklets are also popular.

Ashraf has learned a lot about women and how to properly interact with them. It is important. Indeed, very important. There is one thing Ashraf does not understand. In the same ket lives a strange woman. For a long time, Ashraf even did not realize that it was a woman. Anatkhun Lala. She is middle-aged, with a short men's style hair, and she wears traditional men's clothing and a turban. She aslo carries al traditional gun and an ammunition belt over her vest. Every time Anathkun Lala comes along, Ashraf looks surprisingly and curiously at her. Yesterday, he had asked Baba, but he did not answer. According to Aaj, she is a woman, she just looks like a man. Is it really a woman who wants to be a man?

Every morning, just like the other men from Darpa Khel, she goes to Miranshah to shop. If someone gets married, she is always the one to sing. Ashraf is now certain that she is a woman who just looks like a man. Even so, she cannnot go with the men to the mosque, and she eats with the women.

This morning Aday told Ashraf that Anatkhun Lala is seriously ill. She was admitted to the hospital in Miranshah. There she stays in the women's ward. Ashraf hear the latest news from his younger brother Tarik. He is in Miranshah and went to the hospital. He heard that Anathkhun Lala got into an argument because one of the staff members addressed her as a woman while she wanted to be addressed as a man. When Tarik tells the story, the men shake their heads in silence. What is the secret of Anathkhun Lala? Ashraf can't let it go.

He decides to ask Aday. She looks seriously at Ashraf as he asks her the question. At first, it seems as though she wants to walk away without saying anything, but then she turns right to the boy and looks at him thoughtfully. It takes a long time before she answers. She looks sadly towards the ground. That is not like Aday. Then she tells her sad life story. At an early age, her parents were murdered. Anathkhun Lala was shortly after, at a very young age, forced to marry someone against her will. He was an older, cruel man who abused her for years. After a long time, she fled. She escaped the atrocities of the scoundrel who did not deserve to be called a Pashtun. But he pursued her and overtook her during her flight. Then he shot her and left her for dead. Everyone thought she was dead, and the villagers wanted to bury her, but miraculously she survived. Now she was a broken woman. Mentally and physically broken. When, after a long period of recovery, she was back on her feet, she threw out all of her woman clothes, cut her hair, and began to live as a man. She never wanted to be reminded of her old life as a woman. The pain of her past was too large for her to carry."

Aday stops her story and looked Ashraf straight on. "Son, nobody has the right to treat a woman like that."

Silent and in awe, Ashraf walks back to the mosque. He slumps to the ground with his back against the wall. Suddenly, he has even more appreciation for Baba and Aday. Suddenly he understands why there are so many women often rescued and protected by Aday. The incredibly sad feeling that had taken possession of him gives way to pride.

Ashraf watches Aday from a distance. She looks at Ashraf and smiles at him. She is not aware of what Ashraf is thinking. The secret of Anathkhun Lala. Ashraf has never loved his mother more. A broad, grateful smile appears on his large round face. His nearly black eyes shine as he lifts his hand slightly and waves to his Aday.

# BALODAI

Ashraf has been excited for a few days. It is almost time for the annual festival of the wheat harvest. It's the middle of the summer. Actually, it's a little too hot and dusty, but that's not what matters now. Ashraf is not the only one who is anxiously waiting for things to happen. Together, with a large group of boys and girls from his sub-tribe Lama Khel, they go from door to door singing songs to the other people of the tribe. Well, the boys do not actually sing at all. The girls do, while the boys protect them, like real Pashtun warriors, against the rival Balodai groups and also against guard dogs. Ashraf and his friends are armed with long sticks and surround the girls. They look dangerous and seem to be ready for every violent incident that could affect these innocent girls. It's almost disappointing that there are no fields or roads or a dog from their rival Balodai group. They sing at various people's doors, praising their men and women, and wishing them wealth, good harvest and beautiful brides, grooms and sons.

Ashraf enjoys this annual spectacle. His great feeling of responsibility to protect the girls brings him closer to his Pashtun heart.

The girls carry a large doll with them that is prepared and loaded with gold jewelry that they have borrowed from their houses. It's part of the tradition. What is means exactly, everyone seems to have forgotten. What does it matter? Ashraf doesn't feel like thinking about this any longer. The girls hop around in their beautiful traditional clothes back and forth from house to house. The boys plow through the sandy and dusty paths with the doll, doing their best to keep up with the girls.

They stop at every house in Darpa Khel. When the gate or door opens, it is an inaudible signal for the girls. Their bright, sometimes giggling, voices start, slowly but surely, to merge into a beautiful song that conjures a smile on the faces of everyone who hears it. After singing, the boys and girls get some money or wheat. Ashraf and Aaj drag along with the group, going throughout the whole village for the next few days and nights. This whole thing ends with the traditional festival with one big food item called *khoza posthi* (sweet bread). Sadly, the girls sing their last song about the doll dying. While the melancholic sounds of the song slowly fade, it seems as though everyone is drowning in a deep depression as the doll is stripped of all its decorations. When all the gold is taken from the doll and given back to people who lent it, the saddest part has been reached. And yet, happiness quickly comes! The sadness surrounding the death of the doll is quickly forgotten when, a moment later, everyone from the village is laughing and chatting incessantly about the banquet. Ashraf and Aaj stuff themselves with treats and roll rambunctiously along the ground.

The khooza posthi are made outside in in the open ground. The village's drummers have the responsibility to prepare this bread with help from others. The thin large round bread are about a meter in diameter are backed from unfermented dough on large metal sheets which are supported by a few layers of bricks. A fire, made from the wood brought from the surrounding mountains, is started beneath. When they are done baking, groups of men shred the posthi into small pieces and then spread into large round brass or aluminum flat pots which are about one to one in a half meters in diameter called *thools* or *thaals*.

Once the large thools are two-thirds full with the shredded posthi, a very liquidy curry is poured over them so that the posthi are soaked well. Meat is spread towards the periphery. Then ghee used for cooking or oil heated is poured over that. Lastly ground or powder sugar is sprinkled over in a thick layer. Now this sweet and spicy dish is ready to be had.

Men gather outside in an open space, while the women and girls stay inside. After the meal, the men start the traditional Ataan dance where the group of drummers stand in the middle, and the men make a large circle and start slowly to dance, with the circle moving anti-clockwise and the individual men dance at the same time individually in clockwise and anti-clockwise motions. Their moves get faster and faster as dictated by the drummers and towards the end, it turns into a frenzy. Then the second section of the Ataan dance starts when the drummers go to one end of the room and the men to the other end. In groups of two, starting with the most experienced dancers of the village, the men slowly and gradually move to and fro towards the drummers, getting faster as time goes on. Then another group of dancers start. During this portion of the dance, people also pour money over the dancers and the drummers. All the money though goes to the drummer's reserve. The girls also dance and sing inside.

Some of the men are sitting on the *charpais*, the wooden beds. A soft snore betray that a few have fallen asleep. A few men sit together and whisper something over and over again. The smoke from the water pipe spirals slowly into the night on the way to an unknown destination. Baba looks serious. But why?

Ashraf is thoroughly enjoying himself, and it is sad that the party is almost over. When the banquet is almost over, and the first people begin to leave, Ashraf shuffles towards Baba. The men lie and sit in a large circle with the sad remnants of the once-lavish delicacies in the middle. Ashraf crawls against Baba. Silently and unnoticed, he curls up on a pillow next to Baba's broad, strong back. He heard the men talking about the battle between Darpa Khel and the Bura Khel tribe. Nearly a hundred years ago, some people of the Bura Khel tribe arrived in Baba's village, Darpa Khel. They asked the elders for permission to allow their camels and cattle to graze in the Danday fields north of the village at a place called Taabai. They got permission, so they put down their tents down and stayed there. During the last hundred years, the tents disappeared, and the Bura Khel built houses and turned the place into a village called Taabai, and the residents are now called Taabiwool. One of the men in the circle raised his voice, "Now they seem to be taking over the whole area." His eyes spit fire. Here and there, sleeping men wake up and come closer. Everyone talks together. Another is told the whole story, and then another, and another. Clearly what happened was against all the wishes of the Darpa Khel residents. The typical steadfastness and stubbornness that is such a part of the Pashtun people, rose up in every man. Baba looks thoughtful, but is not saying much. It is around 1965, and on this Balodai evening, it has been decided that the whole Taabiwool people of the Bura Khel tribe must leave the area.

The days go by as if nothing special is going on. The men are meeting more often than usual, and sometimes there are sounds of heated discussions. First, the leaders of the Bura Khel tribe are asked nicely to leave, but when they indicate that they are not intending to leave, the atmosphere changes rapidly. In the following days, the village elders of Darpa Khel come together a few times to discuss it. It is not long before the decision is made to go to battle against the Bura Khel. Every home must provide at least one fighter.

In a few days, everything has changed. The fighters gather on higher ground. Baba is the only one in the village with a car, a brown Opel with the unforgettable registration number BU38. He needs his car to supply the fighters. From the upper area, is a road to the village. The road is just outside the village at the base of a small mountain called Tarakai-saar. Ashraf has been one time with Baba and has seen a multi-colored Bedford truck being loaded with *naghaans* by people from the village.

Naghaan is traditional bread in Waziristan. It is a kind of bread that, unlike naan, is baked on a stone plate and not in a tandoor. The tandoor is used in Pakistan and is a kind of oven with a hole in it where, in a special way, the bread is spread against the inside walls of the oven, and then baked. It is a beautiful sight to look at, but not here in Waziristan. Here, the naghaan, is baked on a stone slab. The dough for the bread is made from wheat flour usually the night before and left to ferment. Ashraf, Aaj, and the other boys from the village have to help carry the bread. Women bake the bread and the boys and men walk the baskets to Tarakai-saar, to the beautiful multi-colored Bedford truck. Ashraf finds it exciting. It is the first time he really helps in battle, even if it is only helping with the supplies for the warriors. That truck looks so strange with all that nagaahn.

The fight that follows is like any battle in Waziristan. Hard, grim, and violent. There are dead and wounded on both sides. A cousin of Baba, Malik Akhbar Khan, son of Uncle Barkat Shah, is also injured. Ashraf and Aaj look curiously but also with dismay at the huge amount of blood. Akhbar Khan is a malik, a village elder. He was hit by a bullet. Baba takes him as soon as possible to the hospital in Miranshah. The doctors look worrisome at the huge wound caused by the bullet. They shake their heads. They cannot help him. Baba has that unyielding look in his eyes again. He does not give up and takes his cousin to a hospital in Bannu. They are more optimistic and able to surgically remove the bullet from his body. Ashraf and Aaj whisper to each other. Aaj is talking a lot about the brave warriors, the heroes, that manage to drive away the men of the Bura Khel tribe through a hail of bullets. Aaj would prefer going to help the battle. Though be it with his slingshot. Ashraf doubts. On the one hand, he wants to be like Aaj. As soon as possible, he wants a large gun with even larger ammunition belts and to join the brave warriors from the village. On the other hand, he thinks about the doctor in Bannu. The man who has saved Uncle Akhbar Khan by removing the bullets from his body.

The battle between the Darpa Khel and Bura Khel tribes continue unabated. None of the stubborn Pashtuns know when to stop and admit defeat. Then the Pakistani government intervenes. They mobilize village elders and tribal elders from other villages in order to urge both parties to peace. A jirga follows.

Both warring parties must cease fire and agree to a ceasefire and give a large quantity of weapons as collateral. Ashraf tries to follow the conversations. He does not understand many things at all, but it is his first experience with corruption. The Bura Khel tribe bribes the government officals, who, as a gesture of thanks, give them a big portion of the Dandey, the area that is the main issue of the conflict.

Grinding their teeth, the residents of Darpa Khel observe these developments. Sometimes Baba talks with the other men of the village about the corruption. Ashraf can hear pent-up anger and frustration in his voice. According to Baba, corruption destroys everything that is good and beautiful. He says corruption is the worst and most dangerous poison that threatens humanity and the world. Piercingly, he looks at Ashraf. A real Pashtun never does that, never ever partakes in corruption. Again, those same dark, unyielding eyes ensure that this lesson will forever be etched in his memory.

# THE DAMOON AND DRUMS

Thankfully, there are times when there is no fighting. In the villages in Waziristan, most conflicts are resolved through a meeting of the maliks and elders. At such a meeting, called a maraka or jirga, other people come to watch and listen. Many Pashtuns do that. It is a popular form of entertainment and also a form of involvement and education. Everyone gets informed about all the latest news from Waziristan.

Uncle Barkat Shah is one of these wise maliks. He often narrates history and storytells in order to arrive at a solution of the conflict. Every time, Ashraf is impressed by the wise men of the maraka. Although most maliks are illiterate, they prove themselves again and again to be wise and prudent. They are wiser than many people who have studied long and hard. Wisdom and intellect are two very different things. Baba has said that before, but it has been proven again and again by the marakas. Also during this maraka, Uncle Barkat Shah sits in a circle and gives his opinions about all kinds of situations. Ashraf understands that these discussions and decisions can save lives during a conflict.

Ashraf always tries to be present at a maraka when he is on school vacation. Every conflict, every discussion, and every conclusion, fascinates him. After hearing the story of the conflict, a wise malik will start to talk about a random situation. In the beginning, Ashraf always thinks that the malik does not understand the issue, but as he continues to talk, he gradually comes to the current conflict.

Baba's uncle, Barkat Shah, is known by the name of Ket Baba, Ket being the name of the large housing compound with the huge walls that was built by him and his brother Malik Ahmed Khan, Baba's father. According to Sharif Khoon, Uncle Barkat Shah is the most respected malik throughout Waziristan. He has a great beard that has been dyed black and the scent of snuff always surrounds him. The huge pistol that he always carries makes him seem very impressive and dignified. Uncle Barkat Shah does not say much, but when he speaks, everyone is highly focused on his words. In that sense, he seems a bit like Baba. There is always a large group of men carrying rifles and ammunition belts surrounding their vests. Uncle Barkat Shah never carries a rifle, but always a big pistol. He walks with a cane because he thinks that is fitting for his stature. Sharif Khoon has said that he really does not need that stick at all. Whenever Uncle Barkat Shah is visiting, Ashraf tries to see and hear him. It never takes long before Uncle Barkat Shah inhales a big sniff of tobacco powder called *naswar*. A sniff of naswar gives a special sensation to the body, where, after inhalation, it feels as though your nose is traveling through your whole body. You can't detect this happening with Uncle Barkat Shah. One only notices the typical sweet, and a little sickly, scent that always lingers around him. Even if he has been gone for hours, this distinct scent remains in the air, as if it has trouble saying goodbye.

Uncle Barkat Shah, like Baba, also has a day house in Miranshah. The boys call this day house Bangla. Before Baba had his own day house, he shared Bangla. Bangla is more of a large roof terrace above the shops in the middle of the bazaar, with four rooms and a kitchen. One can stand on the terrace against a small wall and look down the various tributaries of the bazaar and the hustle bustle going on. It is always enjoyable to stand over there and watch. There are large, impressive woven Iranian and Afghani carpets on the floor accompanied by many cushions.

Uncle Barkat Shah also has a fixed routine that resembles that of Baba. Every morning, Uncle Barkat Shah receives people at the day house who want his opinions and judgments regarding business and personal matters. Afterwards, he always goes to Miranshah Qila, north of Miranshah, where the government officials reside and where the Tochi Scouts are stationed. After visiting the officials, he returns to Bangla for lunch and then for a nap. Then he receives people again and then goes back to Darpa Khel in order to be home in time for the late afternoon prayer.

While Baba is still talking with Uncle Barkat Shah, they hear the first sound of the damoon drumming. Ashraf recognizes the sounds of the drums even now, though the sound is faint. It's an emergency. Ashraf climbs the roof of his house and in the distance he sees smoke in the air, down in Darpa Khel village. He screams, "Fire! Fire! Hear the damoon drumming! Fire! Fire!" A few seconds later everyone runs towards the fire to help put it out.

It is cold outside and Ashraf quickly grabs his brown *chadar* from the ground. A chadar is a type of garment made from cotton or wool and wraps around the body and is used in many ways. Chadars for summer are made from cotton. Chadars for winter are made from wool. Ashraf's chadar comes from the Swat Valley, which lies in the north between Pakistan and Afghanistan. They make beautiful chadars of good quality there. Everyone in Waziristan uses his chadar to dry his face after washing, for prayer, and also to sit on, to eat on, or to wrap around himself when he is sitting outside relieving his bowels. This time, Ashraf uses his chadar for protection against the cold. Along with the men, he helps extinguish the fire. Buckets of water are passed, and men try with sand and other things to get the fire under control.

Exhausted, the men stare at each other with black faces. It is an unfair fight. The fire has, in no time, destroyed the house. Disappointed, the men and boys stand around the charred remains of what was once someone's pride and joy. Fortunately, the surrounding houses were spared. A few elderly men stand together and deliberate what to do with the family that now has nothing. The busy chatter and even busier hand gestures suddenly fall silent. The problem is solved. Ashraf and Aaj want to know what will happen but everyone is silent. Soon after, peace has returned. Ashraf puts his now black, smokey, stinking chadar back on the ground. Aday will probably see if it can still be cleaned.

Some days later the damoon drums sound again. This time it is not an emergency. It is a call for the annual dredging of the canal. The irrigation canal accumulates mud, and once a year every household sends someone to help dredge the canal. This calls for the use of special tools. The damoon beat the drums with a rhythm that sounds quite different from the rhythms that signal a fire or a call for chasing thieves and robbers. While Uncle Barkat Shah and Baba are still talking about the big and small problems in Waziristan, Ashraf is listening to the increasing rhythm of the drumming by the damoons who are trying to energize those who must clear the canal. Along with Aaj, they slip through the large gate to the outside. It is nice to see the hard working men in the river who are gladly excited by the drums. They work hard, but there is also a smattering of laughter. The strange throbbing rhythm of the drums makes this hard work a wonderful, festive affair.

As night falls, the drums are silenced, making room for the night sound. More and more, Ashraf starts to love all these known and lesser-known sounds in Waziristan. More and more he sees, he understands the beauty of his country, people, his faith, and his culture. At the same time, he also learns to understand the occasional darker side of Waziristan. Gradually and unintentionally, Ashraf departs from the innocence of his little childhood and becomes injected into the reality of the complex and hard, but also strangely righteous, life in this unique part of the world.

# LANDAA & MICHAGHNAA

Even though there is a large orchard of various fruit trees surrounding Baba's house, and Baba almost always goes daily to Miranshah to get fresh fruit, Aaj and Ashraf regularly go out together to steal fruit from other people's orchards. Though it is not necessary, the boys theorize that a real Pashtun must do brave things every once in a while. Around the orchards are often high fences topped with sharp objects. Aaj is very agile and is a master at climbing walls and fences.

Like always, Aaj also goes first this time. Just like accomplished robbers and burglars, they climb over the high walls, pick the fruit, vanish, and find a quiet place to eat and talk about their heroic deeds. Usually it goes well. Sometimes they get spotted, but they are a faster and always manage to escape. Ashraf knows that if they are caught, the owner will recognize them and later confront Baba about it. But the excitement and fun outweigh the risk of punishment and Baba's dark glaring looks. It is going well. Nobody sees the two boys and later they will sit and feast. It was almost too easy.

Aaj has gotten his slingshot back. The adventure with the camel is far behind them, so they can start again with their numerous experiments. It is spring, and it is nice to try and shoot birds from the air or from a tree. Again, Aaj is the best. He always has the best slingshot. Baba has forbidden the shooting of birds. He considers it cruel and unnecessary. Ashraf's shrug was almost undetectable, but Baba caught it. He softly and ominously called Ashraf's name and just stared at him until Ashraf averted his eyes and bowed his head.

There are two types of slingshots. There is the *landaa*, the traditional slingshot, and the *michaghnaa*, which is a sling where you put a stone in, swing it around, and then release one end which releases the stone into the air.

The boys mostly make the landaa slingshots themselves. First they cut a nice Y-shaped acacia branch and then tie the two top points together. Then they light a fire and hold the tied branches in the smoke. This makes the branches hard. Then they can untie the points, cut into proper size and what's left is a perfect slingshot frame. They call the frame of the slingshot *khasnaai*. The boys then fasten a piece of rubber on each side of the frame and then tie a piece of leather between them, called *guthmaai*.

The boys use round stones and clay balls for the ammunition of the landaa. With the michaghnaa slingshot, they use all sorts of stones. The michaghnaa is by far the most dangerous slingshot because the stones can launch from the sides if the shooter is not adept at using it.

Sometimes Aaj and Ashraf go to an old woman who makes very good small round slingshots, like small canon balls, for them. She does this in exchange for the birds that they shoot and kill. Baba has said that it is unnecessary and cruel to kill birds, but those words don't apply now. Naturally, he cannot take the dead birds home because Baba has expressly forbidden the shooting of birds and other animals. But now Aaj can take the slingshots and give the dead birds to the old woman. These smart Pashtun boys think they can solve all adult problems in this manner.

Sweat drips from the boys' faces. It is hard to hit the birds that fly over the meadows. So Ashraf tries to drive the birds into the trees while Aaj crawls as close as possible to the trees. Ashraf knows this ritual like no other. Once Aaj is under a bird and takes out his slingshot, the bird is doomed. Aaj is so good with the slingshot. Less than two seconds later, the bird falls dead out of the tree. Triumphantly, the boys bring the bird to the old woman.

Ashraf is proud of his friend Aaj. Sometimes they fight with other groups of children in the village. They use their slingshots to chase these children away. Thanks to Aaj and the fact that Ashraf's ket just outside Darpa Khel is on higher ground, they almost always win against the other guys.

Aaj and Ashraf are in a good mood. Waziristan taunts them with all its birds and wild animals that just seem to be waiting to be caught or slain by these young hunters. They quickly decide to go on the hunt for quail. The major population of quail originates from Russia, Siberia and other Central Asian states and moves towards the warmer regions of the world, including Pakistan and the tribal areas. The migrant birds are usually hunted with the help of big nets and a recording of their own voice. Sometimes people keep quails as pets and breed them round the year and then hang them in their cages at specific places where migratory birds would come.

The quails are normally found in the corn field, but it is difficult to shoot them. Aaj picks up a large net from his house. Over the course of time, they have developed a perfect method to catch quail. Quickly and methodically, they hang the net on one edge of the corn field and then go hunting from the opposite side by herding the quails rowing a rope over the cornplants. This is their lucky day because not too much later there are three quails entangled in the net. Aaj decides to take two quails home to eat. They keep the other one alive to use in future quail fights. Unlike cockfighting, quails do not fight to the death, but rather until one of them flees. The boys have more quails which they have caught and keep them in Kurarai cages made from some type of reed. Some of these cages are very nicely decorated.

Aaj and Ashraf are excited today. After quail-hunting, they quickly make a blowpipe made from the Wala tree branch. It's apparent that they have done this hundreds of times. Each grab a branch from the tree and beat gently on the bark until its skin is loose from the bark. Gently, they pull out the inner layer and then use the outer skin as a blowpipe which just looks like soft drink straw. They quickly run to the wheat field and search for the bragatai. It is another small bird that can only really be caught if the wheat is quite high. The male bragatee birds are the most beautiful, with black and white wings, a white brown chest, and a black head with white stripes. The females are dull gray. The boys know that the bragatee cannot be shot with a blowpipe, but they try anyway. Rather this bird can be caught with an ingenious trap made of a long stick with a sharp point. A kind of mousetrap which entangles the legs of the bragatee. Such a trap is called a *landekai*. Ashraf can also never take home a landakai because Baba must not know that he is trying to capture birds. Fortunately, Aaj always take that kind of stuff to his own house.

The boys wander home. It's late, and they have hunted enough. The bragatee has been forgotten. Tired and happy, the boys walk towards their houses in the ket. The beautiful life in Waziristan seems to smile at them.

Just before the ket's gate, two large rough-looking men forcefully push the boys aside. They hurriedly walk down towards the main Darpa Khel village. Their dark turbans, heavy weapons, and large ammunition belts stocked with bullets make the two young hunters anxiously recoil. The men have a wild look in their eyes. They are dirty and look hungry and tired. The boys have never seen these men before. From a distance, the boys keep watching and follow them. Then the men quickly slip inside to the ket of Ashraf's maternal uncle, Malik Zamin Dar Khan, down in Darpa Khel.

It soon becomes clear. It is the pashtunwali, the unwritten laws of the Pashtun people. *Panah*. They ask for protection. Baba explained it long time ago. Panah is to take someone in personal protection. Even if a notorious criminal or an outlaw asked for panah he will definitely be granted asylum and duly protected. In the tribal areas it happened that the man, who had just committed a murder, asked for panah from one of the powerful families, and they had to give him. During panah he enjoyed equal rights and status.

The men are also from a powerful and known family of Bannu. They are fleeing because they killed many people from another family. Their names are Sheroon and Khesroon. They are not fleeing from the victims' family, rather they are fleeing from the police. They fled to Waziristan because the police will not be able to follow them there. In Waziristan, there is no police. Instead, there applies the unwritten laws of the Pashtun people, pashtunwali. According to the code of nanawatai, Ashraf's family must offer them shelter. Nanawatai is a sort of honor code whereby Pashtuns help protect each other against their enemies. Baba has explained this to Ashraf several times.

Ashraf's uncle asks the men a few critical questions. Then he lets them inside. Nanawatai. The two men will have shelter, food, and protection for a long time. In due course the men will participate and help in various chores and tasks in order to pay a little compensation for their long stay. Ashraf does not find out exactly why they had killed somebody.

Did it involve the relationship between a boy and girl? If the relationship becomes known, the girl's family will ask the family of the boy to let him marry her. If the boy's family refuses, the girl's family will kill both the boy and the girl. This is to save the nang, the honor, of the family. He heard this once from Sharif Khoon. Could this be the case with these two men? Have they killed the boy and girl in order to save the nang of the family? Ashraf does not know.

He stares at the dark sky. Baba has explained it all. He has forbidden him to shoot birds. He considers it unnecessary and cruel. He has also explained pashtunwali. There is no place in the world where the crime rate is so low. Blood revenge, honor, and protection go hand in hand. Over the years, the Fakir of Ipi has disappeared from the thoughts of Ashraf. Instead, the struggle to understand the beautiful and dark sides of life in Waziristan has taken over.

# HALF A RUPEE

For years, Ashraf firmly believed in this mythical night called Shaqadra. Legend has it that on one night every year, there is a moment when everything turns upside down. When this happens, you can wish for anything you want, and all your wishes will come true. The children eagerly wait for the moment when everything turns upside down, and they do everything they can to stay awake as long as possible. Their families help them. Eventually, they fall asleep and miss the big moment, again. That great, magical moment.

Ashraf doesn't believe in it anymore, and he realizes that he is getting older. There are things of his childhood that can never come back. Never again will he wait for that great, magical moment of Shaqadra. Nevertheless, the day before the party is no less fun. The anxious faces of the smaller children put a smile on his face, and, if just for a moment, he doubts again. But soon, his knowledge overtakes the magic of the moment.

Now that Ashraf is older, he will occasionally go with his cousin, Farid Khan, son of Malik Akbar Khan, to the bazaar in Darpa Khel to buy a slingshot, kite, or candy. He pays either with cash or with wheat, since wheat is also an accepted means of payment in North Waziristan.

Ashraf goes with his cousin to buy from Taif Shah the shopkeeper. The shopkeeper is a smiling, friendly Pashtun who does not take life too seriously. He enjoys every day and makes a small chat with everyone. He has delicious candy that the boys go crazy for. Today Ashraf doesn't have any money or wheat with him. Farid has a few rupees in his pocket. Farid knows what he wants. Candy. He digs into the pocket of his kameez. He looks, counts, and looks again. Again he asks the smiling Taif Shah what the candy will cost. For the fourth time, the shopkeeper states the amount. Farid counts the money in his hand one last time. He has half a rupee too little. With big sad eyes, he looks at the shopkeeper. "May I get a half rupee credit?" he asks with an insecure tone in his voice. His eyes goes from the shopkeeper to the candy.

Taif Shah looks at the boy gravely. "Half a rupee credit, eh?" He looks as though he is deciding about three years' salary. Tension hangs in the air, but then he emits a deep sigh. "Come on, then, half a rupee credit. But you will repay, eh?" Farid nods quickly and pushes the money into the hands of the shopkeeper while, with his other hand, he snatches the candy from the narrow counter. It worked. They have candy. Laughing and clowning around, the boys walk through the narrow streets of Darpa Khel.

Farid does not pay back the half rupee. At the moment he doesn't have the money to pay. From that day on, he takes a detour when he comes near Taif Shah's shop. Weeks, months, even years later, Farid still takes a detour as he walks to the bazaar in Darpa Khel, hoping Taif Shah will not see him. Over time, everyone in the ket knows this story. Farid is plagued almost daily with jokes that Taif Shah the shopkeeper is still looking for him and has even been waiting at his front door. Farid always smiles back in a friendly manner whenever jokes are made about his half-rupee debt. He never says anything in response though.

Years and years later, Farid has become a well known surgeon and earns a lot of money, and yet he is still the victim of the same jokes. But is it true that that half rupee was never paid back and Taif Shah is still looking for the man whom he long ago lent half a rupee?

There are more beautiful stories in Darpa Khel, old stories that men tell each other when they sit together in the dark evenings of Waziristan. There is a very old story about when Sharif Khoon was young. One of the older men wants to tell this story, and Ashraf is listening along together with the other men and young boys in the courtyard. It is an amazing story about Sharif Khoon that happened long begore Ashraf was even born. The storyteller looks very serious when he begins.

"It happened many many years ago. When I was near my home, I saw Sharif Khoon walking. He looked orderly. His neat, white salwar kameez and beautiful turban caught my eyes. The donkey trudging beside him looked strange. All the men and women who were at the village at that moment could not pinpoint what it was, but something was not right. They all looked at Sharif Khoon. Then he disappeared from sight. Some of the men followed him quickly in the direction where they last saw him on the road. There he was, standing near a group of some older boys. His shoulders looked wider and his chin proudly protruded out from his body. He stomped proudly along with the boys. The donkey was strangely decorated. Bewildered, the men's eyes focused on the legs of the donkey. They stared in disbelief, first at the donkey, then at Sharif Khoon. The donkey had been immaculately cleaned and now lumbered along with his head down behind Sharif Khoon. His front legs, down to his feet, were decorated with many, many watches."

The story teller stops and looks around. The older boys are

laughing and joking. Ashraf and Usman look at each other in amazement. They know Sharif Khoon. There is only one man in the world who was able do to something like this. They shake their heads, grab each other's hands and, laughing, walk back to their house.

# HAJI SALEHDIN

Haji Salehdin lives at Ashraf's house. He is the elder brother of Ashraf's mother. Haji Salehdin has inherited a lot of land near Boya in Lund Village, about fifteen miles to the west of Miranshah, which is near the border of Afghanistan. The land is beautiful and fruitful. However, Haji Salehdin resides the vast majority of the time at Baba's house. Every year he sells his country harvest, often long before it can be harvested. With his earnings, he goes traveling a few times a year. For about ten days, he treks through several towns and cities on a pilgrimage, visiting the holy shrines. When it is time for his return, everyone is on the lookout because he is always bringing back wonderful gifts.

Ashraf likes to sit by Haji Salehdin when they eat. He is always telling jokes. Before they are even sitting down, the jokes have already begun. After breakfast, Haji Salehdin usually goes out of the ket into the fields and sits on one of the few spots on the pathway to Miranshah and tries to entice someone on their way to sit and gossip with him. Towards midday he walks towards the day house where he will have lunch and have mischievous exchanges with Makan, the cook. Then he will take a nap until the early afternoon prayers which he performs in the main mosque near the day house. After the prayers, he comes back to the day house to have a cup of tea. Everyday he brings messages from Ashraf's house for various items that he needs to take back with him. But before he heads back to Ashraf's ket, he goes through the Miranshah bazaar and sits for a while at one of the tea houses where he chats with various people and gets up-to-date with all the latest news. Loaded with all this information and news, he takes the daily grocery items back to the Ashraf's house where he will, again, take a cup of tea and head for one of the spots on the pathway and try to enlighten others with the news and information he has gathered in Miranshah bazaar. Because of this habit, he has naturally become the messenger between Ashraf's ket near Darpa Khel and the day house in Miranshah.

Aday gives Haji Salehdin a shopping list almost every day when he goes from the Darpa Khel to Miranshah. Haji Salehdin faithfully gives this shopping list to Makan the cook who takes care of buying the groceries every day. This system results in fresh vegetables and meats being purchased in Miranshah and therefore good, healthy, fresh vegetables and meats are eaten every evening.

But as simple as this system seems, it is not. Haji Salehdin is not an easy and funny Pashtun to everyone. He has a unique and strange habit to completely ignore people that he does not like. He simply does not talk to them. Even if they say something to him, he acts as if the words are just air. He especially does not like his relatives from his Lund Village to visit the day house in Miranshah or Ashraf's ket near Darpa Khel. He enjoys peace, and if many guests come into the day house, it is a recipe for a disaster. Haji Salehdin tends to act quite unpredictably in such circumstances. What he will do, no one knows, but it will be something strange for sure. Ashraf loves these surprises.

Today Haji Salehdin quarreled with Pirgai, his nephew from Lund Village. No one knows why. When Pirgai entered the day house, he greeted everyone with the words "As-salamu alaykum." Everybody replied with "Wa alaykumu salam." Nothing seemed wrong. Without looking, Haji Salehdin pensively rubbed his gray beard and muttered automatically, "Wa alaykumu salam" as well.

Then, completely unexpectedly, he jumped to his feet as if stung by a wasp. His head was red and his eyes were spitting fire. He looked at the unsuspecting Pirgai as though he were about to attack him. Then he seemed to change his mind. "No wa alaykumu salam!" he cried while spit flew from his mouth onto the face of Pirgai. Pirgai shrank back a bit and looked surprised. "No wa alaykumu salam. No wa alaykumu salam." Then, with an uncontrolled jerk, Haji Salehdin turned and stormed furiously out of the day house. For almost a minute, an uncomfortable silence remained in the large room. Then there was an enormous explosion of laughter that was so loud that it reached Haji Salehdin all the way outside.

The following day, something happened again. Ashraf was bored while sitting in the day house, that is, until the moment when Haji Salehdin arrived. Haji Salehdin and Makan the cook have a complicated relationship and often have complicated interactions. So complicated that they become angry for weeks and no longer talk to one another. Ashraf is already relishing in the hope that something interesting will also happen this time. He knows that Baba can get really angry when these old, stubborn men argue about childish stuff. When these two don't talk to each other, all sorts of things go wrong, for Haji Salehdin is the daily messenger between Aday and Makan the cook for the daily provisions.

The two men are, again, not talking with each other for some time. Haji Salehdin has found a solution. His pearly white salwar kameez, his dark turban, and his black dyed beard give him a strange appearance today. Like a big Pashtun ruler, he comes with his head into the kitchen. Makan looks up and says nothing. The men have not been talking to each other for days, and so also not today. Haji Salehdin solemnly walks to the big white wall. As if

Makan is air, he ignores him and doesn't give him the time of day. When he arrives at the wall, he has a friendly smile on his face, like he has just met up with an old acquaintance. "As-salamu alaykum, Wall." He seems to be waiting for a reply from the wall, but instead he mumbles the shopping list and tells the wall all the groceries that need to be purchased for the village house. After a friendly nod to the wall, Haji Salehdin stately turns back around and leaves the day house, all without giving Makan a glance. Ashraf looks at him with his mouth wide open. Makan acts as if this was the most normal thing in the world and says nothing. He goes about his work, unfazed. Shaking his head, Ashraf leaves the kitchen. He must make sure he is there this afternoon when Haji Salehdin comes to pick up the groceries. He must know how this ends.

The day flies by, and Ashraf has made himself comfortable in the kitchen. With his back against the wall, he is extremely happy in anticipation for the second part of this Pashtun theater performance. In the late afternoon, Haji Salehdin enters. Makan is still at work, and both men walk stoically passed each other and completely ignore one another. Without giving Makan a glance, Haji Salehdin looks around the room, apparently irritated. Makan walks to the big white wall that, this morning, Haji Salehdin had spoken to. "As-salamu alaykum, Wall," mutters Makan in a dark voice. Then he rattles off the list of groceries and asks the wall to take it to the village house. Haughtily, and without a word, Haji Salehdin takes the groceries and walks out of the kitchen. The two men don't look each other in the eyes at all, not for a single moment.

Surprised, Ashraf looks again towards the disappearing Haji Salehdin and the imperturbable Makan who has just continued to move on with his daily work as if nothing has happened. Shaking his head, Ashraf walks out. He has never seen so much stubbornness in his young life. Then, a broad smile appears on his face. Actually, those crazy, stubborn old men are very amusing.

Baba is not as amused with this though. He is done, and not for the first time. These stubborn attitudes infuriate him. Whenever Baba argues with Haji Salehdin, Haji Salehdin flees angrily to his home in Lund. Then, after a few weeks, he is suddenly at the door and wants to speak with Aday. He tells her that he only came to check if everything is well with the family. This is all an unwritten ritual with Haji Salehdin. Aday asks him, like a pre-rehearsed play, if he would please come back because everyone misses him so much. And how big is the surprise when, every time, after some fabricated unwillingness, he appears remorseful and returns to normal life in Darpa Khel.

But this time Baba is angry in a different way. In addition to the silliness between the two, Baba is convinced that Haji Salehdin is sick. He coughs a lot and everyone is afraid that he has tuberculosis. Haji Salehdin knows that people with tuberculosis are ostracized out of fear of contamination. That is reason enough for him to not go to a doctor. This way, the doctor cannot diagnose him with tuberculosis and as a result, nobody will have to avoid him like the plague. That is his clear, but simple, explanation. Meanwhile, the cough is getting worse, and is sounding more like the barking of a mad, wild dog.

Baba is tired and angry. He wants, at all costs, for Haji Salehdin to see a doctor. It is one of the few times that Ashraf has witnessed Baba loose his temper. He roars angrily at Haji Salehdin, saying that he is the stubbornest Pashtun in the history of Waziristan, and if he does not go to a doctor, he will infect the entire village with tuberculosis.

The obstinate Haji Salehdin clenches his fists, stumbles over a tree root in fury, and stomps with great strides across the courtyard toward the gate. The women are startled. They have gathered around the corner of the house and look curiously at Baba roaring and angrily pounding away at Haji Salehdin. Again, the old, stubborn, harshly opinionated Haji Salehdin runs away to his home in Lund. But Baba does not leave it at that. After a few days of pacing back and forth, Baba gathers some things together. He goes after Haji Salehdin to his house in Lund.

In Lund, Baba finds Haji Salehdin gravely ill, lying on a wooden charpais in the corner of his house. His breathing rattles, fast and irregularly. His face has an unhealthy bright red color, and the sweat shines peculiarly in the incoming sunlight upon his face. The trip from Darpa Khel to Lund has robbed Haji Salehdin of his last strength. Without a struggle, Baba takes him to Miranshah to get treated for tuberculosis. Suddenly, Haji Salehdin seems years and years older than what he really is. His narrow, sunken face with his gray beard and dark circles around his eyes give him the appearance of a fragile old man. It takes a few weeks before Haji Salehdin gets a little better. He, himself, speaks nothing of it. His hard, hallow coughing becomes a less severe cough. The color in his face slowly comes back, and the black bags under his eyes disappear. The whole incident seems to go past him. He gives no response to anyone who asks about his health. From the first day, he speaks not a word about it to anyone. Not even Baba.

Ashraf gives Haji Salehdin a firm handshake when, after a long time, he comes home again. Again, just like before, Ashraf directly starts laughing. Haji Salehdin feels, for the thousandth time, that Ashraf may be missing a bone in his thumb. He does that with everyone. Long ago, he heard that there will come a holy man called Khizer, and by him you may wish anything you want. And that holy man? He will be recognized by a missing bone, just above his thumb.

# PESHAWAR

The years pass. Ashraf grows into a teenager. He becomes increasingly inducted into the secrets of the Pashtun culture and its intertwining rules and traditions with Islam. Baba has taught him, but the additional lessons from the imam, the mullahs and his tutors have polished his thoughts and actions and built an indestructible foundation for the rest of his life.

Step by step, grows an awareness in him that the God of the Muslims is both transcendent and personal. During this process of character refinement, Ashraf learns to pray. Five times a day may seem like a lot, but together, these prayers take no more than an hour. Muslims do not see this requirement as a burden. It's quite the contrary. They give God an hour of their day back, realizing that Allah has given them twenty-four hours to begin with. Prayer is an opportunity to join others in the immediate presence of God and to communicate with him without any interference. The five times of worship are in the early morning, the middle of the day, the afternoon, the evening, and during the night.

Parallel to these issues of faith and culture is the unfolding of the daily routines in Darpa Khel and Miranshah. After the early prayer, the entire family will have breakfast. Then they will wash, change clothes, and then head to the day house in Miranshah. There they pick up their books and go to school. Ashraf remembers his first day of school precisely. Full of uncertainty, he wondered what he was doing among these strange children. They sat upon mats on the ground, and when it got too hot inside the classroom, they all moved to the outside.

His third-grade teacher was Khan Mohammad Ustaad. *Ustaad* is the Pashtun word for teacher. He was a very nice man. However, the boys were, at times, able at to push him to his limits. If Khan Mohammad Ustaad found it necessary to discipline the boys, he would, pinch the skin around their navels and would, without hesitation, turn it around hard.

His fourth grade teacher was Khunam Gul Ustaad. He was also a very nice man who was very dedicated to his work. He had a strange way of disciplining though. When Ashraf thinks back to those times, a painful grimace appears on his face. The normally friendly, kind teacher would roughly grab the hand of the student to be punished and would wrestle a pencil between his fingers. A few seconds later, he would unmercifully squeeze this hand until the student would scream out of pain or tears would stream down his cheeks. Ashraf didn't know what was worse, the pencil or having his navel tweaked.

However, the discipline and pain were quickly forgotten as soon as the school day ended, and they would go to buy some candy. Every day, an old woman would sit near the school and sell homemade dry, thin-layered caramel, called *paaprri*, in a large shallow round pan. Baba had forbidden them to spend money on those caramels.

Luckily Baba was not always there to watch the boys. He was often busy receiving people in the house. Frequently, their impressive collection of porcelain tableware was brought out for lunch time to serve notables or members of the government who visited him. Every now and then, a big lunch for many people was made. Ashraf found those lunches wonderful, especially when important people were visiting. Such people included the Division Commissioner who was responsible for all of Waziristan and Bannu. In addition to the commissioner, other higher military and civil government officials, doctors, headmasters and elders from other tribes came.

But all this was already in the past for the growing Ashraf. Now that he is older, Baba takes him every two weeks to Bannu and a few times a year to Peshawar and perhaps maybe even to Lahore. They travel along long and arduous roads in Baba's car. Ashraf sees the envious glances of the men and boys from the village. Baba is still nearly the only one in the area with a car. Even the administrator, a highly ranked official of the Pakistani government, occasionally borrows Baba's car if he wants to take a trip with his family to Bannu. Baba goes from Miranshah to Bannu, where Baba possesses a large building compound that is filled with shops that he rents out. Above this building is a living area that he uses when he is in town. Sometimes, if they do some shopping in Bannu, they will even sleep there.

Proudly, Ashraf looks to Baba sitting behind the wheel, as a huge cloud of dust kicks up behind them as they leave behind North Waziristan. With these rides, Ashraf seems to become carefully detached from his familiar and protected world in Waziristan. These new experiences are like bricks being laid upon the firm foundation of the Islamic and Pashtun traditions.

There are two good hotels in Peshawar. Baba often stays at the Greens Hotel with Ashraf and his older brother Usman. Ashraf likes to sit on the balcony of the hotel to look at Sadar Road. There are the frequent passing of nicely decorated *tangas*, horse driven carts.

People sit on the front and back seats of the tangas while the tanga driver, at times, sits on the right side bar in front of the seats. Often they are on their way to Qisa Khwani Bazaar in the main city of Peshawar. This path is frequented by the odd cars, rickshaws, double decker buses and bicycles like an immense theater play. The site of the hundreds of camels between Darpa Khel and Miranshah doesn't compare to this. It is an impressive entanglement of people, animals, carts and vehicles that Ashraf cannot stop watching. Magnificent birds of prey and large vultures circle high in the air and find their hideout on the huge tall trees opposite of Ahsraf's balcony. Peshawar is remarkably clean. Cleaners walk around everywhere, putting trash in the wicker baskets that they carry on their heads. Ashraf sits for hours on the balcony, watching these scenes and never becoming bored.

Ashraf's life seems like a fairy tale. His seemingly beautiful and protected life in Waziristan is punctuated by periodic trips to the big city. These trips make him more mature and give him a glimpse of a whole new and different world. It is a life that is so different from the life and rhythms of Darpa Khel. These people are so different from Aday, Baba, Haji Salehdin, Sharif Khoon, and the others. The rhythm of this city is so different from the rhythm of the village, where the daily queues of mothers and children and shouting Talibs wait for food at the gate. The sounds are so different from the mooing of the cows, the bleating of the sheep, and the occasional ominous sounds of the damoon drumming throughout the Tochi Valley, echoing in the surrounding hills. Even the call to prayer from the mosques sounds different here.

Ashraf finds the city and outside world beautiful, but at the same time he is happy to see the hills around Darpa Khel and Miranshah appear when he is in the backseat of Baba's car, driving home.

Ashraf gets a chill down his spine. Baba has decided that Ashraf and his older brother Usman are going to attend school in Peshawar. In one way or another, Baba is being pressured by his surroundings so much that he decides to send his two eldest sons to this boarding school. The school is called The Islamia Collegiate, later known as the Univeristy Public School. According to Baba, it is a very reputable school. It is a boarding school. Ashraf and

Usman do not really like it. They go to sleep with knots in their stomachs in anticipation of what is going to happen. Their faces divulge their doubt and fear. The beautiful city of Peshawar has transformed into a hostile place of danger that silently and insidiously creeps closer with every minute that ticks by.

Usman and Ashraf are sitting in the backseat in Baba's car riding to Peshawar. Again there are boys, girls, and men everywhere, with their slightly envious glances, watching the car pass them by. Normally, Ashraf is radiating with pride. But now he looks at the ground. The boys do not say a word. One more time, Ashraf looks at the ever shrinking Miranshah. A strange feeling in his stomach and chest overtake him. He looks at Usman. He doesn't seem to be faring any better. Ashraf looks at Baba. His firm gaze on the road rob Ashraf of the courage to ask if he could stay home. Wouldn't it be a lot better and easier to stay and study at home? Driving the boys to the big city of Peshawar is part of Baba's dream for them. This morning, Ashraf briefly spoke with Aaj. Proudly, he let Ashraf see his new gun. An old, nearly worn-out gun, but nevertheless, impressively big in the hands of the petite Aaj. Full of admiration and respect for Aaj, Ashraf examined the gun.

Pashtuns are fond of firearms. Like water to a fish, is a gun to a Pashtun. Rifles, pistols, or revolvers, it doesn't matter. A Pashtun has a strong, impressive firearm for his personal protection and for the defense of his honor and that of his country. Actually, a Pashtun is almost never without a weapon. In the house, it is located in a prime location. When a Pashtun goes out, he wears it either visibly or out of sight, but always within reach. Conflicts between tribes or families are almost a welcomed opportunity to show their prowess with their weapons on the battlefield. With their love of weapons, the many opportunities to practice, and jumping at every chance to fight in the tribal areas creates a unique environment for every Pashtun to become a legendary hero. In particular, the tough Pashtuns from the Afridi, Mehsud, Daur and Waziri tribes are described as being the best guerillas of the world in their own hills.

Aaj is left in Darpa Khel with his gun. Ashraf and Usman are at the boarding school in Peshawar. Everything is new. The school, the city, the food, the dormitories, the lessons, the people, the other boys. Everything is different. Ashraf misses Baba. He misses Aday and Sharif Khoon and Aaj. He misses the hills.

Baba pays the school fees for four months. At this English school, there are all sorts of different kinds of dormitories. Usman and Ashraf are placed in a dormitory named Harding Hostel. They have to share a room with two or three other students. They are real city boys, smooth talkers with lot of bravado. It is quite obvious that Usman and Ashraf are not from the city. They talk differently, act differently and are, quite simply, different. Before the boys have settled in, they are already bullied. They are rendered as being farmers, backward boys from the countryside.

With a serious face and a sharp voice, one of the city boys asks them where their goat is. "If you don't have your own goat, little farmers, then there's no milk here for you at breakfast." Usman and Ashraf look at each other in despair. Tears of frustration and anger emerge. Ashraf almost takes a bite of his lip. They will show these city boys once and for all the worth of a Pashtun. Baba has said they cannot fight. With a jerk, the boys return to silence.

The Pastun boys find the English school to be of no interest. After one day, they have already seen everything. They want to go home, away from the city, away from this school, away from those arrogant city boys. Away, away, away. Back to Waziristan where they belong.

Even before the second class began they ask the teacher for permission to buy books in the city. With big brown honest eyes the boys look to the older teacher. The man looks at the two boys intently. The doubt in his eyes will just not disappear. It seems as though he is going to say no, but then, unexpectedly, he gives his consent. Once outside, the boys take the double decker bus straight to the Greens Hotel. If it goes well, Baba is still there and can bring them back once again to Darpa Khel. Panting, the boys arrive at the hotel. But Baba is not there. They clamor up the outside of the hotel and reach the balcony and wait. Without a word, they sit on the balcony and look blankly at the swarm of traffic. They are certain. Baba will come back. He has not gone back to the village. The minutes and hours silently tick by. The doubt and near desperation is evident in their brown eyes, eyes that cling to an invisible desire whose fulfillment seems to be moving farther and farther away.

And yet, unexpectedly they see Babs's car coming. Baba parks the car in front of the hotel, comes out and looks up and sees the boys. Usman starts crying like he has never cried before. He sobs and stammers that he wants to go home. Ashraf adds to the misery. Giant tears roll down his cheeks. Through the tears, Baba looks strange and surreal. Is he mad? Or Sad?

It works! Baba's often unyielding eyes are soft and mild. He envelops the boys in his arms and says in a whisper, "I also want that. I miss you already. We are going home." Baba sends his driver to the English school to pick up the boys' belongings. They spend the night at the hotel and early next morning they are all sitting in the car, driving back home. Usman and Ashraf are struggling to keep their sad faces from smiling. They are really very happy.

Ashraf blissfully watches the stars. It is wonderful to be back in Darpa Khel. The familiar sounds of the village and the night make him at peace. The sounds of the last call to prayer fade away. Satisfied, he tries to penetrate the darkness with his eyes.

# EDWARDS COLLEGE, PESHAWAR

The brief but dramatic adventure in Peshawar has left small, yet deep, scars in Ashraf's mind. Never before has he been so aware of the outside world of Waziristan. Never before has he been so aware of the fact that a quick and abrupt end can come to this familiar, secure, albeit sometimes harsh, existence in Darpa Khel.

The daily rhythm feels like it never left. The early morning prayer followed by breakfast with the whole family seems nicer and more intense than all previous years. Unknowingly, Ashraf views daily events with different eyes. Female servants dry the dishes on the rough wooden beds in the courtyard. The same pile of dishes that slowly accumulate on those same beds after they have been rinsed off of the ground. The smallest children play in the brown dust, the little girls in their colorful salwar kameez and the boys in their usual dark brown ones. Women and men sit upon the ground, rocks, rugs, or simply on their haunches in groups far away from each other.

After showering and changing clothes, Ashraf, deep in thought, saunters behind Sharif Khoon to the day house in Miranshah. Aaj remains behind in Darpa Khel. The hundreds of camels near the

Khwar River have chosen this day to plant an indelible memory in Ashraf's head. The beauty of the hills, the river, the birds of prey high in the air are slowly being locked in his brain and soul. The voices of the other children hardly get through to him. This hike to Miranshah through the river, jumping from stone to stone, shapes the last chapters of this young boy.

There is a period in which nothing seems different from previous years. Darpa Khel, the school in Miranshah, the day house, Sharif Khoon, Haj Salehdin, his best friend Aaj with whom he hunts, the mischief, and the big and small adventures. The boys are officially adolescents. They get their first wet dream. Similar to when a girl gets her first menstruation cycle, it is a indication of maturity and the need to participate in the traditions of prayer on a regular basis. Ashraf undergoes the local tradition of having water poured over his head in the pool located next to the local mosque. The adult men and older boys tease him with jokes and comments. However, Ashraf knows that something fundamental has changed in his life.

From this moment, he must, for the rest of his life, pray five times a day. If he is rich enough one day, he must make a pilgrimage to Mecca at least once in his life. From this moment, he must think like an adult about *zakat*, the giving of alms. This involves donating yearly two and a half percent of one's possessions to the needy. Soon it will be Ramadan, the month of fasting. Also at this moment, Ashraf realizes that he has entered the next phase of his life. The earlier jokes of the men and boys have not even occurred to him. However, the moment he joins the men for one of the five daily prayers at the mosque makes an indelible impression on him. Here again, is a turning point in his life. When he enters the mosque between the men, he looks back. Against the courtyard wall, is his younger brother. He has the same expression that Ashraf has had his whole life up until this point. Ashraf will never look the same. This chapter of his life, with one small step over the threshold of the mosque, is closed. There is a wistful look in

Ashraf's eyes. Soon it is replaced by a look of pride. A look that says he is not a stranger here.

The pressure for Usman and Ashraf to attend another school is still present. Sometimes Baba talks about it briefly. Whenever Baba is talking about it and Sharif Khoon is within earshot, he glances with a distrustful look at the boys. The boys have passed the tenth grade with good grades. Baba has found an English college in Peshawar. It soon becomes clear that Baba has enrolled the boys. During one of the many trips into the city, everything is bought: the uniforms, the bedding, the school supplies. Again, the boys sleep in the Greens Hotel. Again, Ashraf looks from the balcony, enjoying the secrets of Peshawar. However, this city has changed. Everything has changed. The fairytale has shifted into an unknown and even occasionally frightening chapter in their lives. Nobody knows what the next day will bring. Certainties have evaporated like a pot of boiling water. Again, the boys feel a knot, similar to the one before, in their stomachs. Again, there is the feeling of nostalgia for their safe land of Waziristan.

Until the eighth grade, Usman did very well in school, though Ashraf's grades were disappointing. Baba had previously decided that Ashraf could skip two grades, but that was too much. There was a period when Ashraf's grades suffered. But then, suddenly, the tide seemed to change. Ashraf seemed to enjoy school. His grades increased significantly, and he seemed to have a talent especially for mathematics. It even went so well that he regularly outsmarted his teacher. Even before the math teacher could write everything on the board, Ashraf would blurt out the answer. The silent, envious glances from the other boys, and the peculiar, nondescript look from the teacher, provided Ashraf with some chuckles. The teacher made it increasingly difficult for Ashraf. With a strict, uncompassionate look in his eyes, the teacher raised the bar daily for Ashraf. Although Ashraf had skipped two grades, he rose to the top of the class in no time. Baba was very proud. He did not say much about it, but Ashraf could see it in his eyes. And sometimes, unbeknownst to Baba, Ashraf could sometimes overhear him bragging to the other men in the village or day home.

In the ninth grade, the boys had to choose a career direction. Each were called to see the principal of the school to make their choice. Usman and Ashraf discussed together what they would like, but they couldn't figure it out. This was a choice Baba must make. However, Baba was away for a week on business. The boys did not make a decision. Instead, they waited. When Baba returned after the week, the choice was made quickly. Without thinking for even a second, and with a slightly reproachful look in his eyes, he gave the boys his answer. Ashraf looked at Baba. Shall he ask? He already knew the answer though. It had everything to do with Baba's own story and his dream that every Pashtun in Waziristan should have access to education and healthcare. His dream was to be a doctor. Thus Baba had chosen!

Now that they have finished the tenth grade, Baba will take them back to Peshawar, along with two of their cousins, Farid and Suleman. This time it seems that this trip to Peshawar is final. They are going to study medicine. Baba has a serious conversation with the boys, telling them that they are almost men. He tells them that they are responsible, proud Pashtuns who have a unique opportunity to work on their future. Baba is not usually a man of many words, but this case is an exception. One thing was clear. This time, Peshawar is the final destination. Non-negotiable.

They are going to Edwards College, an institution with a big reputation. It is a leading college managed and run by a missionary. The principal of Edwards College is Phil Edmunds. He is a tall man with a protruding chin. He is originally from Australia and speaks with a strange Australian accent. Ashraf, Usman, and their two cousins Farid and Suleman feel equally excited and confused. The campus is located on a site where a large military garrison is housed and lies in a part of town where there is also a provincial museum, a train station, the airport, and a few other colleges.

It is a beautiful campus. The English-style, red-colored bricks divulge a part of its history. To further confirm this, the boys discover a Christian chapel on the campus that has been erected almost a hundred years ago in 1888. Later, a mosque was built beside it. The two faiths go hand in hand here. Ashraf finds the old library one of the most beautiful and impressive places. It has a large, wide wooden staircase and dark bookshelves with large glass doors that are like big fragile hands caring and protecting the precious knowledge and wisdom. The heavy wooden tables with their enormous green tops and the rows of wooden chairs stand invitingly, waiting for the fledgling students. The serenity that hangs here makes Ashraf and the boys nearly afraid to speak or to make a sound. The tall, lean Phil Edmunds, with his strange, protruding chin, starts to speak. The boys think he is the only one who dares to raise his voice in the library.

All four of the boys want to be in enrolled in pre-medicine courses, but there is not a place for them all. Which of them must choose a different direction? But this cannot happen, for that is contrary to the very reason the boys were sent to this school.

They feel like they are not being treated fairly and make a plan. This will not happen. These four young boys will not be driven apart so easily. With the stubbornness and intransigence of real Pashtuns, they protest against this unjust judgment.

The pensive principal looks to the agitated boys. His thoughtful blue-gray eyes wander towards the ceiling. For minutes, he stares at the ceiling without saying a word. His chin looks possibly even larger than before. The young boys, determined though with a bit of doubt in their eyes, look to this large, tall man from Australia.

He looks back at the boys, and, just when they expect to hear 'no,' he replies, "Come back after three or four days." Through his Australian accent it sounds as if he said, "Come back after three or four dies." Bewildered, the boys look at the stately principal who, with a frown upon his forehead, walk away. The boys are convinced that four other students have to die before they can all join the pre-medicine studies. Shocked, and with slouched shoulders, the boys walk to their rooms. Do many boys here die? Can they bear that on their consciences?

They all sleep in one room. After this strange incident, the boys keep a sharp eye on Principal Edmunds. You never know what lies in a man's character after he rules that four boys must die first before they can all study in one group.

Despite their suspicions, the boys know that the principal is strict but fair. He usually appears suddenly and unexpectedly. Usually in places one never expects, so no one dares to sneak out of the college lest he be caught. Principal Edmunds has his eye on everything. And, when someone is caught, it is already clear in advance what is going to follow. Hard and business-like, the offender is publicly reprimanded. And in every case, the parents are later informed. This is obviously the worst part. Punishment from Principal Edmunds is one thing, but the additional punishment from Baba is another!

Every night, the boys eat in the large dining room with all the other students, the warden Jilani, and Principal Edmunds. No one can touch his plate or eat a bite until the liberating words of the principal have sounded. Just before he opens his mouth, he stands up, towering over everyone. As like a custom, he sticks his pointy chin forward and speaks these words, "For food, friends, and fellowship. God make us truly thankful. Amen."

As his words, strangely spoken, are still ringing, many students launch into their own prayers and start eating. Everything is disciplined. Eating, studying, exercising, cleaning, yes, everything is coupled with strict discipline. After dinner, the boys are required to study in the study room for two hours.

The boys miss their families. Farid and Suleman decide together that they are going to call their father. Begging and crying, they ask him if they can be allowed to come home and go to college at Miranshah. Ashraf and Usman witness the entire scene. They've been through this a few times and do not dare to call Baba. The two cousins succeed. The drama also worked. Farid and Suleman are overjoyed. Away from college, away from Peshawar, away from the discipline, and away from Principal Edmunds. It will not be long before their Baba also comes to pick them up.

Ashraf and Usman feverishly discuss what they should do. It makes no sense for them to stay behind since their cousins are returning to Waziristan again. A plan begins to develop in their minds. They cannot ask for themselves this time, but perhaps it will work if Farid and Suleman ask Baba. Farid and Suleman smile. They have already considered doing this for their cousins who have to remain in this terrible place. Hopeful, Ashraf and Usman look at the boys as they are picked up to go home.

The problem of them all studying medicine is dissolved, in any case. No longer will anyone have to die. Even better, the boys are able to go home now. Everything is solved.

A few days later, when the boys are playing soccer in the nearby field, Baba suddenly appears on the sidelines. His dark eyes reveal nothing good. He is angry. Very, very angry. The boys can see it. A big swarm of mosquitoes hang over Baba's head. Ashraf and Usman do not dare to look at him, nor stop their game of football. A wave of panic rushes over the boys. Baba is really very angry. In their minds, they hope their soccer game will last forever. It makes no difference, just as long as Baba goes away without saying anything.

But the game is quick. Way too quick. Baba doesn't need to call them. Reluctantly, the boys go to him. With their heads slightly bowed, they ask Baba how he is. This is courtesy with which every Pashtun greets one another. First they ask how it is with him, then they ask about the family, their village, his work. Perhaps this will work with Baba. Baba does not respond. He looks straight at the boys. Without flinching, he snaps at the boys, "Even if you die here, you must stay here! Understood!" The words were louder than the worst thunder and lightning in the history of Waziristan. An ominous silence follows. Ashraf doesn't dare to say anything. Usman either. The boys stare at their brown shoes. Baba stands there and says nothing. The boys continue to stand, with bowed heads, before Baba. They do not dare to speak. Peshawar holds her breath. For a moment it seems as though the world has stopped and all of its sounds are silenced. Minutes seem like hours. With a jerk, Baba turns and disappears towards the big city of Peshawar.

# THE UNIVERSITY

Gradually, Ashraf and Usman begin to find Edwards College in Peshawar more and more appealing. During vacation times, they go to Darpa Khel and enjoy all the ordinary things that now seem more special because they moved away and began their studies at the Edwards College. Sharif Khoon's stories, the eternal feud between Haji Salehdin and the cook Makan in Miranshah, the camels by the river, Aday who tirelessly cares for the many children and women who seem to move with the rhythm of the rising and setting sun to get their daily portion of food. The familiar cry of the Talibs and the invitation to prayer that sounds near and far throughout the hills of Waziristan.

Waziristan is no longer the center of their world. The whole world is no longer the same as living in Waziristan and Darpa Khel. Ashraf quickly gets familiar with another world. A world that is much more complex than life in Waziristan. A life in Peshawar where the history of Pakistan is a reality that determines the news of the day. Where the eternal fight between Haji Salehdin and the cook Makan is not newsworthy and where no one is interested in the old tales of Sharif Khoon.

During this period of political turmoil in Peshawar and the whole of Pakistan, one feels the consequences of the division of India and Pakistan that occurred in August 1947. A division by which it was decided that the area should be divided according to religion. The predominately Hindu areas became India, and the predominately Muslim areas became East and West Pakistan. East Pakistan was the more populated of the two, but the power was in the hands of the people in West Pakistan. This resulted in great tension between the leaders and people of West and East Pakistan. At a mass meeting of a million people, Sheikh Mujibur Rahman demanded the independence of East Pakistan. Zulfikar Ali Bhutto, who had the most followers in West Pakistan, opposed this demand, and a huge conflict came about as a result.

Not many years before, Pakistan had wars with India over the disputed Kashmir region. Now India founds it chance to help divide Pakistan and create Bangladesh.

Ashraf does not concern himself much with politics, but in Peshawar, it is a reality that one can not escape. Baba talks a lot about the events in Afghanistan. Pashtuns feel still connected to the Pasthuns in Afghanistan. They constitute the largest ethnic group in Afghanistan. Yet many Pashtuns also live in Pakistan, mainly in the western provinces. The man-made border, called The Durand Line, separates Afghanistan and Pakistan. This Durand Line came after a contract between the Afghani Emir Abdur Rahman Khan and the British Sir Durand. For Ashraf and many Pashtuns, this is a relatively old and complicated story that means, more or less, that the tribal areas and Waziristan are theirs.

Last night, when the men were sitting together in the courtyard, Ashraf and Usman shared the latest news from Peshawar with the men. They shared the news about school and about the war on the eastern border of Pakistan. At the same time, there were problems in Afghanistan with the deposition of the king, Mohammed Zair

Shah. While he was away in Italy seeking medical treatment, his cousin and brother-in-law, Daoud Khan, made himself president.

Then, just like before, the men go on about the news of Darpa Khel and the happenings in Miranshah. Haji Salehdin has everyone are laughing, and a few minutes later, all the problems of the world have disappeared under the immense spectacle of the starry sky and the nearly unceasing buzz of the swarming mosquitoes that are the familiar sounds of the Waziristan night.

Ashraf enjoys his stay in Darpa Khel, but, at the same time, he wants to return to college, as strange as it may seem. He misses his friends and life at Edwards College. There is no trace of nostalgia this time in Ashraf's eyes as Baba drives Usman and him back to Peshawar. He loves these two different worlds in their own, incomparable way.

Ashraf is happy having his nose in his books. He is eager to learn. He wants to know everything. He continues studying when others stop. Usman finds studying boring. In the evening, after the compulsory study time, Ashraf goes to his room and wants to study a little more. Usman does not. He wants to sleep. While Ashraf is trying to figure out the letters and texts by the last bit of light, Usman is trying his best to make it as dark as possible so he can sleep. The boys care about each other a lot, but they are very different. Usman fails the final exam, and Ashraf passes with flying colors.

Ashraf is ready to move on to the university. The spots for the medical program are limited. At the Khyber Medical College in Peshawar, there are only two places available for students from North Waziristan. At the King Edwards Medical College in Lahore, there is only one place available. Three of Ashraf's uncles have studied medicine in Lahore: one of Baba's brothers, Fakir Khan, and two of his mother's brothers, Ayub Khan and Mohammad Khan. That is reason enough for Ashraf to want to go there too. Because he has the best academic grades of all the students from

North Waziristan, in fact the best in all the seven tribal units, he may choose. King Edwards Medical College in Lahore it is. The two places in Khyber Medical School are quickly assigned to two other students from North Waziristan. One of them being his cousin Fardid Khan. Baba is proud.

The ride to Lahore is long and tiring, but also beautiful. It's not the first time Ashraf is making this trip. He's gone with Baba before, from Waziristan via Peshawar, through the rugged hills and outstretched fields via Rawalpindi along the famous Great Trunk Road through the plains of Punjab up to Lahore. It is a long, bumpy, and sometimes dangerous road that crosses through many busy towns where donkey carts, pedestrians, and pushcarts compete with each other to safely reach the other side. Small children, barefoot and wearing no shirts, play in a world of their own among this swarm of vehicles, unaware of the many dangers around them. Stray dogs also try to find something to eat or to steal amidst this hustle and bustle.

The beautiful hills, the hairpin turns, the flat green stretches, the towns and rivers ensure that the long road between Peshawar and Lahore is never a boring spectacle. Large herds of sheep block the road. Ashraf notices that as they near the eastern border of Pakistan, the salwar kameezes of the women look more colorful. Here, many women and girls wear cheerful, multicolored scarves and clothing that signifies a different culture. Ashraf enjoys this different world.

It is hot and dry in Lahore, unlike in Waziristan and in Peshawar. Drought, dust, and extreme heat can quickly result in a dry, hoarse throat. Heat with temperatures above 110 degrees Fahrenheit suck all the energy out of one's body. Lahore is located in the Punjab. It is Pakistan's second largest city and the capital of West Pakistan. It is not far from the border of India. It is a beautiful old town with the beautiful, impressive Badshahi Mosque that was built by Mughal emperor Aurangzeb somewhere between 1658 and 1707. Ashraf looks at the ancient mosque. It is swarming with people. His thoughts wander to the small and familiar mosque in Darpa Khel. Ashraf sighs. Though proud, he is also anxious as he goes towards this new period of life at the King Edwards Medical College in Lahore.

LIke so many things in life, everything goes differently than planned. During his first days at Lahore, Ashraf falls ill. Years earlier, during a family trip to Lahore, he had the measles, so now from the first day, he associates Lahore with illness. He wants to leave. The feeling of loneliness creeps up slowly and eventually overtakes him. Although he is older and wiser, history seems to be repeating itself. Ashraf wants to leave Lahore, away from this place that at first seemed so beautiful, away from this new step in his life. He wants to go back to Waziristan. Or back to Peshawar. Two worlds are enough. There is no room for a third. Lahore makes him ill, and not for the first time.

Baba, who can always arrange everything, must arrange it this time too. Baba looks at Ashraf's condition. Sick, frustrated, and disillusioned, Ashraf waits. Baba looks, with his typical inscrutable gaze, out the window, as if the solution is to be found out there, somewhere far away. He looks once more to Ashraf. Baba looks distressed. One more time he looks out the window and then makes his decision.

A few days later, everything is arranged. Ashraf can switch places with a student from Azad Kashmir. The student from Azad Kashmir will now go to King Edwards Medical College in Lahore, and Ashraf will take his place at the Khyber Medical College in Peshawar. Baba has arranged an impossible feat. Ashraf has questions but will not ask them. He does not know how Baba has arranged this, and Baba stays silent.

Shortly after, Ashraf begins his studies at the Khyber Medical School in Peshawar. Soon, he also becomes sick there. This time, it is caused by prolonged work dissecting cadavers. This happens to many students. It is a part of the program. It is for each doctor a way to get to know the human body inside and out. It is a matter of getting used to it. Ashraf also gets accustomed to this, and soon he gets better. After some time he is no longer bothered by it anymore.

It does not take long before Ashraf settles back into his old rhythm. He loves studying. He loves books and investigating cases. But once, he gets a failing grade in medical jurisprudence. It was unjustified. Dr. Zaman, a teacher at the medical school, has something against students from the tribal areas. Ashraf shrugs. He can't fight against it. His study in Peshawar is progressing well and in December 1976, he graduates as a doctor. Shortly thereafter in 1977, he begins with his first internship.

It is during this time that it is extremely turbulent in Pakistan and Afghanistan once again. Under the leadership of General Mohammed Zia-ul-Haq in 1977, there is a coup in Pakistan. The incumbent Prime Minister Zulfikar Ali Bhutto is imprisoned. In Afghanistan, there seems to be no less agitation. Daud Khan, who declared himself as the first President of Afghanistan in 1973, and most of his family are assassinated during a coup by members of the People's Democratic Party of Afghanistan (PDPA). The coup happened in the presidential palace on April 28, 1978. It is the start of the Saur Revolution that finally leads to the 1979 intervention by the Soviets and the 1979–1989 Soviet–Afghan War against the *mujahideen*. These events would change Afghanistan, Pakistan, the tribal areas, and even the world, for decades.

Ashraf hears and reads about the news concerning the world around him. Though it is not his native Waziristan, he must deal with it. Due to all the turmoil in and around Pakistan, the army begins to recruit physicians. It is not a voluntary choice. Every doctor must serve in the army for two years. Officers of the army are sent out to draft young men like Ashraf for such a period.

## CONSCRIPTION?

Ashraf's knowledge of the army and military does not extend much beyond the images and stories about the Tochi Scouts near Miranshah. Baba has done business with them for years. Ashraf knows that the Tochi Scouts in the tribal areas along the border of Afghanistan are particularly responsible for controlling the border. Additionally, Ashraf's former school, Edward's College, was located on the site where a large military garrison is housed. Much more than that, Ashraf's never really learned about.

Ashraf is harshly confronted with a world he does not know. Every newly qualified doctor must serve in the army for a period of two years. It is a matter of waiting until an officer from the army comes to enlist Ashraf. Ashraf discusses this with Baba, and again, he hears Baba discuss this matter with his friends who hold influential positions.

The Pakistani military was formed out of a division of the Indian army after the independence of Pakistan in 1947. The constitution of Pakistan contains a provision for conscription. According to insiders, conscription has never been imposed. That sounds promising, but Ashraf is not so easily reassured. Since its founding in 1947, the Pakistani army has been involved in three wars with neighboring India and in several skirmishes near the border with Afghanistan.

The Pakistani army is a big player in the land. That was evident after the first coup in 1958 by General Ayub Khan. Ashraf knows it is not limited to just this one time. Only very recently, in 1977, a coup was organized by General Zia ul-Haq, and the government was overthrown. After a while this led to the hanging of Zulifkar Ali Bhutto after he was tried and found guilty of conspiracy to murder a politician named Kasuri.

Everything is unrestful. The Pakistani army is putting pressure on numerous fronts, all the while Ashraf wants only one thing, to continue to work on his career. Baba has the dream that all his children will become doctors and that medical care in the tribal areas will advance. Right now, this dream is like the seeds of a flower whose first buds are visible in the early spring. These fledging buds must not be destroyed. They must grow. The dream must continue.

There is a lot of talk. The army, the unrest, Ashraf, and many more matters are discussed. Baba speaks to one of his friends, Mr. Sikandar, who is the director of the Labor Employment Exchange in Peshawar. This is the place where all newly qualified doctors are registered after graduation and from where warrants are issued for conscription of doctors to the army. Baba asks Mr. Sikandar to give him a warning prior to a warrant being sent . He promises to warn Baba and Ashraf when an army representative is coming to enlist Ashraf. Ashraf is worried that serving in the army may hinder him pursuing his postgraduate studies and training. He thinks seriously about hiding. Waziristan is large, and the government has no involvement there. The army does not go out of their own large military complexes and, with exception to the main roads, nobody interferes with the events in the villages or countryside. There are enough possibilities. After a few attempts, the army officers will give up and forget that Ashraf must go to the army.

Yet, Ashraf remains at the hospital in Peshawar for his studies. He assumes that Baba or Mr. Sikandar will give him enough warning. Days go by, and nothing out of the ordinary happens. During a break one day while working in the out patient department, Ashraf goes outside and calls Mr. Sikander, asking if there was any news about the warrants. Mr. Sikandar is astonished and asks in scratchy voice, "Are you still there? Two days ago I told your uncle that you have to disappear."

Ashraf puts the phone down without replying. The words repeat themselves in his head over and over again. What should he do? Where should he go? Ashraf doubts. Does his career as a doctor end here? Now? Hunched over and in despair, he walks back to the hospital to finish his day. A plan evolves in his mind, and he makes the decision that, after today, he will go into hiding in Waziristan for a while. Back at the hospital, the other doctors look alarmed and disconcerted. An army officer has just been through. He was looking for doctors and has already enrolled a number of them.

Now Ashraf has to make a move. He drops everything and goes straight to Baba, who always knows the right solution and who always makes the right decisions. Baba listens to Ashraf's whole story. Deep wrinkles appear on his forehead. He rubs his increasingly graying beard. Then, abruptly, he gets up and takes Ashraf to see Dr. Ali Sher, a friend of his in Peshawar. Dr. Ali Sher is the director of the Provincial Health Department and long ago had served as the medical superintendant at the Agency Headquarter Hospital in Miranshah. In fact, he was the man who had circumcised Ashraf when he was three years old.

Again, Baba has a long conversation. Dr. Ali Sher and Baba finish their conversation. The doctor's dark eyes look at Ashraf. He has not forgotten this boy. He has heard what the boy has to offer. Together the men decide to find him a job through the Provincial

Secretary Health, a job which would allow him to bypass the two-year army duty.

As they are all walking together towards the simple, yet stately, office of the secretary, Ashraf can see from a distance a man sitting behind a large wooden desk, and, to his horror, he recognizes this man. This is the man who gets to decide. Dr. Zaman. The man who gave him his only failing grade ever in his third professional exam in medical jurisprudence! The man that everyone knows hates boys from the tribal areas. Baba and Dr. Ali Sher look at this man indifferently. Do they not know how this man views the people from the tribal areas?

In an authoritarian manner, Dr. Zaman first demands a "no objection certificate" from the army before he will even consider giving a job to Ashraf. Baba smiles. He thanks the man amicably, and then practically drags Ashraf down to the Provincial Martial Law Administrators Office.

While they are waiting in the personal assistant's office, Ashraf sees through the slightly open door a man with an impressive personality. Adorned on his stately green uniform are numerous stars and memories of past exploits. Soldiers and junior officers fly with every move to the left or right. They apparently have one mission, to serve General Sawar Khan, the Provincial Martial Law Administrator. He is not a Pashtun.

While Baba and Ashraf are still waiting for an opportunity to speak to the general, the personal assistant comes in. He is also a high ranking officer, a major. A few soldiers and officers stand up straight. He gives a somewhat indifferent greeting in return and wants to go into the room of the general. Then he spots Baba and Ashraf. There is a smile on his face. It quickly becomes apparent to Ashraf that Baba knows this major. Baba is friends with a certain Colonel Gulsher. His son, Jawed Malik studied years earlier at the Military Academy in Abbottabad. Baba used to visit him and had always brought fresh fruit and sweets along. There,

Baba also met Jawed Malik's friend, who is now this major they are meeting.

Baba tells Ashraf's story to the major. He looks, thinking. "It is General Sawar Khan's last day of work as he is moving to take over the Marshal Law Administrator of Punjab Province. He is very busy." He mumbles. But then, a smile comes across his face. "I'll arrange something," he mutters still in thought and disappears into the general's office.

Baba sits and waits. Ashraf looks at him from the side. Baba exudes calm and self-confidence. After waiting for some time, the major invites Baba to come into the large office of the General Sawar Khan. Baba goes alone. With a wave of his hand, he gives Ashraf a sign that he must remain seated. Just before the big door shuts, Ashraf sees the dignified general greet Baba. Then the door closes.

After some time, Baba comes out of the office. Ashraf is trying to read the expression on his face. Does he have good news? Baba nods to the officers who are also in the room. Quietly, he sits down and waits again. Imperceptibly, he touches Ashraf's hand. Ashraf is silent. It is not long before the friendly major comes in with a letter. Baba takes it and lets his eyes slowly slide along the words. He nods, stands up, and embraces the man as a sign of farewell.

Outside, Baba says that everything is settled. The man asked Baba to write an application addressed to the Health Secretary. Ashraf's eyes fly over the letter that he practically snatched from Baba's hands. Next to all kinds of administrative terms at the bottom, in red ink, states "Health Secretary, give Ashraf Khan the job of his choice!" Puzzled, Ashraf looks to Baba. This is so much more than he had hoped for. Much more than he ever expected. So much more than what he thought would be possible. Deep in thoughts, Baba looks towards the horizon. He seems to already be busy with another problem.

For Baba, it is just a formality. He takes Ashraf to Dr. Zaman, the man who does not care much for the interests of the people from the tribal areas. Without a word, Baba gives the man the letter. The color visibly drains from his face as his eyes wander along the text. He nods politely and gives Baba a hand.

Ashraf chooses a job at the Khyber Teaching Hospital. He is the youngest employee ever. His short adventure with the Pakistani army seems to finally be behind him.

# MARYAM

People are excited in Lamakhael, a subtribe of Darpa Khel to which Ashraf's family belong. After all these years, the family has finally taken revenge. It was more than eight years ago that Ashraf's maternal cousin, Syed Mohammed, was shot at the bazaar in Miranshah. The reason was due to some trivial business conflict. Anyway, it ended in murder. The local security team, called Khasadar, can only intervene in situations that occur on the main roads and at important places. The bazaar is such a place, and so the Khasadaar were able to intervene and to arrest the culprit. He was sentenced to fourteen years in prison. Coincidentally, a half hour after the murdered cousin Syed Mohammed was buried, his younger brother, Sher Mohammed Khan, was brought in from Peshawar dead. The young man had died falling from a bus. He had no identity documents on him but was identified by another Darpa Khel resident. He identified him by the traditional tattoo on his arm which read Sher Mohamed Darpa Khel. It was a day of great tragedy.

In Darpa Khel, Baba and the men often talk about this awful tragedy. But now the time has come. The murderer of Syed

Mohammed was released after spending his prison term and now he has been killed by Ashraf's family side. For a few days, all kinds of people from the village and surrounding areas come by to congratulate the family. Pashtunwali and badal have done their job. There is eating, talking, and laughter. The old law has prevailed.

While life in Darpa Khel continues and the world around him is unrestful, Ashraf himself is busy with his training. The years slip by and Ashraf becomes a more experienced doctor. He wants to specialize in the field of ear, nose, and throat diseases. He works in various hospitals, and his world becomes larger and larger. More and more, he becomes aware of the vast differences in cultures and religions, and is exposed to how healthcare is managed throughout the world.

Ashraf gladly spends his holidays in his native home of Waziristan. Things there remain as they were. The Pashtuns in Darpa Khel, Miranshah, the tribal areas, and actually throughout the entire region of Waziristan, do not change. The call to prayer sounds the same throughout the hills. The damoon drums still regularly sound. Pashtunwali is still the guiding principle, and all the quirks and little adventures of the Pashtuns are still chuckled at.

During his time in Waziristan, Ashraf often thinks about the problems in the countries around him. In one year, the leaders of the two neighboring countries of Pakistan and Afghanistan are killed. The situation in Pakistan and Afghanistan is extremely restless and unstable. Unwillingly and, for a large part, even unknowingly, the Pashtun people in the tribal areas get more and more involved with the unrest in the region. It remains an issue for both neighboring Pakistan and Afghanistan, but more and more, dark clouds of violence and unrest gather over the tribal areas. Increasingly, the conversation is about the events in Pakistan and Afghanistan. There is talk about the big players behind these conflicts, namely the Soviet Union, the United States, and the West.

Despite all the worries, Ashraf enjoys his time when he is at home in Darpa Khel. Even now, it's as though the clock, for a short time, is reversed. Baba, Aday, his brother, and his sisters sit on the carpet on the floor in a circle around steaming food. The familiar smell of curry and meat mixed with the odor of so many people in such a small space has not changed over the years. Ashraf looks at the small circle. Usman and the younger brothers sit, happily chatting, as the enormous pile of food slowly shrinks. For a moment, all the major problems of the world seem to be forgotten.

Baba does not say much. Then, suddenly, he clears his throat. It's a signal that something important will follow. Suddenly there is silence. The boys look at Baba. Then Baba's voice sounds while he kindly, yet sternly, looks at Ashraf. "You are now an adult, son. Have you ever thought about marriage?" Ashraf does not know where to look. He gets hot and feels that he is turning red. He did not expect this subject. Everyone looks at him. Baba is thoughtful and looks pensively ahead. Ashraf's thoughts run at full speed. What should he say? He is studying, that he has no time for marriage? A wave of panic seems to overtake his thoughts. Must he give a name? Must he say that he would not know which woman to marry? Then he answers, much louder than he wanted to, "I will discuss it with Aday." His voice sounds shrill and cracks. His face was red and his eyes quickly turn towards the ground. To hide his insecurity, he quickly puts a huge bite of food in his mouth. He does this as nonchalantly as possible, doing his best to show that the subject is now finished. Baba looks at him thoughtfully. His gaze wanders off to Aday. She nods to him, in such a way that no one else notices. The boys look back and forth at Baba and Ashraf.

Baba shrugs and nods. The subject is closed for now. Under his eyebrows, Ashraf looks at Baba, who Is calmly eating, as if nothing special has happened. The other boys are also already chatting and laughing. Only Aday is still looking at Ashraf. Her sweet, gentle eyes seem to want to reassure him.

Baba's question remains a whirlwind raging in Ashraf's mind. He can get no peace. What should he discuss with Aday? What should he say? He doesn't know which woman he should marry. He reviews all the girls he knows. A deep furrow on his brow confirms this spiritual struggle. Invisible to those around him, he shakes his head whenever a young woman comes to mind. There is only one that, whenever the thought of her returns, he delicately smiles. Would she want to marry him? She is clever and intelligent. Whenever there is a family occasion, he would see her. Ashraf has known her all his life. "Maryam" he inaudibly whispers her name. "Maryam." A broad smile appears on his face. This is the woman he wants to marry. His relief and joy quickly changes into a nagging uncertainty. Suddenly, she is the only woman in the world that he wants to marry. But would she want to? Would her father and family consent? What would Baba think?

Ashraf discusses everything with Aday. She is a very good listener. She knows her son. Silently, she listens to Ashraf's whole story. A bit shyly, he shares with her all of his questions and uncertainties. Maryam is his cousin. It is very common within the Pashtun and Pakistani culture that you marry someone within the family. However, this is also often a problem. Family ties are strong, but, at the same time, there is always turmoil, whether about relationships, possessions, land, money, or other small things. Minor conflicts, which sometimes cause families to not talk to each other for years. Ashraf is silent as he looks at Aday. For a few moments, her dark eyes look into nothingness. Lost in thought, she nods gently, then lays her hand on Ashraf's arm. With a reassuring smile, she gets up and slowly walks away.

Ashraf sighs with relief. He knows that Aday will discuss it with Baba. Now, everything will be fine. He slowly reclines back onto the creaky wooden bed. It is hot outside. He looks up at the starry sky. Nowhere else is it as beautiful as in Darpa Khel. When he closes his eyes, he sees Maryam's face. A smile appears on his face. Uncertainty and embarrassment has gone. Baba will probably arrange it. Moments later, you can hear the gentle roar of the peaceful, sleeping Ashraf.

The next morning, while Aday speaks with Baba, he gently nods his head up and down. Even as he stares, he nods again. Now, convincingly. Without another word, he walks out. With his hands on his back, he walks towards the gate and then in the direction of Miranshah.

Maryam's father is an electrical engineer and employee of the Water and Power Development Authority. Her family had to live in various cities and towns as government employees are routinely transferred from one place to another every three years. Ashraf only sees her on holidays when the entire family gets together.

At this moment, it is all a bit complicated. There are some small disagreements in the family, small family conflicts over ownership. Fortunately, Baba's younger brother, Atta Mohammad, who is an ophthalmic surgeon, is still on very good terms with Sardar Khan, the father of Maryam. At the day house in Miranshah, Baba has a long conversation with his younger brother. Atta listens well and then leaves to go see Maryam's father.

A few weeks later, Baba's brother is back. He meets with Baba, and then shortly thereafter, they call Ashraf. It is settled. Ashraf will marry Maryam. But her father has one condition, that Maryam would finish her studies before marriage. Maryam also supports this marriage agreement. She has known Ashraf since childhood through many family visits. Right now, Maryam is studying medicine at the Fatima Jinnah Medical College in Lahore. If everything goes according to schedule, her studies will take another five years.

Ashraf sighs. He is relieved. It's settled! Waiting five years for marriage is not a problem for him. He also wants to study. He realizes that getting married at this moment would change his life completely. Though he is engaged, he will not see Maryam. They must wait until they are married.

Time goes on. Ashraf continues to study and work. The unrest in the area continues. After the bloody palace revolutions in Afghanistan in which president Taraki is killed, the Soviet Union makes a decision in 1979 to take matters into their own hands completely. The Red Army of the Soviet Union enters Afghanistan, resulting in the execution of the incumbent President Amin. Charging forward, they make their marionette Babrak Karmal president of Afghanistan. After the invasion of Afghanistan by the Soviet Union, Karmal takes some non-party ministers in his government and tries to restore Islamic dominance in the country. Despite this, there is a growing backlash against the government. The opposition to the presence of the Soviets in Afghanistan is called mujahideen. Mujahideen literally means "warrior" or "zealot" in Arabic. This is someone who is committed to be a holy warrior for a cause. Nowadays, the term mujahideen is used by the media to describe various armed fighters who espouse fundamentalist Islamic ideologies.

Ashraf wants to further specialize. He can do this in England, but before he can, he must take an entrance exam. This exam will ensure that he can practice medicine in England and also that he can continue his study of otorhinolaryngology. He passes his exam and begins his specilization studies in England.

During his first few weeks in England, he cannot make sense of the country or its people. Luckily Ashraf's uncle Dr. Faqir Mohammad is living and working in England for fourteen years already. He is a great source of help and guidance in Ashraf's first years in England.

Ashraf has studied English for years, and he feels he speaks the language fluently. Yet, he has trouble communicating. He finds that he cannot finish his sentences. Often his native audience would reply with "Excuse me?" or "Pardon me?" No one seems to understand him. What is wrong with his English? What is wrong with the Englishmen?

Soon, it becomes clear that the unique accent and pronunciation of Pakistanis and Afghans is difficult for the English to understand. Sighing, he realizes that he has an unexpected task in addition to his studies. He will have to pounce on the English language. His pronunciation must improve dramatically as he wants to have a future here. Step by step, he progresses in his studies and language learning. He works and studies, and it does not take long before he can call himself an otolaryngologist: an ear, nose, and throat surgeon. Meanwhile, he hears "Excuse me, Sir?" less and less. Apparently his pronunciation is greatly improving.

When Ashraf is in Pakistan, in the neighborhood of Lahore, he goes with his cousin to visit Maryam. He really shouldn't, but he can't resist. In one way or another, he has been thinking about her more and more. If he is unable to sleep at night, he thinks of her beautiful face, her light eyes, and her lovely smile. Then he dreams away about a life with her. About a family, about happiness, about love, and more. To avoid problems, he always takes his cousin Javed with him, for he is studying at the Engineering University in Lahore. Ashraf does not want to embarrass Maryam. The etiquette of relating to women is a very sensitive subject in the Pashtun culture. Javed finds it funny to accompany the shy Ashraf to the girls boarding school. In the great hall of the girls boarding school are several benches and seats. There are many people in the hall, so they are not alone. Maryam is politely waiting. Ashraf shyly shuffles back and forth on his chair. Maryam gets a cola and a traditional samosa snack for the two young men. Ashraf peeks beneath his dark eyebrows as unobtrusively as possible to Maryam. He does not say much, and neither does Maryam. Maryam peeks back. When their eyes meet, they both turn beet red. Javed fires a barrage of cheesy jokes about the couple, and Maryam doesn't miss an opportunity to get up every time to get a cola and snack for the two. Whenever they are nearly sick from the cola and snack, they part ways.

It is a ritual that repeats itself several times in the coming years as Ashraf and Maryam wait for their marriage to each other, and not one of the three wants to miss out on these secret visits.

# MARRIAGE

*Wadah*, the Pasthun word for marriage. The bride and groom actually have no say about their wedding, for in the Pashtun culture, everything is arranged for them. Far before the marriage, the two sets of parents have made all the negotiations. A variety of arrangements are made for the future bride and groom. It is a deeply rooted tradition. The highly conservative traits of the Pashtuns and their traditional views regarding women and marriage are such that few Pashtun men and women ever think to deviate from these traditions.

Ashraf's and Maryam's arrangement went a little less strictly by the rules. Baba had asked Ashraf if he knew of a woman with whom he wanted to marry. Maryam was also asked if she thought Ashraf should be her future husband. Uncle Atta Mohammad had done the negotiating, and now the time is finally here. A few more days and Ashraf and Maryam will marry. The past differences between the two families have been settled. Several days of celebration with old customs and traditions are at the door. Ashraf is nervous. He has been to several weddings. But now? Now it is about Maryam and him. He has not seen her for a long time. She did not complete her studies and returned to her parents' home. In his dream and thoughts, Maryam has become more and more beautiful.

Ashraf has already experienced more of the world and knows that all the traditions of the Pashtuns are foreign to outsiders. Ashraf has taken leave from his job as a junior registrar at Walsgrave Hospital in Coventry, England for this moment. It is wadah, the moment of the wedding ceremony. It takes three days before the real formalities of the wedding occur, but the party has already begun. Ashraf knows that it will be a several day feast in which he and Maryam are the center of attention. Maryam is nearby at the home of her family's ket in Darpa Khel. Ashraf's house is full of relatives and guests from Darpa Khel and other far off towns. They will stay for a week until the celebrations are over. There are the continual sounds of drums, singing and dancing which are only interrupted by feasts. Haji Salehdin makes his normal jokes, and stumbling Sharif Khoon tells his tales as if he were sharing them for the first time. During these days, all the problems of the Pashtuns seemed to have disappeared like snow in the sun.

It is Wednesday. There are three days of proper full celebrations, visits, laughter, congratulations, and talks. Ashraf yawns. He is tired and realizes that the real party has yet to begin. His face does occasionally hurt from the smile he wears on his face the whole day. The men are inside the walls of Ashraf's ket. They sing and dance in the usual form of Athaan. Ashraf thinks of Maryam. How is she doing? Occasionally, he hears the music and laughter of the women off in the distance from her house. Traditionally, the girls sit inside and sing and dance together. Most likely there are candles everywhere and the other girls will decorate Maryam's hands and arms with henna. As a child, he was allowed to be with the women whenever there was a wedding. He would like to sneak around the corner to see how she is doing over there. In a few days they will officially be husband and wife. His thoughts wander. Again he sees the beautiful face and light eyes of Maryam. It's been a long time since he had last seen her. She has sweet, gentle eyes. In this way, they resemble the eyes of Aday.

This evening, women of all ages from Ashraf's house are visiting Maryam's house in her family's ket. Aday is also going. Maryam's hands and feet are beautifully decorated with henna. Aday makes three beautiful braids in Maryam's brown hair. It is customary that the braiding is entrusted to a woman who has many sons. The idea is that this will help the bride give birth to many children herself. It goes without question that Aday will braid Maryam's hair. Aday has many sons, including Ashraf. The women laugh and Maryam turns red.

Ashraf's family delivers the bridal gowns and jewelry this morning. It is a beautiful red wedding dress with lots of jewelry and ornaments. Shyly, Maryam looks to the fine decorative work on the dress and then to her visitors. For the second time, a great meal in Maryam's home is served to the villagers and relatives. The women sing and dance. Maryam's thoughts are also filled with the days yet to come and of her future husband, Ashraf. Unnoticed, she slips her hands through the three beautiful braids created by Ashraf's mother. She knows her well. She is a sweet and caring woman. Would Ashraf be like her? Her thoughts wander to the quiet young man with brown, often pensive, eyes. Another few days, and he will be her husband. A gentle, yet uncertain smile appears on her face.

It will be a wonderful day. Maryam is up early and Ashraf is awake much earlier than usual. The hours and minutes creep by. It is still long before the real party starts. Even the morning prayer has yet to take place. The sun is not even up yet. Today is *Wru* day, the real wedding and bridal procession. Then the amazing voice of *chargerai* souds like a dance of waves on the oceans. It is the voice of some eldery women who have climbed together on the rooftop of Ashraf's house. They are all incredible artists, singing an incredible song in an incredible way. No combination of words can describe the effect that these women with this song have on Ashraf, Maryam and all the people inside the circle of their voices. The women sing, in a very high tone, the story of a little chick. Every word is extended as much as possible. The song tells the story of a little chick, a chick that is not supposed to crow this morning. It is the story of Ashraf who will become a man today.

This chargerai is a signal for the whole village. Women and girls are busy putting on their best clothes and jewelry. The men are even busier with their guns. During tribal weddings Pashtuns seize every opportunity to shoot in the air and to have shooting competitions. Ashraf pretty much knows what awaits him, yet it is still very exciting. Now the time is really near, and it will be all about Maryam and him.

The hard, sharp crackling of gunfire rips the silence. The tribal Pashtuns are born shooters and fighters. This is their life and entertainment. Almost all of the villagers have gathered, and the men have divided themselves into two groups. One group is on the behalf of the groom, and the other group is on the behalf of the bride. The sheer number of men with their turbans, dangerous-looking rifles, and ammunition belts almost make a bystander forget that this is simply a game during a wedding celebration. Ashraf views the entire scene from a distance. He cannot see very well what the men are using for their target. They stand a bit further, on the rocks, in a place where no one can be hit by a stray. The target must be hit before Wru procession, then the actual wedding may begin. Ashraf sees a few women peep around the corner of a building. Maryam is ready and waiting for the bullseye.

Then loud cheering. One of the men hits the target. There is laughter and cheering. Later, the winner will get a beautiful turban. Shooting at a target is part of the *Naksha Wishtal* tradition. Ashraf cannot recognize the winner from such a distance. Then the group surrounds him. Everyone pounds on his shoulders and congratulates him. In almost a ceremony of its own, the winner is presented with a magnificent turban as a sign of his victory and shooting skills. The women are gone, and the first sounds of drums can already be heard. The last note of the drum is a signal for the start of the party. Wru has begun. Ashraf's heart is beating in his throat.

For the women in the house, everything has seemed to reach a high point. While the men were busy with their traditional shooting game, the women were having a sort of competition with singing and folk dancing. Divided into two groups, they sing in duet-style. Eventually they form a circle and sing and dance the last song in unison. This spectacle is called *balbala*. Then, it is quiet. The sounds of the singing and dancing are silenced. The father and mother of the bride come forward quietly and modestly. They stop just before they reach their daughter. It is a solemn and emotional ceremony of the parting of the bride. Maryam emits a suppressed sob as her father and mother embrace her as a sign of farewell. Everyone is silent.

Then the bride is transferred to the groom's family. One of Maryam's younger brothers carries her to the beautifully decorated horse that is waiting outside. While leaving the house, a woman holds a Quran over her head. It is a symbol of good luck and happiness in her marriage. Maryam is helped onto the horse. Before her sits a child in brightly colored clothes. The youngest brother of Ashraf, Arif, is sitting on the horse, which takes them to Ashraf's house. It is a magnificent, strong brown horse. Most of the people of Darpa Khel are attending the wedding, dressed in their best clothes. Maryam wears a lovely, bright red dress. The wedding dress is modest but incredibly decorated with fine embroidery. The wedding party starts by a group of drummers which is now followed by a huge crowd of women singing and dancing accompanied by young boys. They now go to Ashraf's house. Baba pays the boys who soon allow the couple to pass through the gate leading to Ashraf's house. It is an old tradition.

Through her translucent veil, one can see the radiant and exquisite face of Maryam. Sometimes she has her eyes downward. Sometimes, for a moment, she flashes her gaze forward, towards the direction of Ashraf's house. Her hands, decorated with henna, are like valuable art work. The horse is decorated with flowers. The sound of the drums leads the procession from Maryam's house, through the ket, to the house of Ashraf. Little village girls look breathlessly to the dignified, impressive, joyous procession. Their brightly-colored, festive sawlar kameez makes it an artistic and colorful spectacle.

Handfuls of money are tossed over the bride and horse. That too is part of the Pashtuns tradition. The drums are heard again. The women sing happy songs while the men shoot their rifles and revolvers in the air. It is not long before the procession arrives at Ashraf's house.

In a beautifully decorated room, Maryam is set upon an even more beautifully decorated charpais. All the women are anxious to see her face. Cautiously, the veil is lifted. Aday must see her face first and therefore must be the one to lift the veil. This too has the symbolic meaning. The first woman who lifts up a bride's veil and looks at her must be a woman with many sons. It is another special and emotional moment. Tensely the women gather around the charpais on which Maryam is now standing. After Aday has seen her face, the other female relatives now look at her face. This is called *makh katal*. Maryam receives gifts in the form of money and clothing from her relatives and the other guests who come to see her. In the beginning of it all, Maryam feels embarrassed and shy, but after a while, she begins to enjoy the attention, the kind words, and the presents.

While this is happening, a large feast is being served outside. On the floor is a thirty-foot long rug covered with meat, chicken, curry, rice, and more. Selected guests from the surrounding villages and most of Darpa Khel are invited. Everyone will eat. Again, there is talking, dancing, laughing, and singing. Sometimes, an overeager

Pashtun empties his ammunition cartridge into their air. Everyone comes to shake Ashraf's hand. Everyone wants to talk to Baba. The time flies.

At an appointed time at night, three older male family members go to the room where Maryam and the women are. As the men enter the room, everyone gets quiet. Maryam is sitting on the ornate bed. Around her are gathered a few of her girl friends and female relatives of her age. Then, the deep male voice speaks. Everyone knows what he is going to ask. "Do you accept Ashraf as your future husband, and do you want to marry him?" It is still quiet. Nobody speaks, however there are the sounds of suppressed giggles. One of the girl's whispers to Maryam that she better wait with answering. "Are you sure about it?" whispers another girl. Again, the laughter and giggling is suppressed. It's part of the game. It goes on for a few minutes. And then, it has gone on long enough. Harder than intended, the eldest man clears his throat. He takes a breath to say something. His dark eyes and black beard make it more ominous than it is probably meant. Just before he opens his mouth, Maryam says, "Yes." The man looks surprised. Again, Maryam says yes. The man looks pensively at her for a moment and then suddenly turns and leaves. He seems to have forgotten about the two other men and is already at the door before they rise to their feet. Then he seems to remember that he was not alone here. Abruptly, he stops and turns around. When he sees the two other men get up and walk towards him, he nods and goes outside.

It is not long before the three men return to Ashraf. The feast has concluded and the imam is reading a few verses from the Quran. After the reading, the imam asks the men if the woman gave her consent. Even though Ashraf knows the answer, his heart is still beating in his throat. Those seconds seem like hours. Then, the three men nod and say that the woman has given her permission for the marriage. Ashraf heaves a sigh of relief. Only the Imam seems to hear it. He quickly glances at Ashraf, then continues.

The imam looks at Ashraf and asks him three times if he wants to marry Maryam. Ashraf knows the traditions of his people. Some men do not answer. Some do, but they show doubt, or wait to answer. Sometimes they wait so long that the imam becomes angry, leaves, and the ritual has to be repeated the following day. The grooms want to appear tough, so they make sure that they are not too quick to say yes and wait as long as possible to give their answers. They will brag about this moment for years. The older men find this childish and get grumpy if it takes too long. Ashraf is now waiting. Carefully, he looks from under his eyebrows at the imam. A little further on is Baba. No one seems in a hurry. Ashraf waits a bit longer. A couple of his friends laugh. Then, Ashraf finds the waiting to be long enough. Maybe it is too fast for a real Pashtun, but he says yes. The imam nods and the marriage contract is closed.

Ashraf may finally see his wife. He cannot take his eyes off of her. Her beautiful, elegant red dress. The red veil. Her jewelry, the henna, the flowers, her beautiful light eyes. From under her veil, Maryam peeks at her new husband. She is blushing. How long has she been waiting for this? Her heart is beating in her throat.

The days after the wedding ceremony are still festive but on a smaller scale. Maryam wears her red wedding dress and sits on the beautifully decorated bed for two more days. People still come with gifts and money. Ashraf sits with the men and also gets a lot of visitors. But then, it all ends, and normal life begins.

Ashraf and Maryam are now together. They leave for England where Ashraf works and studies. A year after their marriage, Ashraf's first daughter is born in Coventry, England. He has never been so proud. He is so happy and cannot keep his eyes from his daughter. Her name is Aishah. A few days after the birth, Ashraf gets a call from his old college and village buddy, Dr. Shahidin who is working in Ireland. Laughing, he congratulates Ashraf on the arrival of his daughter and tells him that one of their other friends,

Dr. Jan, told him that he should, perhaps, not send a congratulatory card. "He had a daughter, not a son? Maybe you shouldn't send him a card. Maybe he would get upset?" The Pashtun men laugh. It does not matter to Ashraf. He is just as happy with his daughter as he would have been with a son. Now comes a new period in Ashraf's life, the responsibility of caring for a family.

# A NEW JOB

When he gets the opportunity, Ashraf travels back and forth from England to Pakistan. Sometimes he travels with his family, sometimes alone. He always visits Waziristan, whether it's a quick visit or a long visit. Darpa Khel and Miranshah are slowly changing. Every time he visits Waziristan, there are new people in the Darpa Khel. Along the way, he sees them entering the area, coming on donkeys or arriving in cars or mini trucks. There are so many Datsun pickup trucks that in later years, everyone refers to a truck as Datsun no matter the actual brand of the truck. On every trip, Ashraf always encounters a flow of Pashtuns that are coming from Afghanistan. They are fleeing the Soviets who have now occupied Afghanistan.

It belongs to the Pashtuns and their culture that refugees are warmly welcomed. *Melmastia*, hospitality, is one of the basic principles of pashtunwali. The refugees may live in empty schools and empty houses. They can build huts and mud houses on the land around Darpa Khel and Miranshah. Everyone knows that they will return back to their homeland in Afghanistan once peace has returned there.

Many of these young Pashtun refugees join the mujahideen, the freedom fighters who must liberate the Afghan people from the Soviets. The Soviet Kalashnikov makes its appearance in the tribal areas. Many international powers intervene in the conflict. There will come more weapons and more money, and a large portion of it will go to the mujahideen. The local Pashtuns and the tribal areas still hardly involve themselves with everything that is going on around them. They offer the refugees hospitality. They share their homes, their land, their school, and much more.

As an insider, it is not difficult to distinguish the groups. The refugee men wear their turbans differently, and their dresses are different too. The Afghan refugees do not wear the Dastar turban that comes from the tribal areas. Instead, they wear turbans that are not dyed, but rather are some type of print with stripes. Aslo, the Pashtuns in the tribal areas wear their turbans differently. The long part of the turban goes just behind the left or right ear and then hangs over in front of their shoulder.

Ashraf was just in Miranshah when a Soviet MIG of the Afghan army landed at the airport. Regularly, one can see fighting between military aircraft of the Soviets and Pakistanis. The Soviet MIG's pilot is an Afghan Pashtun who fled from the Soviet regime and is now looking for a safe place in the tribal areas. His plane is confiscated by the Pakistani army. The pilot will live near Ashraf's family home in a small house in Darpa Khel. The pilot's family has already arrived.

It is a strange time. More and more refugees arrive in the tribal areas. Generally, they are poor Pashtuns. The rich refugees move to major cities like Peshawar or Islamabad. Many of them get on planes to Western countries such as America, Canada, and England. At this time, it is not hard for them to get a visa, and therefore the planes are filled to the brim with Afghan refugees who will probably never return to their homeland.

For the poor Afghans, it is a different story. They are trying to survive in the tribal areas or in the huge refugee camps near Peshawar and Queta. The madrasas, or religious schools, in the tribal areas are nearly overcrowded with the children of these poor Afghan Pashtuns, for these madrasas are their only alternatives to sending their children to school. These children are the new talibs and charain who stand at the doors of the houses in Darpa Khel and call out for food. At first, there seems to be no difference between the talibs of now and the talibs of the past. But there is indeed a great difference. This is a new generation of talibs that is entering the tribal areas. They come directly from Afghanistan. Upon their retinas burn the image of the Soviet ruler, the true enemy of their country. Their people must be redeemed. It is not long before these young talibs are recruited as freedom fighters to help drive out the Soviets from their country. Step by step, the religious madarasas that once followed age-old traditions, change as a result of this uprising of young freedom fighters.

Despite that his entire focus is on developing his skills as a doctor, Ashraf sees the worrisome situation and sees that the terms mujahideen and Taliban are slowly but surely being misused. It is an unfair fight against a complex world of superpowers and their enormous interests. Everywhere it is said that the mujahideen are mostly being financed, trained, and armed by the United States, Pakistan, and Saudi Arabia. They are told that this is jihad for Islam. But actually, they are being used to get rid of the Soviets from Afghanistan. World leaders from the West call the mujahideen Ronald Reagan, former President of the United States, called the mujahideen; "freedom fighters, who defend the principles of independence and freedom that form the basis of global security and stability. " In the West, the mujahideen are being positively portrayed in popular action films such as *The Living Daylights* and *Rambo III*.

Ashraf sees the poor Afghan boys who have only just escaped from Afghanistan being recruited, tempted by big money, weapons, and military-related training. One day the young talibs and charains are going among the houses in Waziristan, asking for food, and the next day they are being trained to fight the Soviets. Without explanation, some Afghan elders in the tribal areas gain large sums of money for all sorts of dubious favors in the opaque battle for Afghanistan. They are seen as mentors of the mujahideen. Heroes is a big word, but supporters of the freedom fighters, they are. Abroad, they are respected. Some men are even invited by the incumbent President of the United States to come to the White House.

At the same time, Mikhail Gorbachev, head of the Soviet Union, decides to replace Afghan President Babrak Karmal and gradually withdraw Soviet troops from Afghanistan. Gorbechev wants to end the expensive and hopeless battle in Afghanistan. On February 14, 1989, the last Soviet troops leave the country. The battle for Afghanistan was not a struggle of the Afghan people, but rather a struggle between the rich West and the Soviet Union. The Afghan refugee freedom fighters from the madrasas fight under a new name, the Taliban. Inadvertently and unintentionally, this part of the Afghan Pashtun population was orchestrated as mujahideen in the run-up to the collapse of the Soviet Union in 1991. Until this moment, they had only been a forgotten people with their forgotten land, used only for battle between world powers.

Ashraf's family continues to grow. His son, Hammad, is born, and also his second daughter, Fareeha. Ashraf is a happy man. Most of the time, he is in England with his young family. Yet in the shadows of Ashraf's happiness, is the unrest, violence, and incomprehensible events in Pakistan, Afghanistan, and the tribal areas.

The next time when he steps off the plane to visit his native land, he decides to visit Dr. Shahkar, a friend who is a heart surgeon in Lahore. Ashraf worked with him a few years earlier in the English city of Coventry, though the two have known each other since they were students at the Khyber Medical College in Peshawar. Dr.

Shahkar has been working for a year at the Shaikh Zayed Hospital in Lahore. The hospital is named after the ruler of the United Arab Emirates, for he donated the hospital to Pakistan. It is a modern hospital, just like the ones in Europe.

The two young doctors are happy to see each other again. It's not long that they are sitting upon the beautiful pillows on the ground telling all sorts of tales about their time together at the Khyber Medical College and in England. After an hour, Dr. Shahkar has a proposal. Ashraf should join him and work at the Shaikh Zayed Hospital. The chairman and dean of the hospital is General Mohayedin. It is quite common that during this period of time, highly skilled military men are also the heads of federal institutions such as hospitals. According to Dr. Shahkar, General Mohayedin is a highly respected and feared man. He was the personal physician to Zulfikar Ali Bhutto and former President Ayub Khan. In addition to his current role as chairman, General Mohayedin is also the personal physician to the current Pakistani president, General Zia-ul-Haq, who, in July 1977, along with his allies in the military, brought down Zulfikar Ali Bhutto.

The hospital is looking for a new head for the Department of Otolaryngology. The previous ear, nose and throat surgeon head has moved back to America after a short period in the hospital. Dr. Shahkar tells Ashraf that General Mohayedin would like to meet him and see if he could be the new head of the department.

Ashraf has thought about it many times over the past years about his permanent return to Pakistan. A few times, he has talked about it with Baba. First, he would gain medical experience in England, and then settle in Pakistan. But this proposal from Dr. Shahkar comes too quickly. Ashraf does not want to return to Pakistan right now and settle there permanently. However, out of respect and courtesy for their friendship, Ashraf promises his friend that he will have a conversation with General Mohayedin.

Not much later, Ashraf sits with the General. He is a persuasive man, indicating his eagerness to recruit Ashraf. Ashraf expresses, that if he takes the position at all, he would want to be involved in all the major decisions concerning his department. General Mohayedin nods affirmatively and agrees more easily than expected to all of these requests.

If Ashraf decides to move to Lahore, Baba and the rest of the family in Darpa Khel will not be happy with the decision. Ashraf's eldest brother, Usman, makes it no secret that he believes Ashraf would find better work in Peshawar when he wants to come back and settle in Pakistan. Baba does not say much. Ashraf's colleagues in England will possibly be even more critical of the decision. His career is going well there. Taking his career to turbulent Pakistan seems an illogical and incomprehensible step. Is it Baba's dream that is pulling Ashraf back to Pakistan? Or is it something else?

Ashraf quietly listens to anyone who wants to give him advice. He carefully thinks about this possible step. Then, he makes a decision. Baba has taught him. Listening to others is good, but one should think and decide for himself. Others can advise, but no one knows you like yourself. So, Ashraf makes his own decision.

A few months later, he starts in Lahore. The salary is not as high as it was in England. To compensate a bit, Ashraf decides to work at the hospital during the day and practice privately outside in the evenings. He is very close to Dr. Mehmood Chaudhary, the chief surgeon and professor at the hospital. He lives in a large house near the hospital and uses a few rooms for his private practice. He is a skilled physician who commands respect by his profession. He invites Ashraf to make use of a room for his private practice. The two men get along very well with each other. Ashraf asks Dr. Chaudhary about the rent of the rooms. Dr. Chaudhary replies that Ashraf should not pay anything. Since Dr. Chaudhary does not have a lot of work outside of the hospital, and because people in Lahore have not yet discovered the new doctor Ashraf, the two men often spend many quiet hours talking together.

Ashraf needs new medical equipment for his department. Because the hospital is a public institution, applications for new equipment is a bureaucratic process. Excessive bureaucracy is a part of Pakistani society. Requests for new equipment go through Sethi, the hospital director. During the next meeting of the department heads, led by General Mohayedin, Ashraf asks about the whereabouts of the requested equipment, such as the much needed operating ear microscope. It is a device that Ashraf urgently needs for an ear surgery. General Mohayedin looks irritatingly, and slightly bored, to Sethi. There is no response. The General then becomes visibly grumpy and tells Sethi that he must provide things of this nature and it must be within three days.

For the following three days, Ashraf expectantly awaits the requested equipment. Three days pass, and then three weeks. Those three weeks turn into months, and still the requested microscope and other equipment have not appeared. Again, there is a meeting of the department heads. General Mohayedin leads the meeting. At the end of the meeting Genral Mohayedin asks if there are any other matter to be discussed. "Can I ask you something?" Ashraf raises his hand. General Mohayedin nods. "Three months ago I asked about the microscope and you said that it will come in three days. Did you mean three days, three weeks, three months, or three years?" Ashraf's voice sounds flat, businesslike, yet reproachful. Everyone around the table is dumbfounded by this unexpected and bold question. General Mohayedin looks surprised at Ashraf. Slowly the veins on his neck swell. His head turns purple, he leans, half standing with his hands on the table, and yells, "You must not address the chair in that way!" Suddenly, there is a true soldier at the end of the table. The head of the hospital has turned into a seething military man. Without flinching, Ashraf looks at General Mohayedin. Again, in a flat, businesslike, reproaching tone he says, "But then, Mr. Chairman, you must not make promises that you cannot keep."

General Mohayedin seems to explode. Everyone in the meeting

room is holding their breath. The few seconds of silence seem to last forever. Ashraf looks at the General quietly and straight in the eye. Then a roaring and shrill voice breaks the awkward silence." Get that microscope here!" His breathing is nearly gasping as he barks his command at Sethi. Trembling, Sethi looks at the General. His hands and lips tremble. He nods, looks down, and does not dare to get up.

The meeting is quickly finished. General Mohayedin is the first to stomp out. His eyes are spitting fire, and his head looks swollen. Once he is back in his office he shouts at his personal assistant to get him some headache medicine.

Despite this collision, the relationship between the General and Ashraf remains well. Ashraf takes more and more after the character of his father. Was his motto not "If you are honest and do your job well, then it goes well. You don't have to speak in such a way that you have to tell people what they want to hear"?

Ashraf works long hours at the hospital and at his private clinic. One way or another, he is tough and able to handle it. During his vacation, he returns to England. He can work as a locum doctor and make some extra money. After this short vacation to England, Ashraf returns to Lahore and discovers that General Mohayedin has hired another ear, nose and throat doctor in his department. Ashraf is upset that this happened without being consulted. Ashraf speaks with the man, and it appears he is an experienced physician. For a moment, he thinks about it, but it's no use. He could use an additional doctor, so he quickly divides the work in such a way that they don't interfere with each other, but rather help each other. He had some post graduate training in England but most of the time he worked in a small private hospital in Saudi Arabia.

After a few months, an official note signed by Sethi arrives. Ashraf can't believe what he reads. The memorandum states that the other doctor has been made the head of the ear, nose and throat department, effective immediately. Ashraf reads the note over and over again, and still his eyes can't believe what he is reading. A deep sense of injustice surges like a hot wave throughout his body. He is stunned. After reading the paper one last time, he rushes to the office of General Mohayedin. But he is not there. He has gone to America and Europe for ten days.

Ashraf takes a deep breath. He thinks it over for a long time but decides to wait. The other surgeon is a happy man. He is radiating and, whereas before he was not busy with work and had little time to do anything, he now is quickly making stamps with his name and department head title on them. Ashraf himself, in the preceding period, had not yet found the time and need to have those stamps made for himself.

The ten days of waiting for General Mohayedin are very long. Incredibly long. As soon as the General is finally back, Ashraf is in his office. His demeanor is calm, but inside he is boiling with anger. Ashraf asks for an explanation. The General summons Sethi and the other doctor who immediately arrive. General Mohayedin gestures for Ashraf to take a seat near to him. Ashraf is stubborn and remains sitting in the second row of chairs in front of his large impressive office table.

In a tone contorted with rage, Ashraf makes it clear that he does not accept the other surgeon as the new head of the department. He reminds the General the promises made to him in the very same room when he was trying to convince him to accept the post. Frustrated, he illustrates his point with the story about the stamps. That, within a few days, the other doctor has had them made. General Mohayedin, overly calm, looks at Ashraf. He is a true military man sitting there behind his desk. Confidently, he explains that the other doctor is older and therefore more senior. This seems to be the main reason for the change.

Ashraf looks at the General fearlessly and dismissively. The determination in his eyes reveals that it does not bode well. "If to be older and more senior are the criteria, then there must also be an older and more senior doctor in Lahore that can take over your job." As if by magic, the General's self-assurance disappears. The veins in his neck swell up again, and his head becomes almost purple with rage. Ashraf looks at him boldly. General Mohayedin abruptly turns to Sethi and yells; "Rescind the decision immediately." Then he turns with a jerk towards the other doctor and says, "And you. You. scrap your bloody stamps!" Ashraf turns with a smile on his face and walks away. He is convinced that another round of headache medicine must be on the way to relieve the General of his migraines.

After the death of Zia-ul-Haq, Ghulam Ishaq Khan becomes the new president of Pakistan in 1988. Three months later, the elections are held and the daughter of Zulfikar Ali Bhutto becomes Prime Minister. Just before he was put to death, Zulfikar Ali Bhutto urged his daughter Benazir Bhutto to continue his political career. Now the man that ousted her father, Zia-ul-Haq, is also dead. The time for her political career has arrived. She becomes the first woman prime minister of the Islamic republic of Pakistan. However, her regime is characterized by corruption and nepotism. During this period of political upheaval, many senior officials are replaced by those loyal to the new rulers of the country. Benazir Bhuttto dismisses many influential generals, including General Mohayedin. The General's position at the hospital goes to Dr. Chaudhary, albeit temporarily.

# THE CONFLICT

Throughout the course of time, and after many long hours together, Ashraf and Dr. Chaudhary become friends, more or less. Dr. Chaudhary is trying to be the permanent replacement of General Moheyadin. Additionally, Ashraf has built his own network of influential contacts in Pakistan. Dr. Chaudhary asks Ashraf to help him with lobbying for the position. Dr. Chaudhary knows that Ashraf gets along with everyone at the hospital and that he is also very close to the hospital's president of the Junior Doctors Association. The president, now an influential man, is also a Pashtun, coming from Waziristan. His name is Dr. Bashir Khan and is the son of one of Ashraf's teachers, Khan Mohammad, from Miranshah.

Along with Dr.Bashir Khan, Ashraf heads out to Islamabad to join the parliament members coming from the tribal areas to lobby for Dr. Chaudhary. It is a new role and task that Ashraf takes on. Parliamentarians from the tribal areas are not connected to the political parties. They are more or less independent and have helped Benazir Bhutto gain a majority. This is reason enough to let the mission of Ashraf and Dr. Bashir Khan to continue successfully.

It does not take long before Dr. Chaudhary is awarded the prestigious position of chairman and dean at the Shaikh Zayed Hospital and Federal Postgraduate Medical Institute in Lahore. Ashraf has had his first lobbying experience within Pakistan's political arena.

Many physicians have a temporary contract. In his new position, Dr. Chaudhary invites many of them to discuss their contracts. Ashraf watches this from a distance. He is still using a room at Dr. Chaudhary's for his private practice. With limited interest, but with some surprise, Ashraf sees how Dr. Chaudhary has changed since becoming the chairman. Ashraf frequently witnesses Dr. Chaudhary humiliate fellow doctors by berating them. Ashraf tries to talk to him and, in two cases, prevents two faculty members from being unjustly fired.

Dr. Chaudhary is changing, but Ashraf gives him solicited and unsolicited advice and has made himself available to help at anytime for anything. Once, they are discussing the losses sustained by by the hospital kitchen and cafeteria. Dr. Chaudhary asks Ashraf to help out. Ashraf quickly seeks the help from his resident Dr. Mubashar, a young, energetic, and honest doctor.

Ashraf and Dr. Mubashar dive into the administration. They start with checking the revenue, expenses and supplies, and soon they can hardly believe what they find. The hospital has a contract with a meat supplier to suppy only male goats. During one of the surprise checks, Ashraf finds that the butcher has supplied female goats because they are cheaper. To avoid the deception, the butcher sewed testicles on the female goats. Ashraf can't believe his eyes when he looks at the hindquarters of the animal. He shakes his head and almost laughs. Then his smile turns to bitterness. It is a sign that Pakistan is slowly being poisoned by corruption and deceit from the inside, something that Baba long ago warned him about. The old lessons of Baba flash through his mind as he looks at the testicles that are practically falling off. If the bigger problem wasn't so dire, Ashraf would laugh his head off about this one instance. Now his eyes keep rattling in his head, exasperatingly focused on this strange goat.

Ashraf and Dr. Mubashar immediately decide to stop allowing the suppliers to pay commission to the administration and accounts department staff, which has become a norm in Pakistan. These amounts are considered to be bribe money for all sorts of suppliers are then allowed to supply substandard stuff rather than what is specified in the contract. This action immediately leads to lower prices of goods and to the originally contracted items being supplied. With a few simple changes, the two men turn the loss into a profit of 200,000 rupees within a month!

But Dr. Chaudhary continues to change. Day by day, he becomes more suspicious and jealous. He quickly sees those around him as threats and then hastily tries to fire them in a clever manner. Ashraf remains loyal to him and is his silent advisor. He remains a skilled surgeon, but it is not before too long that he starts to see Ashraf as an irritant and a threat. There is a small incident between Dr. Shahkar and a hospital driver. The hospital driver picks up passengers from Dr. Shahkar's flat to take to school. The driver honks incessantly until the passengers come out of their respective flats. The constant honking below Dr. Shahkars flat is irritating. Ashraf complains to Dr. Chaudhary and requests that the driver be changed. After a few days, Ashraf asks Dr. Chaudhary again. It seems that Dr. Chaudhary is intentionally not paying any heed to his request. In a way, Dr. Chaudhary is trying to irritate the two men so that they get feed up and leave the hospital because they are the only two faculty members who him in the eye. Dr. Chaudhary has reverted to unscrupulous tactics to get rid of them. One day, Ashraf goes to Dr. Chaudhary's office to discuss this issue once for all. The discussion becomes heated, and Dr. Chaudhary tells Ashraf that he has done a lot of favors for him. Ashraf looks at him in astonishment. He wants to remind Dr. Chaudhary of all the favors he has done for him, but instead, he keeps calm and tells him that the only favor he can think of is that he let him use a room, free of rent, for his private practice. "I offered to pay you rent, but you refused. I will still pay, and even pay retroactively for the use." Dr. Chaudhary is on the attack. His suspicions and jealousy make him blind. "No, I do not mean that. What I mean is that I gave you my friendship." Ashraf got extremely upset and angry and replied, "I have given you the best friendship. And from now on, you will see my animosity." With a jerk, he turns around and stomps out of the office.

It is the beginning of a futile struggle. Ashraf remains the head of the otorhinolaryngology department, but Dr. Chaudhary allows history to repeat itself. He makes Ashraf's colleague, Abdul Hadi, increasingly more important. He assumes that Ashraf will eventually choose to leave. But Ashraf is a Pashtun. He is not going to give up so quickly. He is older, wiser, and has become more intransigent when it comes to injustice. He decides to keep a record of Dr. Chaudhary's wrongdoings.

When hiring people for the hospital, Dr. Chaudhary plays, in his own way, political games in which he ignores numerous rules. In addition to Ashraf and Dr. Shahkar, another Pashtun, Dr. Qamar Zaman, works as a the head of the gynecology department in the hospital. Soon it becomes clear that Dr. Chaudhary wants to fire these three men. Not before long, Ashraf's book of records is full of incidents.

The three Pashtuns are determined to not be fired by Dr. Chaudhary. The three of them journey together on the long road from Lahore to Islamabad, through the changing landscape of the Punjab, and meet with the parliamentarians from the tribal areas. From there, they go with the parliamentarians to the minister of health. They meet with the mother of Prime Minister Benazir Bhutto. She is the head of all the federal health institutions. She has an office in the prime minister's house. After they have told her the entire story, she asks them for the names of people who could succeed Dr. Chaudhary.

Ashraf's second lobbying task seems to be headed for another success. The three Pashtuns are giddy with excitement and call the hospital in Lahore and share the news with their friends. But they should have restrained themselves. It only takes a short time before Dr. Chaudhary hears the entire story. Faster than lightning, he gathers his own political supporters and solidifies his position as the hospital chairman by contacting an inner circle of ministers and party members. The three Pashtuns have learned a valuable lesson and are back to square one.

The relationship between Ashraf and Dr. Chaudhary is completely broken. Ashraf still respects him as a surgeon, but despises his administrative and managerial ethos. He does not know what to do anymore. This is all new for him. Dr. Chaudhary does everything in his power to make Ashraf's life miserable. He is constantly and harshly checking Ashraf's work. Ashraf completed a corrective nasal surgery and put a splint on a patient's nose. Dr. Chaudhary sneaks into the ward and lifts up the splint to check and make sure the surgery was done well. Ashraf hears about this from a junior doctor. Dr. Chaudhary later conspires with a young dietitian to lodge a complaint against Ashraf to say he is making indecent proposals. However, neither the check nor the dietician's complaint ever gain ground.

During the ensuing months, Dr. Qamar Zaman's contract comes to an end. He was on a temporary contract, and it was not renewed. Dr. Shahkar also decides to accept a job in Lady Reading Hospital, so he leaves Shaikh Zayed Hospital and moves to Peshawar. This leaves Ashraf, opposing Dr. Chaudhary alone. Ashraf will not budge no matter difficult the situation is made for him. Ashraf is the last Pashtun consultant left in the hospital faculty. His other consultant friends in the faculty avoid him or turn against him in efforts to please Dr. Chaudhary.

As a last resort, Dr. Chaudhary turns to Ashraf's family. He asks for help from Ashraf's father and Uncle Atta Mohammed. In the sixties, Dr. Chaudhary and Uncle Atta Mohammad worked together in the same hospital in Britain. It is not long before Uncle Atta Mohammed visits Ashraf in Lahore. He tries to convince Ashraf to give up the fight against Dr. Chaudhary and in return he would get any position he desires.

Ashraf doesn't even have to think it over. He is a Pashtun. He can be as stubborn and unyielding as all Pashtuns when it comes to choosing between right and wrong when it is about honor. Ashraf cannot let this happen. Dr. Chaudhary began this fight, and Ashraf will finish it. His mind is made up. Uncle Atta Mohammad knew this before Ashraf replied. He could read the answer already in Ashraf's eyes.

After the departures of Dr. Qamar Zaman and Dr. Shahkar, Dr. Chaudhary sees his chance. He suspends Ashraf and Dr. Bashir because they went to Islamabad without formal permission long ago. As a result of his suspension, Ashraf cannot be at the hospital in Lahore. However, in a strange way it works in his favor as he will have all the time to lobby against the injustices of Dr. Chaudhary in Lahore, Islamabad and Peshawar.

While Ashraf is thinking about his next steps, the Prime Minister of Pakistan, Benazir Bhutto, is fired. Almost immediately, she is succeeded by interim prime minister Ghulam Mustafa Jatoi. Ashraf now sees his chance to campaign for the departure of Dr. Chaudhary. For a third time, Ashraf goes to Islamabad, again with Dr. Bashir and Dr. Shahkar, who joins them. Ashraf makes visits to political parties, political leaders, ministers, and many other influential people. As though history were repeating itself, General Mohayedin is again a candidate for the prestigious position at the Shaikh Zayed Hospital in Lahore. After a short while, General Mohayedin goes back to the advice of the president Ghulam Ishaq Khan that the post would no longer suit him.

In Islamabad, Dr. Chaudhary is also lobbying for himself to keep the position. An interesting episode happens in the MNA's hostel where members of national assembly lodge during assembly sessions. Mr. Sultan is an influential MNA from Multan, Punjab. Ashraf goes to Mr. Sultan's room to seek his support. Suddenly, Dr. Chaudhary enters the room. It creates an embarrassing situation especially when he is polite to Ashraf and offers to give him a ride back to Lahore. Ashraf is surprised at this blatant fake dramatics. Ashraf looks at Dr. Chaudhary and could not believe he is offering him a ride back. Is this the same man who is trying, at all cost, to get him removed from the hospital?

In addition to being a skilled surgeon, Dr. Chaudhary is cunning and clever. He is getting better at his lobbying and political skills. He is acquiring more and more support and the chances of him keeping his dream job seem to increase by the day.

Ashraf does not lose heart. He is combative and determined to put an end to the unjust regime of Dr. Chaudhary. During Ashraf's rounds of lobbying, he mets Tasneem Nawaz Gardezi, the new Minister of Health. Together with his friends, Ashraf apprises him about Dr. Chaudhary's misadministration. The minister listens carefully and gives a positive response. But the game is not over yet. Dr. Chaudhary has good resources within the political field of Pakistan. It is not long before he hears about the minister's meeting. With some arrogance, he brags and lets Ashraf know that he is not worried. "I have Gardezi in my back pocket. I paid for the air conditioning at his Lahore home."

Ashraf is in Miranshah for Eid festivities. After Eid prayers he discuses his predicaments with his father and tells him about Dr. Chaudhary's remarks about the health misnister. Although it is a risky plan, they decide to go see the minister to tell him about Chaudhary's comments. They travel on the second day of Eid all the way on a bumpy road from Miranshah to Bahawalpur about 300 -350 miles.

With Baba, Ashraf seeks out Minister Gardezi in his hometown of Bahawal Pur. Ashraf relays what Dr. Chaudhary has said. Minister Gardezi looks at the two men long and thoughtfully nods in approval. Then he asks them to visit him in Islamabad in a few days. The Minister dismisses Dr. Chaudhary and replaces him with General Dr. Najeeb Ahmed. The moment Baba hears the news, he calls Ashraf to tell him. Ashraf heaves a huge sigh of relief, perhaps the biggest sigh of relief in his life up to that point.

# STRUGGLE FOR POWER

The new chairman and dean of the Shaikh Zayed Hospital and Post-Graduate Medical Institute, General Professor Najeeb Ahmed, was previously the director of the National Institute of Cardio-Vascular Diseases (NICVD) in Karachi. Just as soon as his new role and function begins, he must start making tough decisions. He must now decide whether or not the dismissed Dr. Chaudhary should stay on as the head of surgery at the hospital or be sent to the parent department, Provincial Health Department of Punjab, from where he was on deputation to the Shaikh Zayed Hospital.

General Najeeb cannot foresee the consequences of his decision. He is of the opinion that if he leaves Dr. Chaudhary to continue as a surgeon in the hospital, he will win his support and and also be able to keep an eye on him. Ashraf, however, advised the General to send Dr. Chaudhary back to the Provincial Health Department of Punjab and cautioned that if Dr. Chaudhary were to stay, it will not be long before he starts conspiring and stirring things up to get his coveted position back. Ashraf has to watch this happen. His relief was but brief.

A large group of junior doctors and consultants are working on temporary contracts. To win the loyalty of these doctors, new directors often offer them permanent contracts. General Mohayedin had not done that and at the time of his dismissal, and he had no support from his staff at the hospital. The new chairman, General Najeeb also decides to not give this large group of doctors permanent contracts, against Ashraf's advice, reasoning that this will enable him to dictate his authority.

Dr. Chaudhary sees his chance and announces that people are entitled to permanent contracts. He also reasons that it is much better for the hospital if they pick a chairman from within the hospital's original staff instead of choosing an outlier, such as General Najeeb. How he did it, Ashraf does not know, but Dr. Chaudhary has created a new battle in the shortest of times. He organizes meetings with the consultants and doctors who do not have permanent contracts and is gaining support in his struggle against General Najeeb.

At one of these meetings in the consultant's staff room, General Najeeb shows up unannounced. Dr. Chaudhary sees him and shouts that he was not invited and should leave. His shrill and cracking voice echoes throughout the main hall. "This is a faculty meeting, and you're not invited. Go away!" The color drains from General Najeeb's face. He feels humiliated and seems confused whether to leave or to stay. Then Ashraf says, "Stop! I invite you to stay." It's the small nudge that General Najeeb needs. He stays. It is certainly not a nice meeting for General Najeeb. Dr. Chaudhary incites the doctors to seize this opportunity to attack the General. He has the doctors who are not tenured to put the heat on him. Ashraf tries to counter, saying that they have forgotten how Dr. Chaudhary has treated them. General Najeeb listens to all the comments and accusations and promises improvement. General Najeeb's eyes now sees what Dr. Chaudhary is capable of. But it's too late to dismiss him. He knows better than anyone that he has lost all his authority in this short time.

Dr. Chaudhary can smell the victory. He feels that General Najeeb's chances are over. He is on the warpath and wants a large group of consultants to settle this fight once and for all. He goes with a large, rambunctious group towards the General's office.

The chaos seems complete. Dr. Ashraf sees this and swiftly calls Dr. Bashir, the Pashtun who is the son of his former teacher in Miranshah, to arrange for counter action. He mobilizes an equally large group of junior doctors, paramedics and other hospital staff to intercept Dr. Chaudhary's group before they can arrive to the General's office.

The sound of screaming men, hard knocks, and moans overwhelm the hospital corridors and grounds. In a short time, there is a brawl. Dr. Chaudhary, with a bloodied head and torn shirt, looks at what he has done. The sounds of approaching police cars and military police can be heard. Forcefully, they put an end to the brawl.

Dr. Chaudhary is cunning and decides to inform the Ministry of Health about the unrest, spinning the story in his favor. Before the end of the day, General Najeeb is transferred. Dr. Chaudhary is, for a short time, the hero for his group at the Shaikh Zayed Hospital in Lahore. He proudly slaps the shoulders of the consultants and junior doctors that were involved. His torn shirt and still bleeding wound on his head seem to affirm his temporary hero status.

The flush of victory is short-lived. Unexpectedly, a temporary replacement for General Najeeb appears on the doorstep. He is Dr. Ghayur, a surgeon of the Pakistan Institute of Medical Sciences (PIMS) in Islamabad. Dr. Ghayur is a Pashtun! The disillusioned Ashraf cannot believe his luck. Without any hesitation, Ashraf informs Dr. Ghayur about the mishaps in the hospital and the dubious role Dr. Chaudhary has played.

Ashraf advises Dr. Ghayur to send Dr. Chaudhary quickly back to the Punjab Government where he originally comes from. Dr. Ghayur nods during the talk and says that that was his plan and that he will make a recommendation in that regard. He asks Ashraf to have some patience. Those final words leave Ashraf unrestful, and for good reason. Instead of transferring Dr. Chaudhary, Dr. Ghayur puts him on a throne. Ashraf is stunned and doesn't know what is happening. Then he finds out from his sources that Dr. Ghayur visited Dr. Chaudhary's home in the evening. Ashraf can't believe his eyes and ears. How is it possible that there is no end to this? Is it the odd combination of a skilled surgeon and a destructive administrator who puts people on the wrong track? Ashraf wrestles with himself. Is this his fight? Why is he even worried about this?

After a few weeks, a permanent replacement for General Najeeb arrives. He is a retired general. Ashraf also unsuccessfully tries to warm him of the dangers and injustices lurking in the Shaikh Zayed Hospital. It is wishful thinking. This retired general uses the hospital for his own financial gain. He comes from a particular religious sect and puts people from the same sect in high positions in the hospital. He appoints a recently appointed doctor, the son of someone with a high hierarchical position within the sect, as the new hospital administrator. This doctor is single. He moves into an apartment near Ashraf, excpet these apartments were designed to house families. For these family apartments, there is a long waiting list, but that does not seem to apply to him. It is insidious corruption by which everything and everyone is for sale.

This doctor soon starts bringing all sorts of women to his apartment. In this Pakistani culture, and also for Ashraf's Pashtun beliefs, the doctor's behavior crosses a line.

The security guard of the apartment building also cannot stand this disrespectful behavior and warns Ashraf when this doctor brings another woman back to his apartment. Along with the other residents, the security guard makes sure that when this doctor brings a woman, they cannot leave the apartment. Ashraf goes and brings the general and makes it clear that it is a shame for a hospital employee to bring ill-reputed women to his apartment within the hospital complex. Ashraf shouts, "Next time it will be your house!" Other residents want to call the police, but Ashraf stops them. He does not want things getting out of hand. The General promises to fire the doctor. But Ashraf doesn't believe it anymore. He doesn't believe anyone anymore. He feels that the whole world is against him.

He is tired and disillusioned. Has his expectations of the doctor been too high? Is he a perfectionist? Is his confidence in his people and country too high? Does he have an exaggerated sense of justice? Should he just accept that there will be a certain level of corruption and injustice in the people around him? What is the point of having dreams for a country like Pakistan? Dreams for a country like Afghanistan? Dreams for his people in the Pashtun tribal areas?

This fight is taking too long. After some contemplation he submits an application for a two year leave. Normally, such a request would take a few months to process, but his request is approved with lightening speed the same day. A record!

Ashraf had lived in Lahore for about four years. Now, without looking back, Ashraf the Pashtun leaves!

# THE DREAM IS BACK

Having obtained his British citizenship earlier in 1987, Ashraf, along with Maryam and their young family, return to England to settle there. He has had enough of Pakistan. Enough corruption, injustice, unrest, and political games. He has had enough of the ignorance and the inability to do anything about it. Enough of everything!

In England, Ashraf is plagued by inexplicable unrest. He works but looks for other opportunities, both in and outside of England. A colleague at work tells him about opportunities in Saudi Arabia. A few possibilities emerge both in Saudi Arabia and England. Ashraf tells a friend of his who has worked in Saudi Arabia and asks for advice. His unrest continues and eventually Ashraf chooses a hospital in the Eastern Province of Saudia Arabia. This is the area where locals are mostly educated and has a large expat population from all over the world. Without one protest, Maryam follows her husband. The young family is getting used to their father's ways. The time in Saudi Arabia is and will be the best time of his life.

For a period, Ashraf works at the Al Fanateer Hospital in the industrial city of Jubail. After a year or so, he moves to the Armed

Forces Hospital at the outskirts of Jubail the town. That was not an easy step. Saudi Arabia has a strict policy about granting visas associated with the company that one work's for. Under the country's rules, Ashraf cannot just switch from one hospital to another. He must wait two years before he can get another visa again. Ashraf has learned that Pakistan is a country of networks, contacts and corruption. Saudia Arabia is a bit different. It is not so much about corruption as it is about networks and contacts. Soon it is clear that only with the right contacts will he will be able to move to his new job at the military hospital. He meets Mr. Abbas, the Sudanese general manager of the company which runs the Al Fanateer Hospital. He is gentleman through and through, having been educated at a university in Leeds, England. Ashraf is able to create a good rapport with Mr. Abbas, whose two daughters were studying at Fatima Jinnah Medial College in Lahore, Pakistan. This is where Maryam also once studied. With a few phone calls, it is all arranged. There is no money involved. In Saudi Arabia, it is only a matter of who you know .

During this period, Ashraf's youngest daughter, Zainab, is born. Ashraf is proud of his family. Three daughters and a son. When he thinks about his family, all the other problems seem so small and insignificant.

From a distance, Ashraf follows the developments in Pakistan, Afghanistan, and the tribal areas. He also continues to follow the events at the Shaikh Zayed Hospital in Lahore. Whether he likes it or not, his old friends and colleagues tell him everything that happens in the hospital. The contract of Dr. Bashir, the son of the teacher from Miranshah, will not be renewed. Dr. Chaudhary seems to be the eternal replacement for all the generals who come and go as chairman of the hospital. And he is becoming more powerful. His career does not go by the book, but eventually Dr. Chaudhary gets a shot at being the Minister of Health in Punjab, the largest province of Pakistan. Slowly but surely, Ashraf's frustration towards Dr. Chaudhary evaporates. Despite their quarrel, Dr. Chaudhary has always been a very skilled surgeon and, in his networking and lobbying, a smart man.

Ashraf is at work in Saudi Arabia. His unrest disappears. During the summer holidays, he goes to England, and in between he goes home regularly to Waziristan. Asghar, Ashraf's younger brother, has also become a doctor. He, however, does not want to leave his homeland and has decided to stay with Baba. Asghar wants to establish a clinic and perhaps later a hospital in Miranshah. He wants to serve the local population. Ashraf knows that this is a great dream of Baba's and helps Asghar however he can.

In England, during a summer holiday, Ashraf meets a group of doctors from the Pakistani province Khyber Pakhtunkhwa who also want to return to Peshawar in order to set up a hospital there. Ashraf thinks of Baba's dream. Medical care for his own people. He decides to join the group, quickly, without hesitation. Along with ten other doctors, they decide to start a hospital. They want to call this hospital the Ghandara Institute of Medical Science. They organize meetings at various locations around Manchester and Blackpool in order to devise a strategy for funding and making preparations. It soon becomes apparent that even the preparations are costly.

During this time, Professor Dr. Kabir, one of their former teachers at Khyber Medical College in Peshawar, meets some members of the group in England as he also intends to start a private medical college in Peshawar. They negotiate the modelaties of cooperation and partnership but not much comes out of it for the group. However, Dr. Kabir does gain from this meeting, as he names and registers his project as the Ghandhara Institute. The group cannot do anything about this as they had not registered the name. Dr. Kabir beats them to it, and his resources give him an edge. He is financially very well off and has solid political connections. He has been the Principal of Khyber Medical College of Peshawar and also the Secretary of Health of the Provincial Government.

The men don't worry themselves too much about it. They want to start their own clinic as soon as possible, but only when they can financially handle it.

Some of the group members during a visit to Pakistan give a presentation to the Minister of Health. By this time, they have a new name for their project, the Abaseen Institute of Medical Sciences (AIMS). The minister offers the group the Rural Health Center at Nahaqi, on Charsadda Road, for joint management as public private partnership. The employees will be paid by the government while the group of doctors must provide the money to run the hospital and, where necessary, adapt and improve. And that is desperately needed. The group receives funding from a health authority in Britain for some joint work. Making the realization of the plan seem closer than ever. Ashraf is proud.

One of the ten doctors gets a job at the Khyber Medical College as assistant professor and as a visiting physician at the Lady Reading Hospital of Peshawar. As it usually happens in joint groups, this doctor wants the project for himself and one of his first activities is to conspire and dismiss all the other doctors in the organisation. Ashraf can't believe what he is witnessing. The reason he gives for dismissing the doctors is that they have not been present at the annual general body meeting of the organization! Even before a reaction is possible, this doctor appoints his family members to the board of directors of the the organization to replace the doctors. Ashraf is furious. The other men as well. They explain this conflict to the government and the governor's inspection team is tasked to investigate. It doesn't take long before it is decided that they are in the right. Yet, in the end, it doesn't solve anything, for the man has good contacts with the local government, and they are unable to dismiss him.

The remaining group decides to withdraw from the Rural Health Center and continue under the previous name Abaseen Institute of Medical Sciences (AIMS). They get funding from the World Health

Organizations (WHO) and two ambulances from another organization for a diabetes project. By this time, a second member of the group has moved to Peshawar, and it is not before long that this time he decides to claim the project for himself leaving the other members high and dry.

This is the final straw that breaks the camel's back. Ashraf is sick. Again disillusioned, he withdraws from the group. What is it about this country and its people? How often should he discover that corruption and self-interest have apparently become the most important values in Pakistan? Tired and depressed, Ashraf withdraws to concentrate on Waziristan. The familiar sounds of Darpa Khel, the people with their ancient Pashtun traditions and occasionally ludicrous obstinacy, let him forget his many frustrations. This time his frustrations do not run as deep as the previous time.

The determination in his eyes is stronger than ever. Finally, Ashraf makes the decision to fulfill his father's dream himself without the help from others. Without outsiders, but ,instead, along with his wife, children, Baba and Hammad. Suddenly, the old fire is back. The dream that he, as a young boy, heard from Baba: quality health care made available and affordable for his people.

This time he's going to do it alone!

# SERIOUSLY ILL

Ashraf alternates living and working in England, Saudi Arabia, Pakistan, and Waziristan. He sees the world around him changing quickly.

Pakistan remains a volatile country whose power dynamics are constantly changing. It is 1999 and General Pervez Musharraf is serving as the chairman of joint chiefs and the chief of the army staff. In October, while abroad, General Musharraf is dismissed from office by Prime Minister Nawaz Sharif. General Musharraf tries to return to Pakistan on a flight from Sri Lanka with two hundred other passengers on board, but Prime Minister Sharif does not allow the plane to land. This is a huge mistake on the part of Prime Minister Sharif because within hours of the decision, the army deposes him in a bloodless coup and allows the plane, which only had enough fuel to fly for a few more minutes, to land. This incident does not escape without consequences. On June 20, 2001 General Musharraf appoints himself as the president of Pakistan.

At the same time, the situation in Afghanistan does not come to rest. The country is divided among many local militias and warlords fighting each other. Mostly as a result of the United States' aid to the mujahideen, the country and tribal areas are up to their necks in weapons. The West needs to help bring stability to Afghanistan. Trained by the West, the Taliban helps with restoring peace and order in the country. Under the leadership of Mullah Mohammed Omar, the Taliban rapidly emerges as powerful group. Back in 1995, they conquered Herat, and in 1996 Kabul fell into their hands. In 1997 and 1998, against much opposition, they took the north. Only Badakhshan and the Panjshir Valley in the northeast remain in the in hands of Ahmad Shah Massood. This Ahmad Shah Massood was an Afghan-Tajik leader who played a role in ousting the Soviets from Afghanistan. As one of the leaders of the Northern Alliance, he fights against the Taliban.

The power center of the Taliban is Kandahar. Initially, the Taliban brought peace and order. Important decisions made in the Supreme Council are made relatively democratically. The ancient principle of 'majority rules' is long-standing. The Taliban are a religious group that strictly adheres to the rules of Islam and advocates Sharia law.

Ashraf thinks back to forty years ago when Mullah Dindar tried the same thing in Miranshah and Darpa Khel. In every village that he visited, he wanted to institute Sharia, the original Islamic law. At that time, most villages in Waziristan did not have so many problems.

Now, instead of Mullah Dindar, it is the Taliban, who were trained and armed by the West. On September 9, 2001 Ahmad Shah Massood is killed in an attack. The last resistance against the Taliban seems obliterated. Then on September 11, 2001, the world is shocked by the events in New York and Washington D.C. Thousands of people die. America accuses the Taliban and Al-Qaeda of the Saudi Muslim fundamentalist Osama bin Laden, of being responsible. The Taliban has, for years, with help from the US, the West and Saudi Arabia, participated in the struggle against the Soviet/Russians, and, according to the United States, has now turned against the Western World. They claim that Osama bin Laden is in Afghanistan and demand his extradition. The following day, the Taliban reject this ultimatum. They want to see evidence and are only willing to accommodate the request as a trial will take place outside the United States.

Because of this, the United States and the United Kingdom decide to attack the Taliban. The Northern Alliance that is bombarding the Taliban receives military aid, and the Americans, along with support from the British, increase the pressure on the Taliban. During these actions, thousands of Taliban fighters and civilians are killed. Soon, only the southern area and tribal areas, including Waziristan, remain in the hands of the Taliban. Osama bin Laden is not found despite all the military deployment.

It is the beginning of a long, exhausting, devastating battle that is fought mainly in the tribal areas between Pakistan and Afghanistan. The maliks are now gone from the land, and the ways of the Taliban rule. This is where Ashraf was born and bred. This is the land where he wants to realize his dream. The country that, years from now, will be plagued by rampant bombings and drone attacks.

In 2003, Ashraf makes a visit to Peshawar. Dr. Shahkar is also there. Like Ashraf, he also currently works in Saudi Arabia at the Saudi ARAMCO.

For some fifteen years, Ashraf has been experiencing some pinching pain on the left side of his chest. It has gradually gone worse. After investigation he discovers this to be a small tumor on one of the intercostal nerves which is usually benign but could be extremely painful especially when touched or pressed. Over the course of time his children have also gradually known not to press against his left side of the chest. This has progressed to a situation where he cannot sleep on the left side as as it stretches the nerve leading to severe pain.

He has already discussed the condition with his friend and decides to have the surgery performed by him in Peshawar. Although, due to the large network that he has established, Ashraf can have treatment and surgery for this anywhere, and for free. In Great Britain, Lahore, or in the prestigious military hospital in Riyad in Saudia Arabia. As usual it is not long before everything is ready. He envisages that it will take only a day or two to recover, and hence he does not inform his wife and children so as to spare them of unnecessary worry. Dr. Shahkar operates on him at the new private hospital in Hayatabad. It is a recently developed residential area of Peshawar that is near the border of Afghanistan. This is where Ashraf also built a house. The surgery goes well, but the wound is painful.

Hours, and a few days, pass, but Ashraf is not recovering. The pain gets worse rather than better. He is running a high temperature. Beads of sweat form on the brow of the ailing Ashraf. He has severe diarrhea as well and is exhausted to the extent that he could not walk to the wash room and had to use a pot by the bed. His wound has become infected. He becomes seriously ill. He is transferred to the hospital's intensive care unit. There are more patients there with the same symptoms. They also had surgery on the same day that Ashraf did. Earnest research is being done. What is the cause? After personal investigation by his relatives and colleagues it is found that the same day when Ashraf had surgery, there was another patient with infected burn wounds. It seems that the infection had spread from this patient to him and the other seriously ill patients who also had surgery the same day. Two of the patients die in the next few days.

Ashraf's health continues to deteriorate. His wound is open and full of pus spreading into his chest and near to the pericardium, the covering of the heart. Usually seventy percent of patients with such chest infection never make it. He loses consciousness. Is this the end? Baba and his sons fervently consult Dr. Shahkar. Is there a cure? Is there something that can be done? Worried faces stare across the table, searching for a solution that no one sees. Baba, Usman, Dr. Shahkar and other relatives make the decision.

They come to the conclusion that here, in Hayatabad, patients are dying. Ashraf cannot stay here any longer. Soon, Ashraf is transported by plane to the Agha Khan Institute in Karachi. It is one of the most famous hospitals in Pakistan, known for its quality, knowledge, and skills. Ashraf hovers between delusion and reality, between life and death. Occasionally he is conscious and confusingly looks around. Lying strapped in a stretcher fixed across three seats, accompanied by Asghar and his nephew Hamid, he ascends into the skies above Peshawar and heads towards the direction of Karachi.

There is an ambulance waiting for him at the airport that swiftly transports him to the emergency room of the Agha Khan University Hospital. Here he immediately undergoes CT-guided aspiration of the pus collection in his chest and around his heart by the highly skilled heart surgeon, Dr. Shahid Sami and his team.

Ahsraf opens his eyes and sees a blurred familiar face. He tries to remember and put a name to the face. After a while he recognizes the face, it is Dr. Mubashar, his confidant from Shaikh Zayed Hospital in Lahore with whom he had brought the hospital's catering department's expenditures in order. He looks at the worried and sad face of his confident. A smile appears on both faces. Dr. Mubashar is doing everything he can to take care of Ashraf as best as possible. For days, he hovers between life and death. His body fights a hard and bitter battle against an enemy that is invisible to the human eye. The infection seems to lose ground, inch by inch. Then, it is over. The infection has been overcome, but the body is exhausted from the struggle. His diarrhea has also stopped after discontinuing the antibiotic Augmentin. The days slip by. Finally, the infection is completely defeated.

After ten days, Ashraf can sit down again, and not long after, he is successful with taking a few steps. The proud Pashtun in him is reawakened, and soon he is unstoppable. Ashraf wants to return to Peshawar and then quickly go back to Maryam and his children in Saudi Arabia. The doctors and nurses are concerned and try to talk him out of it, but the determination of the Pashtun blood running through his veins prevails. Two days later, with sweat on his face and trembling hands, he is on a plane on the way to Saudi Arabia to be reunited with his family. For far too long have they been worried. It is time to reassure them.

At King Fahad International Airport in Dammam, an ambulance is waiting to take him straight to the Armed Forces Hospital in Jubail. He must stay in the hospital for a few weeks so that the gapping open wound in his chest can be cleaned and dressed once or twice a day. All the veins in his hands and arms have become thrombosed and collapsed from the many painful injections. His colleagues from the hospital take good care of him and his family. After a few weeks he is transferred to his house but he still has to take rest for a further two weeks after which he is completely recovered. He has cheated death.

Ashraf has had a lot of time to think. Why is he not dead and the other patients are? Why do some people die young, and other do not? Why did so many children in Darpa Khel die from the plague, but he and his brothers did not? Does God have a purpose for his life? Why has he escaped death again, while other people around him have long been buried? These are questions that he receives no answers for. Sometimes, for hours, his brown eyes stare off into the distance, searching for the answer. Then sounds the last call for prayer. Ashraf stands up and follows.

## KIDNAPPING IN MIRANSHAH - AUGUST 12, 2005

Life goes on. The brief, but intense, period of Ashraf balancing on the brink of death has changed him more than he wants to admit. Increasingly, he is deep in thought, searching for his destiny. Increasingly, the words of Baba return to his thoughts as if asking for a short-term solution. Baba's dream to become a doctor. To make health care in Waziristan and the tribal areas accessible to everyone. An end to the senseless deaths of those who die out of sheer lack of doctors and medicine. But where should he start in this country stricken by the diseases of corruption and self-interest? Where should he start, now that the tribal areas have become the world's battlefield in the supposed fight against terrorism? Will the roar and thunder of bombings and the fear of drone attacks ever disappear from the tribal areas? Will Darpa Khel and Miranshah ever return to the place where the boys of the ancient Pashtun tribes sleep in the courtyard and the young Talibs call at the gates to receive their daily ration?

In the tribal areas between Pakistan and Afghanistan, there is certainly a large shortage of ear surgeons. In fact, ear surgeons are near non-existent. Ashraf still carries a simmering desire to give back something to his country of birth which has enabled him to be a skilled surgeon, and to be able to provide his family a fulfilling environment. So, he decides to try again. He has learned a lot through trial and error. This time he relies on his own knowledge and Baba's dream to help guide him. He is a respected ear, nose and throat surgeon, and he feels that he could have a tremendous input in this scarcely provided field. He discusses his plans with his friends Musheer Hussain, a very prominent ear surgeon in the UK, and David Proops, a famous ear surgeon in Birmingham who was once also the president of the Association of ENT and Head and Neck Surgeons of the UK. They both pledge their support and promise to help in whatever way they can. In fact, it was Musheer who suggested the name for his project, MAKIOSHS.

Ashraf decides to start MAKIOSHS, the MAK Institute of Otology, Speech, and Hearing Sciences. Slowly but surely, the plan develops in his head, and he begins to work out the details. During each visit to Peshawar and Waziristan, he arranges meetings with people from the government to talk about his plans and to assess whether or not he can count on their support. He arranges a meeting with and speaks to the Governor of Khyber Pakhtunkhwa Mr. Iftikhar Hussain Qureshi and tells him about his plans.

He sits in the meeting room of the huge Governor House of Peshawar with its high walls, elegant furniture and pictures of previous governors dating back from the English era hanging on the walls. The governor looks at him, deep in thought. "You're a year late. Earlier, I could have given you a piece of land in Peshawar for your project, but not anymore." Ashraf is silent. Without having too high of expectations, he looks at the man with his brown, thinking eyes. It is an awkward silence that hangs in the room. Both men seem trapped in their own thoughts. "I am not the chief executive of the province any more as there is a democratic government in place, but I do have another offer. A space in the

Agency Headquarters Hospital in Miranshah, which is still under my jurisdiction. You can take any empty plot of land or a wing in the building. Just say the word." Governor Qureshi gives a questioning look to Ashraf. He doesn't react immediately. Then he nods thoughtfully and promises to take a look at it.

Is it safe to go to Miranshah? Ashraf, deep in thought, looks at the traffic that hurtles past him. Why don't they stop with their never-ending, senseless honking? It is typical for Pakistan. Everyone seems to honk their horn from the moment they get behind the wheel. Reason or no reason.

It is a period in which the Pakistani army is very active in Waziristan. The battle against terrorism is at its peak. There are continuous bombings and military operations by the Pakistani army in the tribal areas. The American's unmanned aircrafts are a nightmare for every Pashtun in the area. With their special and worrisome sound, they are nearly invisible and ensure the destruction of every house, village, or convoy in which terrorists are believed to be hiding in. No judge, no trial, just the execution of residents of the tribal areas thought to be involved in terrorism.

Strange, actually, that there is so much resistance when Ashraf explains the principles of pashtunwali. Eye for an eye, tooth for a tooth. What is the difference with drones and military actions that have already slain thousands of people? Both the guilty and not guilty. These are the questions that nobody wants to ask and nobody wants to answer.

Ashraf does not want to get involved in this fight. He has his own battle. It is an uphill struggle to make Baba's dream a reality. A dream that is slowly becoming his own. A friend arranges a meeting for Ashraf with General Safdar, the Corps Commander of the 11th Corps in Peshawar which is responsible for all the military operations in Waziristan. After the usual compliments, the conversation quickly comes to Ashraf's plans in Miranshah. From his first words, General Safdar is enthusiastic about the plans. He shows keen interest in his project and promises to supply funds for a new building of the project at the Agency Head Quarter Hospital in Miranshah. From that moment, everything goes smoothly.

Ashraf leaves Peshawar and heads to Miranshah. Hamid, the son of his eldest brother Usman, is his driver. The young man likes to drive cars and loves to do all kinds of jobs with Ashraf. He is often called upon during Ashraf's visits, when Ashraf has meetings to explain and discuss his plan and arrange matters. Sometimes, it seems as though nothing has changed. Sometimes, the violence has seemed to have disappeared and is no more than a terrible nightmare after a long, hot sleepless night. The drive to Miranshah and Darpa Khel goes smoothly. There are a few common check points with Pakistani soldiers behind sandbags, but even that gives virtually no delay.

In Miranshah, Ashraf inspects the clinic. He is surprised. It is an extremely suitable place in the hospital for his plans. Is everything now coming together? All the lessons he learned, Baba's dream, the experiences and knowledge he had gained, and even the difficult periods of his life? He chooses to temporarily set up in a large unused wing and build on an adjacent piece of land. With his savings, he would make improvements to the wing, and soon, the work will be in full swing.

During one of his visits, General Safdar sends his medical corp head, General Malek, who is also a doctor, along to Waziristan to look at the project. The two men inspect the chosen place for the new clinic. The first steps in making Baba's dream a reality are coming closer by the day. He comes back to Peshawar to complete the official formalities in the Federally Administered Tribal Areas (FATA) Secretary for allotment of the plot in the hospital in Miranshah. He is surprised to find bureaucratic hurdles even though the governor had given direct instructions. During the visit to Miranshah he has also taken with him Mr. Farooq, a famous architect in Peshawar. Mr. Farooq was instrumental in selecting the site. Ashraf's leave has finished, and he must return to Saudi Arabia. He arranges with Mr.Farooq to pursue the matter and to draw the building plan.

Like a virus, the new plans have a grip on him and as soon as his work in Saudi Arabia permits, he goes back to Pakistan. His impatience drives him back to his homeland where he flings himself with full force into the new project. As usual, nothing in Waziristan goes by itself. One hundred and one things clamor for his attention, and quickly he has to return to Peshawar to arrange matters that have to be settled on site. Ashraf usually does not drive, so Hamid takes him from Darpa Khel to Peshawar. The men get into the beige Suzuki Alto and drive out of the gate towards the collection of hills in Waziristan.

About five miles before Mir Ali, they are overtaken. Irritated, Ashraf looks aside to the reckless, speeding vehicle. It is a white pickup truck. Masked and heavily armed men sit in the back of the pickup. They are the kind of Pashtuns that Baba has warned him about many years ago. Loafers who never went to school and are now afraid to work. They are the kind of men who were poisoned by the struggle of the West against the Soviets, and now by the fight against terrorism. They are seen more and more. Foolish, headstrong, loafers who apparently have nothing better to do than drive around, heavily armed. The boys and men who were, in the past, recruited to fight in Afghanistan against the Soviets, now feel that everyone is their enemy. They had been trained and armed by the West. Money and weapons have been abundant. While Ashraf looks annoyingly at the men and shakes his head unnoticed, they are roughly pushed off the road. Hamid steers sharply to the left and slams on the brakes as hard as he can. The men are rocked back and forth, and they nearly slam into the pick up truck. Ashraf feels anger surging like a wave through his body.

Like lightning, the heavily armed men jump out of the back of the truck. Taking a few big steps, they reach Ashraf and Hamid's car. Roughly, they open the doors and drag the two men out from the car. They yell at them, kick them, and beat them. Ashraf resists, but it is useless. Strong hands violently push him back into the backseat of the car. Hamid is brutally pushed through the other side and into the backseat as well. Three of the heavily armed men dive into the small Suzuki Alto. The whole things last only a few moments. The hard, cold steel of the barrel of a Kalashnikov becomes painful as it is pushed against Ashraf's neck. It is a tacit message that Ashraf should keep his mouth shut.

Then they drive away. It is a wild ride. The men drive like crazy. Out of his peripheral vision, Ashraf can see that the criminal has his finger on the trigger of the Kalashnikov that is still painfully pressed against his neck. While both men are slung around in the car, a strange sense of peace comes over Ashraf. He is surprised that the Kalashnikov has not gone off, since the men themselves need to use their hands and feet to brace themselves from being thrown against the roof and sides of the car. Only the finger on the trigger of the Kalashnikov seems to be an exception to this chaos.

Ashraf can't believe it. How cans this happen to them? He can't be kidnapped in his own territory by his own people. Ashraf has a lot of money in various currencies. The armed men are still busy with the road and their surroundings. Despite the constant pressure from the barrel of the gun against his neck, he knows that he must inconspicuously remove his British passport from his back pocket and hide it between the rear seats. Again, he hits his head against the side of the car. Hamid moans. The driver of the car is clearly the leader. The men in the Suzuki Alto are talking about him. The pressure of the barrel becomes slightly less, and Ashraf sees the pick up truck driving ahead of them. After a while, the white pickup disappears. Ashraf and Hamid are not handcuffed. Everything went too quickly for that. What could he do against armed men? All kinds of thoughts flash through his mind. He looks at Hamid, but he is obviously preoccupied with his own troubles.

The men continue to drive like mad men. It works better to look outside. Ashraf does not recognize where they are. They follow unpaved, bumpy roads alongside small streams. The barrel of the Kalashnikov against the neck make the hills and mountains appear all huddled together. After having driven for nearly an hour, they stop. It is going as crazy, as uncontrolled, and as sudden as when they had been pushed off the road. Ashraf hits his head. Anger blazes through his body. Roughly, the men are again dragged out of the car. They find themselves in the middle of high hills with a small pass. There is nothing visible all around but the hills with dark stone rocks and only a few patches of flat areas.

They are questioned and searched. The men ask about their identity and relatives and whom to contact about verifying the facts they have told the men. The armed men find a mobile phone and an i-mate. Everything is torn up and taken. Ashraf quickly realizes that the men do not know what an i-mate is. Surprised, they look at the device. Glancing back and forth between the i-mate and Ashraf, the men ask him in a threatening manner if he is a spy. Though Ashraf cannot see the men's faces as they have covered their faces with their traditional *patkai* cloth, he hears the men's accents and can tell that they are from the Laar Daur tribe and the Wazir tribe. They are men of his own people. Ashraf cannot get over it. Men of his own people. The Pashtun people, who he returns to every time. The people for whom he is building the hospital. How has this country has been poisoned? How have his people been screwed up by all the influences of the past few years? Why has mankind not left his people and traditions alone? Why did they join and fight alongside the international powers? Why were tons of dollars, weapons, and military training given to people who only wanted to do wrong with it? Why could the Pashtuns not be left alone with their own laws, rules, and culture?

Again, Ashraf feels anger surge throughout his body, and he must do everything in his power to keep himself from attacking the criminals. The men still keep their faces covered. Meanwhile, the leader who drove the pickup reunites with the group. They do not look like dignified men. They appear worthless and lazy, idlers who are not worthy to be called Pashtuns. A disgrace to their proud people, faith, and culture.

Fortunately, Ashraf has another bottle of mineral water with him. He's been away from Waziristan long enough abroad that his stomach is no longer used to the hard water here. After some questioning, the kidnappers in the white pick up truck leave, saying that that they will come back in a few hours after verifying the facts and that Ashraf and Hamid would probably be released. Ashraf uses the time to think. He can still not believe what is happening. He feels like it is a dream, but then some military aircraft far in the sky brings him back to reality. He wishfully thinks that the aircraft could have possibly spotted them from the sky. What should they do? Run? Ashraf asks the remaining kidnappers if he can attend to natures call and is allowed go behind a huge boulder nearby. Ashraf tries to break up his credit cards. The men have not yet found these. While he is trying to break them up on the rocks, Ashraf realizes that the men probably don't even know what to do with the credit cards. To be sure, he destroys them anyway and leaves them behind in the rocks. Before he contemplates his next move, one of the men calls for him to come back.

It is a long day, and some how it feels to have stretched out too long, having spent most of the day sitting in the blazing sun out in the middle of no where, surround by very imposing hills. Ashraf gradually gets restless as the day goes on. As it nears sunset, the pickup truck returns and informs them that they could not make any contact with their relatives. Therefore, they have to be taken to some safe place for overnight stay. For the first time reality sinks in. Ashraf realizes they are in for a rough and uncertain time. They are huddled into the front seat of the pickup truck. One kidnapper drives and the rest of the armed men ride along in the back of the pickup truck. An arduous and very uncomfortable drive begins. A large patkai is thrown over Ashraf and Hamid's heads so that they will not be able to identify the location. They drive through uneven terrain, over streams and rocks. Soon it becomes pitch dark. Ashraf cannot breathe well as it it is very hot and humid. He starts making noises in protest for the cloth to be removed from their faces and tries to convince them that it is dark and he will not be able to make out the directions. The pickup stops, the driver gets out and discusses the situation with the other men. The driver removes the cloth from their heads, bringing a sigh of relief for the two men.

Moments later they are driven again back through the mountains and valleys. They see by the light of the pickup's lights that they are driving along zig zag roads, through valleys and mountains, and along some small villages. They pass through a wide river stream and then along the high bank of a river with an undulating makeshift road. After a few hours, they reach a village. The large doors of a house open, and they drive inside. Two traditional beds are ready for them. Ashraf shakes his head. This is probably the first time that a native Waziristani has been kidnapped by his own people!

The kidnappers have even prepared a feast for the men consisting of curry, chicken, and pilaf. There is everything. Ashraf will not take one bite. Surprised that he is not eating, one of the kidnappers wants to know why. Hamid crams some food into his mouth. Ashraf can no longer resist. He explodes and scolds the despicable kidnapper. "Would you eat in my situation, you idiot?" Ashraf calms down and lies on a bed. A few strangers come to him to massage his arms and legs. These strangers seem to have nothing to do with the kidnapping and are just doing their job. Ashraf is tired and gives in. It is a common ritual in Waziristan. It helps to get a little bit of rest and relaxation. At midnight, just as he was going to sleep, two men come in and begin discussing something with the guard in the distance. Ashraf hears them say that this location is not safe. It is not clear why the kidnappers think this is so. They then ask Ashraf and Hamid to get up and follow them. They are taken through the dark, quiet narrow streets of the village in another compound and enter through a big door to a large courtyard. They are escorted to one end of the compound where there is a veranda in front and room towards the back. They are taken a large rectangular room. There are charpais in a row against the wall opposite the door. There is one bulb hanging from the roof. Two electric fans stand on the ground, making the typical buzzing sound that Ashraf still remembers from his childhood. Shabby mats and pillows are on the charpais. The armed men lock the door behind them. Ashraf and Hamid go to sleep.

The next morning, the two men are awakened early for prayer. As if there is nothing remarkable happening, they follow along with the traditional morning prayer rituals. There is a small squarish area in the corner near the door measuring about 4x4 feet with three feet walls and a small entryway which is used for washing up and ablutions. There is bucket full of water and a small pot called a *lota* with a handle and an S-shape nozzle. This lota is filled from the bucket for ablutions. There is a small traditional round clay pitcher, full of drinking water. Just near the entrance to the washing area is a *shkeyr*, a circular woven basket made from the leaves of a *mazarai* plant. This shkeyr is filled with hay upon which a chicken sits over her dozen or so eggs.

Ashraf and Hamid sit together in this room with dark, mud walls. Occasionally they hear sounds, but they cannot understand anything. There are no windows in the room, and they are unable to escape. There is a small one-foot diameter hole in the wall facing their charpais. The hole is high, near the roof, blocked with bags. This, they soon learned, is used for keeping an eye on them throughout the night. In the morning, Ashraf and Hamid are forbidden to talk to each other. The young Hamid is clearly afraid to break this rule. Ashraf's bottle of water is now empty. He is afraid of getting sick from the local water and asks the kidnappers for a new bottle. After many hours they come back telling him that they could not find bottled water but instead bring him 7Up. Because their watches have been confiscated, Ashraf and Hamid have no sense of time. Time crawls, minutes to hours and hours to days.

When it is time for prayer, there is a pounding on the door. The food they are served is very basic. However, due to his anger and frustration, Ashraf will not eat. He is visibly losing weight and getting physically weaker. Hamid eats all the food, including the part that is meant for Ashraf. The most distressing thing they experience is when they need to go for toilet. At night, they are taken out of the room and made to relieve themselves in a large round flat pot filled with stones. During the day they are given this pot to use in the room. At some point, the pot is emptied.

Ashraf can be mean. Often he is angry and thoroughly scolds the kidnappers. The kidnappers try to please Ashraf by giving him massages and trying, in their own way, to make things comfortable for him. They ask Hamid to encourage Ashraf to not to be angry as they are trying to bring their captivity to an end as soon as possible. Hamid shrugs. Ashraf hears the men's request. Their stupidity seems to have no limit. Ashraf is only concerned with one thing. During the long hours of the day, he is constantly wondering how they can get out of there. Baba and his brothers must be working on a plan to rescue them. But if so, where would they be able to take cover to avoid being hit by gunfire? In Waziristan, these matters are resolved with pashtunwali. Eye for an eye, tooth for a tooth. Will they try to free them using brute force? Will they take family members of the kidnappers' hostage and use them as bargaining chips? Does Baba and Usman even know what has happened? Where they are? And does Ashraf's family in Saudi Arabia know what has happened? Questions, questions, questions. Ashraf does not know. His anger and frustration battle with his innate drive to survive. All this while his physical strength is rapidly decreasing due to lack of food.

One of the kidnappers tries to befriend Ashraf and Hamid. He tells them about his burdened life. Only his dark eyes are visible as his broad face is masked by the patkai. The turban on his head lays a bit crooked over one ear and his long hair. He says with a dramatic undertone that he does not even have money to buy alcohol. Ashraf feels a wave of despondency and despair rush through his body. Amazed, they watch this strange alcohol-seeking Pashtun. With the same stupid look in his eyes, the man promises them that he will help the men escape if they, in turn, give him money. This man also tells them about his short stint of employment in Dubai some time ago.

Ashraf and Hamid look at each other. They don't know what to think. It is clear to Ashraf that they shouldn't do any business with this man nor his friends. But his stupidity and ignorance can be toyed with. Ashraf decides to play a little and gives the man the name of his brothers. He tells him that he should get in touch with them and that they will arrange money for him. With a broad smile, the man leaves. Ashraf shrugs. He has no illusions that this conversation will lead to anything. But hey, you never know. Hamid is in the corner of the dark room, cowering. He seems lost in his own thoughts and says nothing.

The days go agonizingly slow. The nesting hen is the only distraction for the men. Hamid is still not talking much. Ashraf is still not eating much and to make the situation worse he has developed diarrhea as well. His strength is diminishing rapidly. Just before sunset the door opens, and the men are given instructions to wash and get ready. Short, snarling words make it clear that they have to get prepared to leave.

Finally! This is it. For the first time in days, Ashraf sees a smile on Hamid's face. They are going to leave. Would they be released? Did they negotiate with the family? Ashraf can't believe it. His anger and frustration has disappeared. Did Baba and Usman and their tribe seize family members of the kidnappers and are now using them for a trade? They are served a delicious meal, and Ashraf eats.

After the meal, however, they are returned to the dark room with the nesting hen. Ashraf didn't expect to see that chicken ever again. In the distance is the sound of a donkey braying. At any moment, Ashraf and Hamid expect to be come for. Then they hear the call to prayer, and then the next call, and the next call, and the next. Nothing happens. The chicken seems to be staring at Ashraf. For her, nothing has changed.

# FREE?

A forceful deafening explosion tears the silence. Ashraf and Hamid grab their ears. The enormous pressure almost ruptures their eardrums and makes the mud houses on the compound quake. The two men wonder if they are still alive. Questioning and fearful, they look at each other in the dark. As if it were not enough. After all the hardships they had been through and survived. And now, being kidnapped. Will this be the place where they are going to die?

There are the sounds of screams and moans. "A missile impact. Another missile impact," says a harsh rough male voice in the Waziri dialect. A woman screams, and children cry. This one was very close. The thick walls seem to still be standing, even though you would expect there to be nothing left of the building after such an explosion. All the villages in Waziristan have endured rocket attacks. The tribal areas between Pakistan and Afghanistan are currently the hard and grim battlegrounds of a struggle between modern Western armies and ancient warriors who are known, at this juncture of time, as the Taliban or Al-Qaeda. "Lie down, Hamid, lie down!" screams Ashraf. All around them they hear the sounds of gunfire, running footsteps, and shouting men. Then the sound of a hard, dull thud. Dust is everywhere. The people outside shoot their Kalashnikovs wildly without aim, and their bullets, impacting the clay walls, add to the horrific sounds penetrating their ears.

A strange silence seems to gain the upper hand. Even Mother Nature holds her breath. Only in the distance, can the cry of a child be heard.

The rockets land just next to the compound. Ashraf and Hamid remain lying flat on the ground. They cannot go anywhere. They are trapped. Captured and kidnapped by their own people. Ashraf dares not to even think about it. If the thought just comes up, flames of fury surge through his body. Kidnapped by his own people. "Are you alive?" whispers Ashraf in the direction of Hamid. The grumbling and coughing on the other side of the dark room is proof that he is still alive. Again there is gunfire and screaming. Both men scramble to their feet. Ashraf feels sick. Rage, fear, deprivation, and exhaustion have left their marks on the two men. The next hours are restless.

The next day, very early in the morning, the thick wooden door opens. They are roughly grabbed and moved to another location. Right next to the building, where they had been trapped, is an enormous crater. A big hole in the roof of the building next to the compound is a silent witness of a successful attack. These are drones. The fear of every resident of the tribal areas. Unmanned aerial vehicles that are controlled by someone somewhere far away behind a computer screen. Like a computer game, young Western soldiers control the unmanned aircrafts and manage to hit their targets, all without having to set their feet on the battlefield. No risk to their lives is involved in such an operation. They are cowards in the eyes of the Pashtun, who have grown up in a culture where man-to-man combat is a way of life. These are highly dangerous circumstances for the Pashtun people. How many innocent civilians have been killed here? Ashraf has no time to think about this.

The captors dress their captives in the traditional burqa worn by the women in this area in order to escape detection. Resistance is futile and will only lead to disaster. They can only look at the outside world through the gauzy, narrow window in the burqas. They walk together with their captors through the village to another compound. In the distance is a woman without a covering over her face holding a Kalashnikov. Her hard, vacant eyes watch the little procession in which Ashraf and Hamid are a part of.

In the new compound, the men are forcibly pushed into a sloping tunnel going deeper into the ground. Hunched over, they stumble into the tunnel until they come to a very small area. It is horribly dirty, humid, and frighteningly stuffy. Hamid and Ashraf get almost no air. They snatch the burqas from their bodies. There is no ventilation. No oxygen. In this manner, they are buried alive. The men realize that they will die if they do not manage to escape. They will suffocate. They shout, scream and yell, until they have no voice left. They will not survive this. The sounds of their voices slowly die. One final time, Ashraf lets out a hoarse cry. It sounds like the creak of a door with old worn hinges. It seems to be a signal for his body. Before his last cry has died, severe cramps seize his body. A few seconds later he has a grueling attack of diarrhea. His body holds nothing inside after his final shout, as if his body had postponed it until this moment. His body seems to want to dispose of anything left in it. In the corner of the dark room, he vomits the last bit of moisture he had in his body. Is this the end? Deafness from the bombing, to gasping for air and being contaminated in a stinking, dirty hole in the ground. Ashraf feels the last of his strength drain from his body. He had so many plans. So many dreams.

Aghast, Hamid looks at his uncle. Will Ashraf make it or is his end near? Hamid continues to yell and roar until the kidnappers come to look. They see how severe his condition is and take Ashraf up from the tunnel. Hamid must stay down. Ashraf is quickly brought to a room in the compound. It is not long before a metal pot with okra, Ashraf's favorite food, is before his nose. But Ashraf cannot eat. The fresh air, however, does make him feel a little better. The vomiting and diarrhea has stopped , but that's about all. Physically, he is a wreck.

Concerned, the kidnappers watch as Ashraf slowly deteriorates. Again, there is shouting and cursing, and a moment later, tea and biscuits are ready for him. Despite his weakness, Ashraf continues to scold the men and says that he would rather starve and die if they do not get Hamid out of the tunnel as well. Not long after, Hamid is dragged out of the tunnel. A boy of about fifteen years comes to massage them both in the hopes that they will be a bit replenished. Ashraf sees that that boy has problems with his hearing and invites him to come to his clinic once he is released. It sounds strange under the circumstances. The boy kindly looks at Ashraf and nods.

Ashraf feels a little bit better. He's still unable to eat. Only small sips of water stay inside. Ashraf is seriously weak. Hamid is sad and scared. That same evening, the two men are brought back to their previous compound, to the mud house next to where the missile had struck. Later that night, the kidnappers begin to dig a tunnel in front of their room in the small courtyard. That work makes a lot of noise, and the two men hardly sleep.

The next day, Ashraf and Hamid are impressed with the results. It is good that Ashraf and Hamid can stay in their room. The electricity fails often, so the fans in their room don't work the majority of the day. If the room gets too hot and stuffy, the kidnappers will allow the men to come onto the veranda. The chicken now has chicks of her own, and the men have their rhythm of prayer and occasional trip to the veranda. One a day, when the electricity fails, and the room becomes warmer, they are not allowed to go outside and get some fresh air. Despite his weakness, Ashraf again feels rage ripple throughout his body. He knocks on the door and chastises the kidnappers for everything that he can think of. The yelling and scolding is so intense that they threaten to shoot Ashraf if he does not stop. One of the kidnappers is apparently ready to do it.

Ashraf sits on the ground, grinding his teeth. He tells Hamid that he is going to act as though he is unconscious. Hamid must then call the men and try to see if they will let them out on the veranda. Hamid is usually brave, but these past days of hardship have made him quite insecure. He has seen the eyes of his abductors and is convinced that they are willing to shoot them dead. Especially now. Hamid is afraid and quietly says that he'd rather not play this game. The familiar unyielding look in Ashraf's eyes gives the answer. Despite this, Ashraf decides to do it without further discussion and is convinced that his nephew Hamid will play along.

A few seconds later, Ashraf lies motionless, as if dead, on the floor. Hamid screams and cries for help that his uncle is dead. A few men rush into the room. They take Ashraf to the veranda. In addition, there is a person with a traditional hand fan made of mazari that blows fresh air. Slowly but surely, Ashraf begins to move a little, and he opens his eyes. Surprised, Hamid looks at his uncle. If he did not know better, he would have thought Ashraf had just beaten his final hours.

The theatrical performance worked. Since then, the two men are allowed to go to the veranda whenever the electricity fails. One time they stay out in the courtyard all night. They do not sleep though. A cloud of mosquitoes seems to have only one purpose, and that is to stab these men as often as possible. The buzzing of the mosquitoes and their constant biting compete with the stuffiness of the environment. It is not a choice.

The kidnappers hardly speak to each other. The reason is not clear. Sometimes when Ashraf and Hamid are sitting on the veranda, a stone from the next building is thrown over into the courtyard. Without saying a word, one of the kidnappers who is guarding them goes to the building and returns moments later. The stupid Pashtun who had previously tried to become friends with them is accompanying them today. The leader of the group calls for him and accidentally uses his name, Eid Mohammad. He's not that stupid because he reacts furiously. He rebukes the leader and shouts that he should not mention his name around Ashraf and Hamid. The leader tries, in a silly way, to rectify the situation and, with much ado and many words, he tries to convince Ashraf and Hamid that he is purposely using these names instead of the kidnappers' real names. In a different situation, this would have almost been laughable. The angry and grumpy Eid Mohammad and his bumbling leader continue to try to fix the mistake. Eid Mohammad still looks angry and grumpy, but now he listens attentively to the words of his leader. Ashraf looks at that men with contempt. So much stupidity he won't quickly witness again.

Hamid doesn't seem bothered by the whole scene. Moments later, the leader of the group tries to act as intelligently as possible. Nearby, a donkey brays. How long has it been it since Sharif Khoon last compared Pashtuns to donkeys? Ashraf looks at the scar from his adventure with the donkey, a memory he will remember for his entire life. Despite everything, a slight smile appears on his face.

Ashraf has already lost a lot of weight and is still sick. Is the water the cause, or the fact that he can't keep enough food down? Every day, Hamid looks more anxiously to his visibly weakening uncle. More and more Hamid talks about it with the kidnappers. It's not good. An end must come. Then Ashraf's health deteriorates quickly. He becomes so ill that he cannot even walk. He becomes less aware of what is happening around him. The kidnappers do not respond to Hamid's pleas. Occasionally Ashraf opens his eyes, but more often than not, he falls into a deep sleep of exhaustion and fever, and his body seems to be giving up the fight to stay alive. Nobody but Hamid seems to making a fuss about this. Here, life is not worth much. The kidnappers seem to have little interest in Ashraf's steadily declining health.

Far away from this sad mud room, mediators have contacted Ashraf's family. Baba and Usman look bleak. Several times a day, the men of the Baba's tribe meet. They are being hard, angry, and unyielding Pashtuns who do not want to negotiate. It is like Ashraf thought, all of the tribesmen's energies are focused on finding out the identities of the kidnappers so that they can kidnap people from their family or tribe. Badal. Eye for an eye, tooth for a tooth. These are the laws of pashtunwali, and they apply to everyone- Ashraf, Hamid, and their abductors. The tribesmen are all heavily armed and ready for badal. They are ready to attack and abduct.

As time passes, Baba gets worried. He talks a lot with Usman. He is the eldest son and is the father of Hamid. Baba thinks that Ashraf will not survive this if they don't act fast. He knows Ashraf. He knows that he has been in the Western world for a long time and that his resistance is much lower than a Pashtun that has lived here all his life. The temperature, the water, the hard life in Waziristan. Sighing, he looks at Usman. "He will not survive if we don't pay, son. He's been away from Waziristan too long." There is a long pause. "We will get the opportunity for badal later."

Baba goes against the judgment of the tribe. He wants to pay and does so.

The moments when he's awake, Ashraf realizes how serious his situation is. His kidneys have just about given up. He realizes that he is going to die. He misses his family. In his final days and hours, he would want to be with them, to feel their love, to say goodbye. How is it going with his family? Do they know what is going on? Ashraf gets tears in his eyes. Hamid's image disappears behind a watery, cloudy lens. The worst thought is that he might never see his youngest daughter Zainab.

Ashraf is on the veranda. High above him, he sees a plane fly over. He should be on that plane. Free as a bird to fly away. Ashraf is jealous of the people on the plane. Would they know what is happening here? With the last bit of strength draining from his body, Ashraf calls to his kidnappers. He tells him that he is a doctor and that he knows that he does not have much more time to live. They look at him indifferently. Then he calls to Hamid, who squats down next to him. Hamid knows that it is going poorly with his uncle. He has witnessed his decline. The idea of remaining alone with the kidnappers terrifies him. Ashraf orders him to tell his family, wife, and children that he loves them very much. Hamid listens without saying a word.

The color of his face has given away to a dull yellowish color. Large dark circles have formed around his eyes. It is the color of death. Ashraf cannot see it, but he knows this better than anyone. He has often seen patients on their deathbed, saying goodbye to all that is dear to them. Hamid sees it. He is not a doctor, but he sees that his uncle has given up.

Ashraf gives some business instructions on what is to be done with his family when he is no longer there, but then he sinks into a deep sleep, or perhaps unconsciousness. Hamid does not know. What should he do? Scream? Yell? Curse? Run? He remains at his uncle's side and does not leave. His final words and instructions ring in his head. He watches Ashraf's laborious breathing. As long as he can still hear it, he is alive.

The kidnappers have told the family's negotiators that Ashraf is sick and does not have long to live. Baba decides to pay immediately. That same day, everything is arranged. Hamid must get ready to leave. Ashraf is hovering between life and death and realizes doesn't believe anymore that he will be rescued.

The kidnappers wash him and put clean clothes on him. Hamid has eaten and is also cleaned up. Then the men have to wait again. Just like the last time. Hamid looks toward the door, hopeful. He does not leave his uncle's side and is hoping for a miracle. Just after midnight, the leader of the group comes with his pickup truck to the compound.

The leader whispers to the other kidnappers and tells them that they must be quiet. They are going to leave. Ashraf has his eyes open again. The leader presses Ashraf's British passport into Ashraf's hands saying "Here is your Russian passport." The stupid leader is apparently convinced that every red passport is a Russian passport. The other items that were previously taken- the money, mobile phones, and the i-mate- are not given back to the men. The little beige Suzuki Alto, which had been at the compound the entire time hidden under a blanket, is pushed out into the courtyard and driven outside. Ashraf and Hamid have to sit in the back of the Suzuki Alto. Hamid helps Ashraf because Ashraf can no longer walk. Ashraf lets himself slide to the side and hangs miserably against the side of the window. The car's ignition must not be started inside the village. Instead, the kidnappers push the car through the village streets. After they have passed the last house, one of the kidnappers gets behind the wheel. He quickly starts the car and drives off into the darkness to an unknown destination in the impenetrable darkness of the tribal areas. It seems like journey with no end. Ashraf is only half conscious. Hamid looks worriedly at his uncle who is being tossed and turned, back and forth, on the seat. Then, they stop in a dark valley.

There is no one there. Suddenly, Hamid understands what is happening. Here, his young life will be terminated. Pashtuns do not pay ransom. In this lonely valley, they will be murdered and left. Here, it will end for good. He bows his head and his shoulders slump down on his frail body. A wave of panic sweeps over him. It does not matter to Ashraf. He is already at death's doorstep.

# FORGET YOUR DREAM

Outside the car, they hear male voices. It's the kidnappers. Hamid can't hear what they are saying. Anxiously, he tries to understand in the darkness. Beneath this dark, starry sky he can only make out a few vague shadows. Two unknown men get into the car with Ashraf and Hamid. The kidnapper gets out.

One of the men turns around and says that the family is waiting for them. The words do not get through. Which family? The family of the kidnappers? Hamid doesn't ask. He's learned not to do that lately. Hamid looks suspiciously at the two men in the front seat of the car. Ashraf hangs against the window. Everything seems to go past him.

The men in the front talk. In a friendly manner, they occasionally look back and laugh. Slowly, an awareness is growing that these men are not connected to the kidnappers. They have been released, but Hamid still doubts. He dares not believe it. Only a few minutes ago he had been resigned to the fact that he was going to be killed. He lives. He is free! They are released!

The Suzuki Alto drives through Mir Ali town. It is Mir Ali, the city near the location of their kidnapping. Ashraf is lucid again. He looks out the car window and smiles at Hamid. "Mir Ali," he mutters. "We are free." They pass easily through all the checkpoints along the way. It is still dark, early in the morning. Only a few men are going to the mosque for morning prayer. A few stray dogs are crossing the road. Time seems to suddenly pass by. Hamid sits straight up in the car and peers through the windshield. They soon pass through the winding road at Eisha and reach the Chashma bridge. No sooner, they are passing through Miranshah town. The sky is gradually getting lighter but the sun has still not come out. "Darpa Khel!" Hamid shouts, his sobs rivaling his cheers. The whole family is waiting. Except Ashraf's wife and children. They are still in Saudi Arabia.

A wave of joy flows through Ashraf's sick body. His kidneys are barely functioning. He is seriously ill and weak. As a doctor, he realizes that it is probably already too late. Everyone fears for his life, but he is home. He is happy that he can die in Darpa Khel, the place where he was born and raised, in the midst of his family. Ashraf is not afraid anymore. He draws comfort the thought that he may die among his family. The pale color of his face and the dark circles about his eyes worry the family. Slowly, the world goes black before his eyes.

The family surrounds Ashraf with care. His face looks pale and worn out. The shadows around his eyes have become deeper still. He does not talk anymore. He does not laugh anymore. He is not angry anymore. Apparently, he does not even hurt anymore. He is just quiet. Anxiously quiet.

Hamid is also watching. He looks a bit better. Worried, he looks at the frail body of his uncle, the man with whom he has been through so much. Tears swell up in his eyes. Nothing seems to help. Actually, they did not dare take him directly to a good hospital in

Peshawar. The ride could kill Ashraf, but what can they do for him here? Baba, Usman, and the men sit in the courtyard with sullen faces.

After two days, Baba decides to take him to Peshawar. Baba looks at his son Ashraf. The usually composed Baba looks desperate. He sees his son hovering between life and death. He breaks out in a sweat. Was it all for nothing? Tears of sadness and helplessness stand in his otherwise determined eyes. This trip is not without risk, but there is no other choice.

Ashraf makes it. The hospital discovers that Ashraf has contracted malaria, presumably from the many mosquitoes that were in the courtyard of the kidnappers. It is critical, very critical. The hours and day creep by. Baba, Aday, and his brother rotate sitting by his bedside. They also attend to the large number of friends and relatives coming for commiseration. When Ashraf opens his eyes, he sees big men all around him. Baba, his brothers Usman and Asghar, and more. The pale color of his face is different this morning. Is this whole ordeal coming to an end? A faint smile appears on his face when he sees the long line of people standing at his bed. Then he sinks again into a deep sleep, but this time it is one of healing and restoration.

Slowly but surely he gets better. Slowly but surely he regains his strength. For the second time, Ashraf has narrowly escaped the jaws of death. As soon as possible he wants to be reunited with his family in Saudi Arabia. They have been through a terrible time. Baba has kept them informed of everything. With the return of his strength, also comes the return of his character. He wants to go to his wife and children.

Ashraf's visa for Saudi Arabia has expired! The moment his body gives even a hint that he might travel, he is on his way to Islamabad. He is still ill and cannot even stay seated on a chair. When walking, he must be supported. The head of the visa department at the

Saudi Embassy is a difficult man. He looks at the British passport that, just weeks ago, had been in the hands of kidnappers. Thinking it over, the man looks at the passport and tells Ashraf that he must go to the Saudi Embassy in London because the original Saudi visa was issued from London. Ashraf sighs. Again he feels anger and frustration through his ravaged body. Has everyone become crazy? One person kidnaps and nearly kills you, and another makes it his life mission to annoy you with bureaucracy.

Ashraf is too tired and weak, but Baba comes to the rescue. He knows people at the Ministry of Foreign Affairs and is also friends with a government officer in a high position. He kindly asks the man to call the Saudi Embassy. It is not long before everything is arranged. Again, Ashraf comes face to face with the difficult man at the visa department. Again, the man looks prudently at the passport. He leafs through the passport, searching for a new reason to be obstructive. Then his eyes light up with joy. He has found something. Ashraf looks curiously and uneasily at the man. "You entered Pakistan on this passport." His reply sounds triumphant. Ashraf suppresses his frustration and anger. Patiently, Ashraf answers, "No. I used my Pakistani passport because I have no Pakistani visa on the British passport, and hence I presented my Pakistani passport to the immigration people at Islamabad airport after arrival." The officer is adamant. He has found something and sees it as his official mission to send Ashraf, once again, home empty-handed. Embittered, Ashraf stumbles out of the office. He does not want anyone's support.

Angrily, he calls his hospital in Saudi Arabia who is already aware of his kidnapping. Disheartened and angry, he tells them the whole story. The hospital director, Colonel Al Qarzai, a very decent gentleman, says he will soon contact the Saudi Ministry of Defense. They promise to contact the ambassador in Islamabad.

The next day, the head of the hospital in Saudi Arabia calls Ashraf and tells him that everything has been settled by a Saudi Military General who had previously worked at the military base in Jubail and had known Ashraf. This time, Ashraf must meet directly with the ambassador. The Saudi ambassador, however, directs Ashraf again to the head of the visa department, and the whole game begins again. That visa officer says that if he could stamp entry on his British passport from Islamabad airport then will renew or extend his old visa. Ashraf is fed up. He goes to the airport in Islamabad where he knows some people. They are very helpful and look up his date of entry into Pakistan. Then they stamp his British passport, although there is still no visa. Let's hope this is enough.

Meanwhile, it's the last working day of the week, and its closing time. Ashraf is tired. He really does not feel like to go back to the visa department again. The officer sees him coming and looks less than delighted when he sees Ashraf. Triumphantly, he says that today it is really late, but that tomorrow he will make an exception and given him a visa.

Ashraf almost collapses. His body gives way. The officer sees that he has gone to far with his bureaucratic theater and, without another word, grants him a visa. "You leave for Saudi Arabia within a week, after that, the visa is invalid." The words don't really register in Ashraf's mind. With the help of others, he stumbles outside of the embassy. Away from that man. Away from the bureaucracy. Away from the stupidity of power-hungry individuals.

He cannot wait to go to his family. At Dammam Airport, an ambulance is waiting to take him directly to his wife and children. The next day, Colonel Qarzai, the head of the hospital where Ashraf works, comes to visit. He knows that Ashraf was busy setting up a private hospital in his native country. A tired Ashraf briefly tells him the whole story of the kidnapping and of everything else that happened.

Colonel Qarzai looks at Ashraf long and thoughtfully. He shakes his head. His eyes seem strange. He grabs Ashraf around the shoulders and holds him a long time. Through his thin shirt, Colonel Qarzai can feel the bones of the emaciated Ashraf. Again he shakes his head. Then he turns around and leaves. At the door, he turns again and says, "Forget your dream. They are not worth it. I hope this experience will make you decide to stay in Saudi Arabia."

# THE HOSPITAL IS DESTROYED

Hakim Khan, a boy from Darpa Khel who grew up in the village and helped work the land, has become a local gangster. He was one of the boys who often playfully fought against Aaj with his slingshot.

Now, Hakim Khan and his brothers have made numerous checkpoints on the main roads and monitors all those who pass by. No one can, or should, pass without paying. They quickly expand their activities to robberies, kidnapping, and theft. They have influential contacts as well. The Seven Agencies in the tribal areas are governed by the Political Agents which is equivalent to Deputy Commissioners in the main, settled districts in Pakistan. They are men of the government who are usually assisted in their tasks by the maliks. They are men of influence. In order to avoid excess or to nip problems in the bud, the Political Agents of the Pakistani government have several options. They may arrest people and also put them in jail if they think it is necessary. They can close shops and markets in the big towns, like the Miranshah bazaar. They are men with power. Hakim Khan has a good relationship with the

Political Agents and also the with the Chief Minister of the North West Frontier Province (NWFP).

Hakim Khan feels untouchable as a local gangster. In 2006, he kills two mullahs and their relatives near the checkpoint he has made on the main road near Darpa Khel. The full story is not known, but apparently they did not cooperate with his gangster activities. So they die. This is the final straw. Ultimately, pashtunwali proves to be stronger than Hakim Khan's gangster ways. There is no police or government involved. Other mullahs stand up and reach for their weapons. People from the surrounding villages quickly join them. In no time, their group is large. So large that it poses too great of a force for Hakim Khan and his posse. After a brief but fierce battle, his notorious brother Sher Alam is caught and hanged near his own checkpoint on Data Khel road near Darpa Khel. Nobody dares to take him down. He lingers for two days as a silent and sinister symbol of the power of pashtunwali. People loot his house and find huge stashes of cash and gold which he had taken from people. Hakim Khan, however, along with some of his other brothers and family manage to escape to Bannu, for a criminal from Bannu or other settled districts of Pakistan cannot be caught by the authorities in the tribal areas and vice versa.

Pashtunwali continues to rule in the tribal areas. Yet, something fundamentals change. The talibs, that have smelled the power, the money and the violence, murder many of the maliks in North Waziristan. It is not long before the role of the maliks has come to a more or less end. They have become invisible or have fled to Peshawar or Islamabad. The Taliban rule over the region between Pakistan and Afghanistan. The world is upside down. The young Talibs, who once long ago approached doors asking for food and recited the Quran when a new shop was opened, have now taken over the role of the maliks and demand money in exchange for giving their protection. The maliks, the once wise men of the country who were always involved in conflict resolution, have been put aside.

In 2007, Waziristan is populated by a large number of soldiers. The area has in recent years, become increasingly insecure and unstable. Pashtunwali has seemed to have lost its force by the interference of many parties. Still, the tribal areas between Pakistan and Afghanistan belongs to the Pashtuns. It is inhabited by the indigenous population. Still, the ancient traditions and rules apply. Still, the same tribes, clans, and families. Still, the many mosques who lead the call to prayer five times a day. Still, the imams and mullahs exist.

But, to the eyes of the world, it is a hotbed of terrorists. The Taliban is the master of the area. Now they have turned against their temporary patron and are angry at everyone and everything. The young Talibs of yesteryear are now grown men. The visceral cry of the Pashtuns in their doings has not disappeared. The poison of the recent history and influence of many outsiders make it a perilous time. A time when the only interest is in violence. A time when terrorists from neighboring countries such as Tajikistan, Uzbekistan, Chechnya and other Arab countries fight against the West and turn the tribal areas into a large battlefield.

Ashraf has been thinking a lot. What would happen if even a fraction of the money that the world puts towards violence and destruction would be put towards reconstruction, health care, education, and work? What would happen if even a fraction of all the political and media attention would go towards the people who are going against the flow and trying to preserve the beautiful things in the tribal areas? The beautiful side of the Pashtun population with their peculiar character traits, culture, and habits.

Will it ever return to the days where men like Sharif Khoon can escort children through the countryside to school without a care? Will the girls and boys go house to house with their homemade dolls strung with gold, singing? And Aday, with all the women of the house, who ensures that everyone who needs food will eat? Yes, there will come a time when the Talibs of yesteryear will come once again to the madrasas and request their food from those more fortunate.

At this moment, it all seems so far away. Unreachable even. Pashtunwali and badal are no match for modern weapons, the drones of the West, and the many bombings and military operations of the Pakistani Army. According to every insider, it is all meant to protect the area from terrorists and to help Waziristan bring stability to Afghanistan. The reality is different. In the West, people are becoming increasingly aware of the futility of this fight. Near Darpa Khel lies a mountain, Theyr Warsak. The army has a large base there. That base is five hundred yards from the compound where Ashraf was born and raised.

There is a lot of shooting back and forth. No one knows who is shooting who. Once the military hears shots, they begin to shoot indiscriminately from their base on Theyr Warsak. This is dangerous. The people of Darpa Khel hardly dare to come out. The children no longer go to school. The chance of being hit by one of these unguided, flying bullets is a permanent threat. Who is the enemy, and who is the friend? The soldiers don't even know but shoot at anything that moves anyway. And the drones, they are controlled by soldiers who are far away and who also do not examine who is friend or foe. The houses in Darpa Khel near Miranshah are full of bullet holes and stand as a witness to this human error.

It is so dangerous that Baba, Aday, and Ashraf's brother Tariq decide to temporarily live in Hayatabad. It is a suburb of Peshawar near the border of the tribal areas of the Khyber Agency at the start of the famous Khyber Pass. Ashraf's brother, Asghar, remains in Darpa Khel although his family has moved with Baba. Asghar is a large Pashtun of an impressive stature with a big beard. He is bigger and more robust than Ashraf. His beard and calm appearance ensures that he commands respect from those around him. He is a man of few words. He continues to believe in Baba's dream. For him, it is simple. He is a Pashtun from Darpa Khel. Just like Ashraf, he is a doctor, and he wants to keep working at the clinic in Miranshah. That sums it up. Baba is behind him all the way, and Ashraf and his brothers support him. He continues on, cares for the house in Darpa Khel, and provides medical care in the area.

Everyone in the region knows Asghar. He is a respected man. Despite all the violence, everything runs smoothly. Patients come and go at the clinic. The house is well-maintained and Baba, Aday, and the rest come regularly to Darpa Khel to visit. The cows, sheep, and chickens in the courtyard provides a peaceful image that is not much different than all those years before. In the courtyard, a donkey brays and makes some strange antics.

Asghar walks with the men to the mosque for morning prayers. Then he eats and goes to the hospital in Miranshah. A couple of heavily armed Pakistani soldiers are at the clinic. They look suspiciously at Asghar's impressive appearance. "Today, our soldiers were shot at from the clinic," the voice of a high-ranking officer sounds. Asghar looks fearlessly at the man and shakes his head. "Nonsense!" And he says no more.

With a jerk, the soldiers turn around and disappear quickly from view. In this area, such a message is a ruling. It does not matter whether it is actually nonsense or not. If the soldiers say it is so, then it is only a matter of hours before everything will be bombed or barraged with bullets. Asghar knows. Everyone runs away from the hospital. They are just in time, for just a moment later, the hospital is razed by the army. This is the final straw for Asghar. His life's work has just been destroyed. He leaves Miranshah and heads to Peshawar. Baba, Asghar, Ashraf, and the rest of the family talk a lot during this time. Should they abandon their dream? Forget it all, once and for good? Should they leave the tribal areas behind?

# WADAH

Despite all this, there is a special moment. Ashraf sits on the carpet on the floor with his wife and children, all of them situated in a large circle around steaming food. The familiar smell of curry, meat and fire reminds him of his past. It seems as though history is repeating itself. Ashraf looks at the small circle. This is his family. Maryam is sitting with their daughters, chatting and socializing. The men eat the delicious, traditional food in silence. For a moment, all of the world's problems, big and small, seem to be forgotten.

Here, Ashraf is Baba. He is the father of his children and the head of the family. He thinks back to the time, long ago, when Baba asked him if he had been thinking about a woman. A marriage. Ashraf looks at his daughters and at his son, Hammaad. The time is drawing near to when Ashraf must have such a conversation with them. When he looks at Hammaad, a smiles appears on his face. The boy will probably be scared out of his wits, just like Ashraf was.

Ashraf realizes that he must discuss these things with his wife, Maryam. In the Pashtun culture, everything is arranged for the bride and groom. Ashraf and Maryam must think about good partners for their children. It isn't for nothing that it is a deeply rooted tradition in the Pashtun culture.

A few weeks pass. Just as Ashraf is about to bring up the subject to his wife, Maryam tells him that she was approached by the family of a young man who would like to marry their eldest daughter, Aishah. Ashraf looks uncertain as Maryam tells the story. He did not expect it to go this way. Ashraf says the name of the young man a few times aloud. Muhammad Sarwar Hassan Aurakzai. He is a twin. He studied to be a doctor and is now a cardiologist. He studied in the prestigious Agha Khan Medical College in Karachi, the same place where Ashraf got the excellent treatment when he was seriously ill in 2003. This young man later on went to the United States along with his twin brother, Raza Aurakzai, to do a specialization and fellowship in cardiology. Dr Aurakzai is the son of a retired major in the Pakistani army. Maryam and Ashraf start to make inquiries to get to know more about the family. In a strange twist, Ashraf's brother Dr. Fida has a colleague Dr. Melvina who had recently got engaged to Dr. Raza, the twin brother. Aishah is already aware of the goings on and, according to Maryam, is enthusiastic. Ashraf does not say much. He thinks. He is Baba, and he must decide.

Ashraf speaks with the father of the young man. They have a long and extensive conversation. The doctor's sister, Hina, is insisting to have the engagement ceremony straightaway and has brought with her boxes of traditional sweets as well, to mark the preliminary commitment. But Ashraf is not yet fully satisfied. A few days later, Ashraf boards a plane to the United States. Upon arrival at the Boston Airport, his suitcase goes missing, so he leaves with whatever clothes he has on and gets a small travel kit from the airline. He ends up getting reunited with his suitcase on the day he is leaving. He meets the young cardiologist who is currently working at the famous Dartmouth-Hitchcock Medical Center in Lebanon, New Hampshire. He stays with him for two nights in his apartment. This is the perfect way to get to know someone quickly. Ashraf listens and asks a lot of questions and learns enough about him. He also discovers that the young man cannot come to Pakistan for some time because the risk is too great that he will be denied re-entry to the United States and have all sorts of problems with his visa.

After two intense days, Ashraf flies to New York to stay for a few days with Dr. Bukhthiar Shah, a brilliant consultant anesthesiologist. He is the younger brother of his friend Dr. Shahkar, the heart surgeon. Dr. Bukhthiar lives alone in a huge house on Long Island and during his stay Ashraf makes trips to Manhattan to explore the city. He has been wanting to do this for over fifteen years but somehow never got time to fulfill his wish. Now he had the chance and visited the Statue of Liberty and other important sites such as Harlem, the Bronx, and Queens. He took a cruise on the Hudson River, visited Time Square and went to a tapping of his favorite television program, The David Letterman Show.

Then it is time for Ashraf to get back on a plane and head to Pakistan. Back in Pakistan, Ashraf talks with Maryam and Aishah. He again talks with the parents of the young man. Will this be his future son-in-law? Is this the right man for his daughter? The future father of his grandchildren? Ashraf feels a strange sensation in his stomach when he thinks about it. He loves his children very very much. This is a choice that will determine the rest of her life. He looks pensively into the dark night. He thinks back to the time when Baba had to decide for him. It all comes back to his mind. Maryam and Aishah are already talking about the engagement and wedding preparations. Ashraf shakes his head. Can he let go of his daughter? How can he know if he will make his daughter happy with his decision?

Then, it all goes quickly. Ashraf has thought long and hard. And then he makes a decision, just like Baba had done. Ashraf agrees and together with Sarwar's parents, the engagement is arranged. But not in Darpa Khel. It is too dangerous. So, it does not go quite according to the old traditions. Instead, the party is in Peshawar. And Sarwar is not there. He is unable to come due to visa problems, so the engagement party takes place without him. There are more than two hundred guests.

Time passes. Aishah and Sarwar call and email each other and get to know each other better and better. Ashraf allows it and turns a blind eye. Maryam is busy with the wedding preparations. It is almost wadah, the moment of the marriage ceremony. This time it is about his own daughter. He feels old. Where has the time gone? His own wedding seems so recent. Can it go according to the ancient traditions, or has that time passed?

Sarwar comes to Pakistan via Canada. It is the only way to bypass the visa issue. It takes three days before the real formalities will take place, but the party has already begun. The party is again in Peshawar. This time it will be a feast lasting several days, with Aishah and Sarwar as the center of attention. Ashraf's house in Peshawar if full of relatives. He can hear the soft, subtle rhythm of the drums and tambourine. In both the men's house and the women's house, there is eating, talking, dancing, and laughing. Salehdin Haj is no longer there, and the stumbling Sharif Khoon has died long ago. No tall tales and jokes as it was long ago at Ashraf's wedding.

There is much that is the same, yet some things are also quite different. There are hundreds of guests. The traditional music at times gives way to disco music. The beautiful horse upon which Maryam came to Ashraf is exchanged for a modern car. Ashraf looks at his eldest daughter. She is glowing. She is happy. She is stunning. He smiles.

Then, Ashraf and Maryam transfer their daughter Aishah to her in-laws. Ashraf swallows a lump in his throat. His little girl has grown up. This tough Pashtun feels small and insignificant now that he has let go of his daughter.

The party is big, different, and intense. Aishah and Sarwar enjoy it to the fullest. They look shy, but happy, together. All the components of the traditional marriage ceremony are completed. Now it is time for the jokes. Some things change. Other things don't.

# AGAINST THE STREAM

It does not take long before Ashraf's brother, Asghar, returns to Miranshah. Again he starts a small clinic in the town. Baba's dream is not going away. It has never gone away. It is a small clinic of a much larger network. Ashraf continues to lives in England but travels every four to six weeks to Pakistan. He has built a large hospital on the border of the tribal areas near Peshawar on Charsadda Road, after his younger brother Arif found a good piece of land. This must become the major hospital of the region, with all different types of specializations and a connection to a network of smaller clinics in the tribal areas. Ashraf calls these smaller clinics satellite clinics. Ashraf has put all of his money into this hospital in Peshawar. A Pashtun is determined and does not run away. A real Pashtun does not give up. Ever.

Ashraf's hospital is almost completed. Again a satellite clinic opens in the tribal areas, and the first patients come to receive care as well. Both places are easily accessible, as they should be. The first test comes when the country is ravaged by a massive flood. The main hospital in Peshawar on Charsadda Roadhas its doors wide open. Everyone receives medical help. Ashraf, Asghar, and the other doctors tirelessly do their good work. Hammaad, Ashraf's son, also helps. He is studying to become a doctor. This is what Baba has dreamed of.

These are the first steps in a much larger plan. Ashraf realizes that Baba's dream is becoming a reality. It will not take long before several small clinics are built in the tribal areas. Ashraf begins with the construction of a school for the deaf near the hospital.

His good and close friend Andrew de Carpentenitier is giving him advice. Andrew is the chairman and one of the founders of World Wide Hearing, a Swiss based organization helping people with hearing problems in developing countries. For over thirty years, he has been the Executive Director of the Holy Land Institute for the Deaf and Blind Children in Salt, Jordan, an organization dedicated to the rehabilitation, education, training and employment of sensory impaired individuals. He has served as an adviser and board member for dozens of international agencies dealing with hearing impairment, sign language, audiology, and special education. He was also an adviser to the World Health Organization (WHO) for hearing issues and hearing aids. As a close friend, he visited Ashraf's hospital in Peshawar on Charsadda Road several times.

Both Andrew and Ashraf dare be different than the rest of the world. It is deep inside Ashraf's character. It is his destiny. Baba's dream. Do not go with the flow! Don't follow the crowd! Even a dead fish can float downstream. It does not take any effort or work to go with the flow and drift downstream. Only a living, brave, healthy fish will swim against the current and travel upstream. It takes a dynamic healthy faith to stand for their convictions, firm against the tide of opinion and the example of unbelievers. The two friends are talking about it. Is there any way out of this mess of violence and destruction? What does it take to be able to swim against the current and move farther upstream? These kind of conversations and advice give new and meaningful strength and perspective to Ashraf and his dream.

Ashraf is also working on plans to make workshops where unskilled boys from the tribal areas and the school for the deaf can come and quickly, but skillfully, learn a new trade. Boys and girls who can and will be the ones who recover and reconstruct the destroyed tribal areas. It's like a virus, but this time it's not a virus of destruction, but one of hope and confidence.

This obstinate Pashtun's dream will be achieved, one way or another. This dream will bring back the Pashtuns to their tribal areas to live among their traditions.

In the distance, a donkey brays. Ashraf subconsciously touches the scar on his leg. His encounter with the donkey long long ago, the adventure that left him with this scar. This wound, acquired in Waziristan, has not healed, and the scar has not disappeared. Likewise, the world will always have its conflicts and will always be searching for its own donkey rides. The world powers have created it's own wild donkey ride in the tribal areas. It will happen in other places. Already, in world news, the struggles in Afghanistan are hardly mentioned anymore. The news is all about new areas: Syria, South Sudan, Mali, Somalia, Libya. The world is apparently needing her wars. The tribal areas between Pakistan and Afghanistan will gradually regain their stability. Waziristan will come back into the hands of the Pashtuns.

Baba, Ashraf, and Asghar recline in the *chappar* on the lawns of Ashraf's hospital in Peshawar. The roof of the chappar protects them from the strength of the sun. The warm breeze that blows through the open sides creates a pleasant coolness. The conversations turn to the topic of Aaj, the old friend of Ashraf with whom he tried to shoot the birds out of the trees. Aaj did not continue his studies and got a clerical job in Miranshah at the municipal committee. In the years since his youth, he was one of the first who moved with his family to a piece of land in Dandey

Darpa Khel, a rugged area to the north side of Miranshah town, after a conflict over it got settled. Gradually many more Pashtuns with overcrowded families living in small houses in Darpa Khel village moved to Dandey. It is sort of an extension of Darpa Khel village, and although not physically connected, it is now known by the name of Dandey Darpa Khel. This is also a place which got numerous drone attacks.

In subsequent years, there arose a quarrel within Aaj's family. One one side of the family, a nephew and a little girl got killed and the other nephew's wife got wounded. On the other side of the family, Aaj and his son got wounded. The nephew's family blamed Aaj. Aaj insisted that the nephew and girl were accidentally hit by their own families. It was long ago. It's almost been forgotten, except that Pashtunwali never forgets.

Lying in the chappar, Asghar breaks the news of a fresh shooting. Yesterday, Aaj, along with his son and daughter-in-law, were gunned down. The traditions in the tribal areas are still alive. Aaj was shot in the stomach. His son was hit in the chest and his daughter-in-law in the leg. There will be no trial in court.

Like the drones. There has never been a trial in court for these unmanned air crafts that cause death and destruction. Just like the Pakistani soldiers who announced that shots had come from the hospital, they act as both judge and executioner. Drone attacks violate human rights because in addition to killing insurgents, they also kill and injure civilians. These are the words of the High Commissioner for Human Rights of the United Nations.

Ashraf jumps to his feet. He goes straight to the hospital. He speaks with the doctors to ensure that Aaj, Aaj's son and daughter-in-law receive the best medical treatment. It is good to know people. The day's drag. Their conditions are critical. Will they survive? Ashraf looks at the pale face of his old friend Aaj. He thinks back to their adventures in the past. It seems so long ago. The camels. The slingshot. Aaj, the sharp shooter. How long has it been? How long since Ashraf last thought about badal? About pashtunwali? About the age-old traditions and customs of the Pashtuns? Was it not when those two heavily armed Pashtuns stormed Miranshah and came looking for Baba, saying that they had just killed a boy? Badal! The boy who was in Ashraf's school? Ashraf shakes his head.

Ashraf intends to do everything he can to help Aaj interact normally with his family again. Badal has been done. Time passes. Aaj, his son, and his daughter-in-law have survived. The scars remain visible, but they survived. This old conflict does not need to claim any more victims. Enough is enough! It is time to move on with Baba's dream!

A year later, Asghar, with the help from Ashraf who is still living in England, opens a small hospital in Miranshah. It is now in the bazaar at the center of Miranshah. It is relatively safe there since the Pakistani army will not be so quick to bomb the bazaar. The drones, also, have not yet caused damage there. Ashraf approves of the place and helps in building the hospital. Asghar runs it while Ashraf is more often at the larger hospital on Charsadda Road hosting medical camps during his visits to Pakistan. Ashraf's son, Hammaad, has now graduated as a doctor and is soon leaving for England to study his specialization. He had helped a lot in the construction and development of the main hospital. Ashraf sees history repeating itself. He is proud of his son and daughters.

Ashraf looks over the Peshawar hospital grounds on Charsadda Road. His brown eyes glide over the large building and the land that lies around it. It is almost on the border of the tribal lands. A school for the deaf is being built on the hospital grounds. In his occupation as an ear, nose, and throat doctor, Ashraf has worked with many deaf children. It has been a quiet, deeply-rooted desire of Ashraf's to help these children especially after meeting and visiting his friend Andrew's institute in Salt, Jordan. This long-time, cherished desire is now being fulfilled. It will be a school for underprivileged children, especially from the tribal areas, who are deaf and have no future in a country like Pakistan. Slowly but surely, the dark clouds above Baba's dream begin to disappear. Will Baba's dream really become a reality?

Ashraf watches the news. His face turns pale. The Pakistani army has announced Operation Zarb-e-Azb. The name is a reference to the sword that the Prophet Muhammad used in one of the battles recounted in the Quran. It soon becomes clear that the army, with the support of the West, will purge North Waziristan from terrorists. Ashraf is concerned for his brother Asghar who remains in Miranshah. Anxiously he follows the news. He is unable to get in contact with Asghar. Miranshah and Darpa Khel are no longer accessible.

The uncertainty does not last long, however, for Asghar, haggard but unharmed, appears at the door. The impressive Pashtun is back in Peshawar. With a sullen face, he tells the entire story. Baba and Hammaad, who has not yet left for England, stand a small distance away. When they hear the deep, monotone voice of Asghar, they come running quickly to hear the latest news. The army has tried to warn everyone in Waziristan. Everyone has to leave their home, village, and town. Large refugee camps have been set up in Bannu. Asghar goes on. He saw thousands of people fleeing. Everyone is on the run. Women, children, the elderly. The cattle is left behind. The first bombing was devastating. The strange and ominous sounds of the cursed drones chased everyone further and further away from their homes. In Asghar's hard, dark eyes are a mixture of anger and sadness.

Silently and somberly, the men sit together. The hospital in the Miranshah bazaar is also destroyed. Again their dream seems to break in pieces. They watch the news. Sometimes, they stare with hollow eyes, long, into the distance, as if the answer were hidden there. A high-ranking Pakistani military officer reports on the news that more than nine hundred terrorists have been slain. Nobody is talking about the numbers of refugees or internally displaced persons, or IDPs as the government and media call them. In the coming days, weeks, and months, it become clearer. Voices from Waziristan let out a cry for help. More than a million Pashtuns have fled. They have been driven out of their towns, villages, and houses. There are many victims. Taliban, yes, but also innocent women and children. Then the world is startled by a cruel and tragic slaying in this senseless, never-ending battle. In Peshawar, terrorists attack a school run by the Pakistani government. They climb over a wall and open fire on the students and teachers. The massacre lasts nearly eight hours. One hundred and fifty-five people, mainly children, have been gruesomely murdered. A rescue operation is launched by Pakistan's Army of Special Forces and they manage to kill all seven terrorists and rescue 960 people.

Demoralized, the three generations stare at the sky above Peshawar. It seems darker and more menacing than ever before. Baba, Ashraf, and Hammaad watch as the planes and helicopters head towards North Waziristan. They are like a large swarm of hunters seeking their prey. It will not be long before the dull sounds of heavy explosions will be heard in North Waziristan. Are all the people from the village and town safe? Almost all of Ashraf's family possessions are there, far away, in Darpa Khel and Miranshah. But what does it matter after all this bloodshed?

Ashraf has never been so disappointed. Hundreds of thousands of people and their animals march from their homes in the blazing heat with few provisions. Children are dying of heat exhaustion on the side of the street. Poor people and children are walking on foot. They look like a human sea, of youngsters and adults. Some people faint, so people pour water on them to revive them. The Taliban and Uzbek foreign fighters disappeared long before the army destroyed everything. The Pakistani government has been shelling North Waziristan with helicopters without actually fighting anyone. They are just destroying the whole area. The families are the ones facing the hardship of travel. Most tribal people could only manage to get themselves out of Waziristan because the Pakistani government had already begun to bomb the villages. They had to leave all their belongings.

The death toll of the cattle is atrocious in and of itself. 1.5 million cows died because farmers were forced to leave them behind. Some of them tried to bring them out of the war zone but the cows died of broken limbs or exhaustion along the way. Why would a government decide to evacuate an area but provide no food, water or transportation along the way? Why do they want the area "cleared out"? For what? Many refugees search for safety in the Khyber-Pakhtunkhwa province. The local people want to help but can they?

The Western world is said to have encouraged these bombings. Why? Ashraf looks to the ground. Is everybody crazy? They are destroying his motherland. Darpa Khel, Miranshah, even the whole of Waziristan. A million tribespeople are on the run. The whole world seems to believe that every Pashtun is a terrorist. Everybody seems to believe that the tribesmen from Waziristan are the main source of terrorism all around the world.

Has everybody forgotten recent history? The global game with Waziristan in the middle of it? History is repeating itself. The war against the British, the war against Russia, and now the war against the United States and NATO. The madrassas which one served as schools for the poor Afghan refugee children were transformed into recruiting agencies with the support of millions of dollars. Poor children and orphans were indoctrinated by hate-spreading teachers from the outside. With more dollars, the Taliban was turned into the Mujahideen and Jihadi to kick the Russians out of of Afghanistan. But hundreds of maliks and mashraan are killed by the same Taliban as a part of the global war game. Step by step pashtunwali is being destroyed.

Without any choice, the tribesmen are in the middle of this global fight. The tribesmen are unpaid soldiers of the nations. Unpaid soldiers between Afghanistan and Pakistan. Unpaid soldiers between the United States, the Western world and Russia. These tribesmen who are lovers of their country, lovers of their traditions and religion. Amazingly brave men and women who only wanted to protect their land and culture.

Pashtuns always win their own fights, for even if they lost, they never admit defeat. It is part of their tradition. But this one? Is this the final battle for the tribesmen? Will pashtunwali be destroyed forever?

What about Baba's dream? Don't go with the flow! Don't follow the crowd! Even a dead fish can float downstream! Dare to be different! Dare to go against the stream!

In Hayatabad, near the house where Ashraf is living with his family in Peshawar, tribal elders from North and South Waziristan have organized a jirga. They ask the government to allow the return of the refugees. Around a million people, driven from their native villages, have been displaced. Almost everything has been destroyed. Houses, shops, businesses. An unprecedented number of Pashtuns have lost their lives. The town of Miranshah has been completely destroyed and flattened. Not a single house, shop or market is standing. There is an eerie feeling when one sees the ruins.

Meanwhile, on December 16, 2014, seven gunmen affiliated with the Tehrik-i-Taliban Pakistan (TTP) launch a terrorist attack on the Army Public School in Peshawar. The militants are all foreign nationals, including one Chechen, three Arabs and two Afghans. They enter the school and open fire on school staff and children killing 141 people, including 132 schoolchildren, ranging from ages eight to eighteen years. A rescue operation is launched by the Pakistan Army's Special Services Group (SSG), who kill all seven terrorists.

The Pakistani government immediately calls for the death penalty for the terrorists. The words of Prime Minister Nawaz Sharif and the army chief, General Raheel Sharif, blare from the television. The Pakistani government will destroy the terrorists to the last man and will make no distinction between good and bad Taliban.

The price is high. Since 2008, almost five million people from the affected parts of Khyber Pakhtunkhwa and all the tribal areas have been registered as internally displaced people, uprooted in various waves because of military operations or the deterioration of security caused by non-state armed actors.

Latest UN figures show that 1,002,002 people from the tribal areas are still displaced and in need of humanitarian assistance and support. In the thirteen years since the September 11 terrorist attacks, the United States has spent a total of 1.6 trillion dollars financing military operations in Iraq, Afghanistan, and other countries for the sake of the global war on terror. The U.S. government's massive spending sum includes the cost of military operations, the training of security forces in Afghanistan and Iraq, reconstruction, weapons maintenance, base support, foreign aid, embassy costs, and veteran's health care. 1.6 trillion dollars is a dollar amount so large it needs more context to understand the scope of U.S. military spending. That 1.6 trillion dollars translates to approximately 337 million dollars per day, 14 million dollars per hour, and 250,000 dollars per minute.

Tom Engelhardt, Teaching Fellow at the Graduate School of Journalism at the University of California, Berkeley described the intervention in Iraq, Afghanistan and Pakistan following the September 11 attacks as a failure. In his estimation, the response in Afghanistan and Iraq transformed global jihadism from "a microscopic movement on this planet" to the number-one foreign policy concern, and "as a result of this strategy it has exploded geographically, while the number of jihadist organizations has multiplied, and the number of people joining such groups has regularly and repeatedly increased." "It has a growth rate that seems to correlate with the efforts of Washington to destroy terrorism and its infrastructure."

The Pakistani army's Operation Zarb-e-Azab in the tribal areas has taken the lives of 40,000 ethnic Pashtun civilians and internally displaced another 1 million. Entire cities and villages have been destroyed forcing people to flee the region. Some 200,000 have crossed over into Afghanistan and the rest are displaced in Pakistan.

UNHCR has tried its best to assist the migrants but because of the onging military operation, it is very difficult, if not impossible, to enter the region and offer any assistance to civilians. International and local media have no access to the area, specifically to North Waziristan, in order to report the massive human disaster occurring.

The Zarb-e-Azab military operation was launched as a renewed effort against militancy. Instead, militants fled to safe havens while civilians get the brunt of the action. The situation created brings about an increase in militancy, insecurity and distrust of the government and army. Who will be the voice of the innocent civilians, orphans and widows of this war waged by the Pakistani government and International forces? Who will assist the Pashtuns in creating a stable and prosperous homeland again? Who is going to tell the wold the truth about these forgotten genocidal activities in the tribal areas between Pakistan and Afghanistan? Will the international community do anything to help the people to rebuild their destroyed homes and lives.

Without a word, Baba, Ashraf, and Hammaad look at each other. Three unyielding Pashtuns. A determined people who will not give up. It does not have to be said. They don't need 1.6 trillion dollars to follow Baba's dream. These three men don't need huge amounts of money to rebuild their land.

With or without help they will be the new microscopic positive movement on this planet with a strategy that can explode geographically. They will be the beginning of a recovery corp, recruiting and training to rebuild all the destroyed areas and bring back the beauty of the men, women, religion and tradition.

The dull roar of the explosions in the distance are like the drums of yesteryear. It is an ancient voice. The voice of the Pashtuns. Baba's dream continues and lives on. No attack, no army, no bombing, no drone nor a completely destroyed land can stop it. A little further on, a donkey with his head bowed waits for an old cart. Again, Ashraf slides his hand along the old scar on his leg. The three Pashtuns turn and walk with their heads held high to the entrance of the hospital on Charsadda Road.

The sounds of the damoon drums are gone. This time, it is the drumming of explosions that speak. The message is the same. A Pashtun does not give up. A Pashtun does not loose a battle. A Pashtun does not bow to violence or misfortune.

The three generations of Pashtuns are already at work, going against the flow. This is Baba's dream!

# BACKGROUND INFORMATION
# PASHTUN ETHNIC GROUP

The importance of Pashtun culture is keen to demonstrate (both to itself and the outside world) its multi-ethnic self-image. Pashtuns have traditionally dominated Afghanistan, so the extent that the term 'Afghan' was originally used as a synonym of 'Pashtun'. Afghan emirs (referred to as 'kings' or 'shahs' since 1926) have all been members of the (Pashtun) Durrani 'tribe', whose geographical heartland surrounds the city of Kandahar.

This Pashtun element is essential to understanding Afghanistan's history, including the last fifteen years' period, dominated by the rise, fall and steady resilience of the Taliban movement. The latter is, of course, perceived as an extremist movement belonging to the totalitarian end of the spectrum of political Islam, but reducing the Taliban simply to its religious driving forces would be shortsighted. Indeed, Pashtun nationalism is a key element of the Taliban movement. Though this fact is well known, it is comparatively unacknowledged by global media coverage, whose main focus is factors that overlap with Al-Qaeda, such as 'terrorism' and 'backwardness', thus amalgamating the two in the common perception.

The Pashto language belongs to the Eastern subgroup of the Iranian subfamily of the Indo-European language family. It is believed to be the mother tongue of approximately 50 million people. Although precise censuses are not available – and in spite of both the numerous native Pashto speakers whose ancestry is largely multi-ethnic (inter-ethnic marriage is frequent in the region) and non-Pashto speakers claiming Pashtun heritage – this number is likely to be a reasonable approximation of the size of the Pashtun ethnic group. Roughly two-thirds of Pashtuns live in Pakistan (known as 'Pukhtuns' or 'Pathans'), where they constitute an important minority (15-20 per cent). One-third of Pashtuns live in Afghanistan, where they often claim to constitute the national majority, although data suggests that though they are the strongest group, they do not make up 50 per cent of the population. The remaining Pashtuns are dispersed in a wide diaspora, with communities in the United Arab Emirates (constituting a cheap source of labour), India and various Western countries.

# BACKGROUND INFORMATION ELEMENTS OF PASHTUN TRADITION

The traditions are discussed with respect to their relevance to cross-cultural interaction and especially negotiation. Some of these features, such as the 'tribal' element, remain very much specific to the Pashtuns. Others, such as the jirga, influence Afghanistan to an extent that they may be seen as a 'national institution'. Pashtun traditions are emulated, at least to some degree, by the non-Pashtun ethnic groups of Afghanistan.

## Tribes

Pashtuns are often described in the academic literature as being the 'world's largest tribal society', and lineage elements do in fact play a key role in Pashtun identity and social organisation. The English word 'tribe', however, connotes a certain primitiveness that does not resonate when used (in English) by the Pashtuns themselves. Rather, the word (in Pashto: قوم; qawm and خيل; khel) is used with pride, and most educated Pashtuns are able to recite their patrilineal list of forebears back to a common Pashtun ancestor. It would, however, be simplistic to consider the tribal element to be the only significant normative parameter in Pashtun society. An insider stresses:

*'...The tribal system is usually not the only structural principle of a tribal society. The example of the Punjab (both Indian and Pakistani) makes it clear that tribe or tribal structure is only one guideline of social orientation in a complex network of different principles and patterns of the social landscape. The society or societies in which Pashtuns live are not much simpler. In Afghanistan which recently has sunk into chaos and turmoil and where tribes have gained considerably in importance, the tribal system is only one component within a much more complex social and political web. This is true as well for areas populated homogeneously by Pashtuns'*

Besides the tribal framework, two other elements play an absolutely central role in the Pashtun social order: Pashtunwali, a code of honour common to all Pashtun 'tribes', and jirga, an important decision-making assembly.

## Pashtunwali

Pashtunwali is an ethical-normative frame of reference that applies to all Pashtuns. The word can be translated as 'pashtunness' and is often referred to as 'the way of the Pashtuns'. The specific term, unlike the concept, is not commonly used by Pashtuns. Pashtunwali is sometimes described as legal system, sometimes as code of honour, and occasionally as the entire tradition. Pashtunwali's fundamental concepts all focus on the central notion of nang, or honour. Pashtunwali is unwritten and comprised of a large set of tenets, rules and concepts, which may be understood as the 'customary law of the Pashtuns'. As customary law, pashtunwali is designed around the narkhcomplex. Narkh is a Persian word meaning 'price', and the narkh system is based on a specific set of compensations to be paid to a victim, or his or her family, following any given offence. The unit compensation is the khun (Persian for 'blood').

The legalistic definition of pashtunwali as customary law, however, is slightly too narrow, however, as pashtunwali comprises more than rules. Rather, it is a moral 'grid of parallels and meridians' to be used by Pashtuns, who, being devout Muslims, attempt to make it compatible with Islam. As a Iranologist points out, '...*today the ideals of Pashtunwali compete with other value systems that gained influence [during the last three decades] ... but there is no doubt that among the competing value systems the ideals of Pashtunwali still continue to present an attractive and sometimes binding option today'.* Pashtunwali's main aspects relate to melmastia (hospitality), nanawatay (forgiveness), badal (revenge), tura (bravery), musawat (equality), bawar (trust) or wisa (trust), ghayrat (self-honour) and namus (the honour of women).

## Jirga

A jirga is an assembly of various dimensions, and thought to be 'one of the least researched aspects of Afghan culture and society'. The assembly can be convened at various levels of the community. An important feature of jirga is that its decision, once made, is authoritative and binding. A jirga takes decisions by consensus, not vote, creating a strong propensity for compromise. A jirga is convened whenever a problem arises and, in principle, is open to all adult males. Jirga is a Pashto word derived from 'jirg' meaning 'wrestling ring'. The interesting etymology of the word is worth noting; jirg is related to a very old Indo-European root (sker) that bears the idea of 'turning; round', illustrated by the Persian (charkh) and Pashto (kharkh) words meaning 'wheel' (Pokorny, 1959). The corresponding Latin circus (derived from Greek κίρκος) became the English 'circle' and originally referred to a 'group of persons surrounding a center [sic] of interest', a meaning which closely approximates that of a jirga. This is relevant not only for the geometry it implies, but also for the symbolic value of the circular, equidistant arrangement in denoting the equivalence of all those (men) partaking in a jirga. This is linked to a core principle in Pashtun culture – musawat, or equality. There is no chairman at jirgas, and all members of the jirga are equal.

## Musawat

(Equality in Pride and Dignity Within a Hierarchical Power Structure)

The principle of equality is highly significant to interacting with Pashtuns. Despite the persistence of social differentiation, understanding the centrality of the belief in the equality of all Pashtuns is critical. This is due to the fact that equality is linked to the idea of brotherhood, which, in turn, is a consequence of the genealogical pyramid (leading back to a common ancestor) that forms the 'tribal' structure. Is it important to note, however, that this sense of equality born of common kinship does not necessarily imply Pashtun society is egalitarian in the Western sense of the term? In the survey of foreign workers with experience in Afghanistan, the overwhelming majority (14 out of 17) stated that they perceived Pashtuns to be hierarchical, rather than egalitarian. This finding seems to contradict the principle of musawat, and may be due to several reasons, some of them inherent to the (not strictly egalitarian) Pashtun social system, and others to recent shifts.

The equality conveyed by musawat should be considered an ideal rather than reflective of some 'really existing egalitarianism'. Equality as conveyed in the concept of musawat is the equality of brothers, but it does not contradict social inequality, difference in age or differences by other hierarchical principles. Equality in dignity (which relates to the right to preserve and defend one's personal honour (nang) does not imply the absence of a power pyramid. Leadership in Pashtun society derives from seniority and experience. As in English, the term 'senior' (meshr) often has a connotation of age or prestige. Pashtuns distinguish between two main groups of elders: a khan (خان) or malik is a hereditary elder whose prestige stems from land ownership and economic strength, whereas a spinzhiray (literally a 'white-bearded') derives his position from personal, 'meritocratic' attributes such as knowledge, wisdom, bravery and rhetorical skills. Respectful and honourable behaviour towards the elderly is mandatory. Other criteria for status differentiation include marital status, wealth, leadership skills and general nang (honour).

Another factor contributing to less than egalitarian nature of Pashtun society is what may be described as the recent, widespread breakdown of traditional social structures in Afghanistan, primarily due to the ongoing conflict.

Traditional social and political relations have increasingly been weakened and dissolved. As a result, the jirga as a major conflict-resolving mechanism of the Pashtuns has lost much of its authority. Might often trumps pashtunwalai and even Islamic law. In many Pashtun tribes, the more permanent shura has replaced the jirga. Most shuras are convened by the new strongmen. This makes them hierarchical in structure, in contrast to the egalitarian jirga where ideally all male members of a certain tribe find a consensus about a certain conflict'.

Last but not least, it is important to distinguish between in-group and out-group behaviour. The survey respondents experienced Afghan/Pashtun society as hierarchical in its interaction (as an aggregate) with foreigners. The presence of outsiders is likely to give rise to behaviour distinct from that characterising in-group interaction.

# BACKGROUND INFORMATION
# OPERATION ZARB-E-AZB

Operation Zarb-e-Azb (Sword of the Prophet) is a joint military offensive being conducted by the Pakistan Armed Forces. An operation against various militant groups, including the Tehrik-i-Taliban Pakistan (TTP), the Islamic Movement of Uzbekistan, the East Turkestan Islamic Movement, Lashkar-e-Jhangvi, Al-Qaeda, Jundallah and the Haqqani network.

Operation Zarb-e-Azb was launched on June 15, 2014, in the aftermath of the attack on the Jinnah International Airport, Karachi, on June 8-9, 2014. At least 33 persons, including all 10 attackers, were killed in the Karachi attack.

Part of the ongoing war in North-West Pakistan, up to 30,000 Pakistani soldiers are involved in Zarb-e-Azb, described as a "comprehensive operation" to flush out all foreign and local militants hiding in North Waziristan.

As a result of the operation, 929,859 displaced civilians were registered by Pakistani authorities. Financial support, relief goods and food packages were being distributed and 59 donation points were established across Pakistan by the army. The Foreign Office of

Pakistan said that the rehabilitation of internally displaced persons is an internal matter and reiterated that Pakistan has not requested international assistance.

According South Asia Terrorism Portal (SATP), between 2006 and 2015, the war against terrorism in the tribal areas thus far killed more than 2.0255 terrorists, 2192 specials forces and 4375 civilians.

Major General Asim Saleem Bajwa, Director General (DG) of Inter Services Public Relations (ISPR), on January 16, 2015, claimed that special forces had killed 2,000 'terrorists' under Operation Zarb-e-Azb, and also disclosed that 200 soldiers had been killed.

Since 2008, almost five million people from Khyber Pakhtunkhwa and FATA have been registered as internally displaced people, uprooted in various waves because of military operations or the deterioration of security caused by non-state armed actors. Latest UN figures show that 1,002,002 people are still displaced and in need of humanitarian assistance and support.

Operation Zarb-e-Azb have failed to destroy the organisational network and leadership of the terrorists. This has repeatedly been demonstrated in their capacity to perpetrate carnage, as in the Peshawar Army Public School attack and the bloodbath of innocent Shias at Imambargah (Shia place of worship) in Peshawar. The linkages of several groups with domestic terrorists operating within the country are growing progressively deeper and more complex. Despite some losses that Tehrik-i-Taliban Pakistan (TTP), has suffered, it is likely to rise again out of the rubble that bombardments and drone strikes have created in the tribal areas of Pakistan.

## BACKGROUND INFORMATION LIST OF DRONE STRIKES TRIBAL AREAS

By most accounts, hundreds of dangerous militants have been killed by drones, including some high-ranking terrorists. But very independent investigation of the strikes has found far more civilian casualties than administration officials admit. Gradually, it has become clear that when operators far away from the tribal areas fire missiles into remote tribal territories on the other side of the world, they often do not know who they are killing, but are making an imperfect best guess.

18 June 2004: The first known US drone strike killed 5–8 people including Nek Muhammad Wazir and two children, in a strike near Wana, South Waziristan. Pakistan's Army initially claimed the attack as its own work.

14 May 2005: 2 killed including Haitham al-Yemeni in a drone strike near the Afghan border in North Waziristan

5 November 2005: A drone strike destroys the house of Abu Hamza Rabia killing his wife, three children and four others.

30 November 2005: Al-Qaeda's 3rd in command, Abu Hamza Rabia killed in an attack by drones in Asoray, near Miranshah, the capital

of North Waziristan along with 4 other militants. Among the deaths are 8-year-old Noor Aziz and 17-year-old Abdul Wasit.

13 January 2006: Damadola drone airstrike kills 18 civilians, in Bajaur area but misses Ayman al-Zawahri, five women, eight men, and five children are among the dead.

30 October 2006 Chenagai drone strike allegedly aimed at Ayman al-Zawahri destroys a madrassa in Bajaur area and kills 70–80 people. Pakistani military officials claim there were militants while provincial minister Siraj ul-Haq and a local eyewitness said they were innocent pupils resuming studies after the Muslim Eid holidays.

16 January 2007: Up to 30 Taliban killed in a drone strike in Salamat Keley, Zamazola, South Waziristan.

26 April 2007: 4 people killed in a drone strike in the village of Saidgi in North Waziristan. Habib Ullah the owner of the destroyed house, said those killed were not terrorists.

19 June 2007: 30 killed i in a drone strike n the village of Mami Rogha in North Waziristan

2 November 2007: 5 killed in a drone attack on a madrasah in North Waziristan

29 January 2008: Al-Qaeda's Abu Laith al-Libi killed in a drone strike in North Waziristan along with 12–14 others, among the dead are two women and three children.

27 February 2008: 12 people killed in a drone strike near Kalosha village in South Waziristan.

16 March 2008: 16–20 people killed in a drone strike in South Waziristan

14 May 2008: 12–15 including Abu Sulayman Al-Jazairi killed in drone strike near village of Damadola, Bajaur.

14 June 2008: Drones fired three missiles at a potential hideout of Tehrik-i-Taliban Pakistan (TTP), leader Meshud, killing one person.

28 July 2008: Midhat Mursi and 5 other people killed in South Waziristan.

13 August 2008: Drone strike on a compound run by Gulbuddin Hekmatyar reportedly killed Taliban commander Abdul Rehman, reportedly along with Islam Wazir, three Turkmen, and several Arab fighters. Up to 25 militants were reportedly killed in this strike.

20 August 2008: Drones fire two missiles that hit a compound in South Waziristan, killing 8 militants.

30 August 2008: Drone missile strike on Al-Qaeda training camp in South Waziristan kills two militants carrying Canadian passports.

31 August 2008: Drones destroy a house in Tappi village in Miranshah, killing 6 people and injuring 8 including 1 woman and 1 child.

4 September 2008: Drones fired missiles at a house in Char Khel in North Waziristan killing 4 people.

5 September 2008: Drones fire three missiles, destroying a house which was potentially hosting Arab foreign fighters, killing at least six.

8 September 2008: 23 killed in Daande Darpkhel drone airstrike, near Miranshah, North Waziristan.

12 September 2008: The Miranshah drone airstrike kills 12 people and injures 14.

17 September 2008: Drone attack in Baghar Cheena region of South Waziristan kills 5 militants including Al-Qaeda operative Abu Ubaydah al Tunisi.

23 September 2008 A US drone is reportedly shot down by Pakistani troops or local militia over a tribal area of Pakistan. US officials denied losing any aircraft.

30 September 2008: Six killed in a done strike near Mir Ali, North Waziristan.

3 October 2008: Two drone attacks hours apart in Datta Khel region of North Waziristan kills 21 militants including 16 foreigners.

9 October 2008: Drone strike killed at least 6 militants including 3 Arabs in Tappi village near Miranshah, North Waziristan.

11 October 2008: Drone strike at a militant compound in North Waziristan kills 5 people and wounds 2 others.

16 October 2008: Senior Al-Qaeda leader Khalid Habib was killed in a drone strike near Taparghai, South Waziristan, along with five other Al-Qaeda or Taliban members.

22 October 2008: 4 killed in a village near Miranshah by missiles fired from drones.

26 October 2008: 20 killed in a drone strike in South Waziristan.

31 October 2008: Two missiles fired by drones kills 7 in Wana, South Waziristan.

31 October 2008: 20 killed including Al-Qaeda operative Mohammad Hasan Khalil al-Hakim (alias Abu Jihad al-Masri) after 4 drone missiles hit Waziristan.

7 November 2008: Drones fire four missiles, killing up to 14 militants in Kumsham, North Waziristan.

14 November 2008: 12 killed in a drone strike near Miranshah.

19 November 2008: Abdullah Azam al-Saudi and 4 other militants are killed in a drone strike in Bannu district.

22 November 2008: British Al-Qaeda operative Rashid Rauf and 4

others including Abu Zubair al-Masri killed in a drone strike in North Waziristan.

29 November 2008: Drone strike on Miranshah, North Waziristan kills 3 people.

11 December 2008: Drone strike in Azam Warzak, South Waziristan, kills 7 militants.

15 December 2008: Drone strike in Tapi Tool region near Miram Shah, North Waziristan kills 2.

22 December 2008: At least 8 killed in South Waziristan by suspected drone strike.

1 January 2009: 2 senior Al-Qaeda leaders Usama al-Kini and Sheikh Ahmed Salim Swedan killed in a missile strike by U.S. drones.

2 January 2009: Drone strike in Ladha, South Waziristan kills 4 people.

23 January 2009: In the first drone attacks since Barack Obama became U.S. president, at least 14 killed in Waziristan in 2 separate attacks by 5 missiles fired from drones. According to the London Sunday Times, 19 people, all civilians, were killed, including four children.

14 February 2009: More than 30 killed when two missiles are launched by drones near town of Makeen in South Waziristan.

16 February 2009: Drone strike in Kurram Valley kills 30, reportedly at a Taliban training camp for fighters preparing to combat coalition forces in Afghanistan.

1 March 2009: Strike by drone attack in Sararogha village in South Waziristan kills 7 people.

12 March 2009: 24 killed in drone attack in Berju in Kurram Agency.

15 March 2009 4 killed in Jani Khel in Bannu district in North-West Frontier Province.

25 March 2009: 7 killed in attacks on 2 vehicles by two missiles in Makin area of South Waziristan at 6:30 pm.

26 March 2009: 4 killed i by drone attack n Essokhel area in North Waziristan.

1 April 2009: 14 killed by drone attack in Orakzai Agency tribal area.

4 April 2009: 13 killed by drone attack in North Waziristan.

8 April 2009: 4 killed by drone attack on a vehicle in Gangi Khel in South Waziristan.

19 April 2009: At least 3 killed and 5 injured in a drone attack in South Waziristan

29 April 2009: Drone strike in Kanni Garam village in South Waziristan kills 6 people.

9 May 2009: Drone strike in Sararogha in South Waziristan kills 6 people.

12 May 2009: Drone strike in Sra Khawra village in South Waziristan kills 8 people.

16 May 2009: Drone strike in village of Sarkai Naki in North Waziristan with multiple missiles kills 25–29 people. According to later reports, the first missile killed a dozen Taliban preparing to cross the border into Afghanistan. At least two more missiles struck rescuers who came to their aid, killing more Taliban, but also six civilians as well.

14 June 2009: Drone strike on a vehicle in South Waziristan kills 5 people.

18 June 2009: Two drone strikes in Shahalam village in South Waziristan kills at least 13 people.

23 June 2009: Drone strike in Neej Narai in South Waziristan kills at least 8 people.

23 June 2009: Makeen airstrike kills at least 80 but misses Baitullah Mehsud in the town of Makeen, many of which were attending the funerals of people killed in the drone strikes earlier in the day.

3 July 2009: Drone kills 17 people and injures a further 27.

7 July 2009: Drone strike in Zangarha in South Waziristan kills at least 12 people.

8 July 2009: Drone strike on a hideout in Karwan Manza area and on a vehicle convoy in South Waziristan kills at least 50 people.

10 July 2009: Drones take out a Taliban communication center killing between 5–8 militants in Painda Khel, South Waziristan.

17 July 2009: Drone strike on a house in North Waziristan kills 4 people

5 August 2009: Drone strike in South Waziristan killed 12, including Baitullah Mehsud, his wife, and his wife's parents. The kill was confirmed after weeks of uncertainty over their fate.

11 August 2009: US drone strike in Ladha village, South Waziristan, kills 10.

21 August 2009: Drone strike on the village of Darpa Khel, North Waziristan, reportedly targeting Sirajuddin Haqqani kills at least 21 people.

27 August 2009: Drone missile strike on the Tapar Ghai area in the Kanigram (Kanigoram) district in South Waziristan kills up to 8 people. One of the dead was confirmed by the Taliban to be Tohir Yo'ldosh (Tahir Yuldashev), leader of the Islamic Movement of Uzbekistan.

8 September 2009: Drone fired missiles kill 10 in North Waziristan. The attack may have killed Al-Qaeda leaders Ilyas Kashmiri and

Mustafa al Jaziri as well as three Punjabi militants and two or three local Taliban fighters.

14 September 2009: Drone fired missile kills four people in a car 1.5 miles (2.4 km) from Mir Ali in North Waziristan.

24 September 2009: Drone fired missile kills up to 12 people in the village of Dande Darpa Khel near Mir Ali.

29 September 2009: Two drone missile attacks take place. In the first, a drone attack reportedly killed six Taliban, including two Uzbek fighters and Taliban commander Irfan Mehsud, in a compound in Sararogha village, South Waziristan. In the second, a missile killed seven insurgents in a house in Dandey Darpa Khel village, North Waziristan.

30 September 2009: Drones fire missiles at a Taliban compound and vehicle killing 8 in Novak, North Waziristan.

15 October 2009: Drone missile killed at least four people in North Waziristan.

21 October 2009: Alleged drone missile killed two or three alleged militants in Spalaga, North Waziristan in territory controlled by Hafiz Gul Bahadur. One of those killed was reportedly Abu Ayyub al-Masri (not the same as Abu Ayyub al-Masri, the Al-Qaeda in Iraq leader), an explosives expert for Al-Qaeda and a "Tier 1" target of US counterterrorism operations.

24 October 2009: Alleged drone strike killed 27, in Damadolla, inside Bajaur tribal agency. The 27 victims were reportedly a mix of Taliban and Al-Qaeda operatives engaged in a planning and strategy meeting. The dead apparently included 11 "foreigners". One of those reported killed was Faqir Mohammed's nephew, Zahid and another was Mohammed's unnamed son-in-law. The meeting was apparently being held to decide on whether to reinforce South Wazaristan against Pakistani forces, which Mohammed advocates, or exploit recent successes in the Nuristan

and Kunar provinces of Afghanistan, which Al-Qaeda wishes to do.

5 November 2009: 2 killed by drone attack in Miranshah town in North Waziristan.

18 November 2009: 4 killed and 5 injured by drone attack in Shanakhora village of North Waziristan, 12 miles (19 km) south of Miranshah.

20 November 2009: 8 killed by drone attack in the Machikhel area near the town of Mir Ali.

8 December 2009: 3 killed by drone attack in a car near Miranshah in North Waziristan, reportedly including 2 Al-Qaeda members. Senior Al-Qaeda planner Saleh al-Somali, from Somalia, is believed killed in this strike.

9 December 2009: Six killed by drone attacks in Tanga, Ladha, South Waziristan, reportedly consisting of four Al-Qaeda and two Taliban members.

17 December 2009: 17 killed in 2 separate drone attacks in North Waziristan in an area controlled by Hafiz Gul Bahadur. In the first attack, two missiles hit a car near Dosali, killing two. In the second attack, 10 missiles fired by five drones hit two compounds in Ambarshaga, killing 15 people. Unnamed sources stated that seven of the dead were "foreigners." The attack was aimed at Sheikh Saeed al Saudi, Osama bin Laden's brother-in-law and a member of Al-Qaeda's executive council, but al Saudi survived. The attack did kill Abdullah Said al Libi, the commander of, and Zuhaib al Zahibi, a commander in, the Lashkar al-Zil.

18 December 2009: 3 killed in a drone attack in Dattakhel region in North Waziristan.

26 December 2009: 13 killed in a drone attack in Saidgai village in North Waziristan.

31 December 2009: Four killed in a drone attack in Machikhel village in North Waziristan. According to The Frontier Post, senior Taliban leader and strong Haqqani ally Haji Omar Khan, brother of Arif Khan, was killed in the strike along with the son of local tribal leader Karim Khan.

1 January 2010: Drone missile strike on a vehicle near Ghundikala village in North Waziristan kills 3.

3 January 2010: 5 people including 3 Arabs killed in a drone attack on Mosakki village in North Waziristan.

6 January 2010: 2 separate drone missile strikes one-hour apart kill approximately 35 people in Sanzalai village, North Waziristan.

8 January 2010: Drone missile strike in Tappi village in North Waziristan killed 5 people. It is alleged that all the militants killed were local and were attached to Taliban Commander Hafiz Gul Bahadur.

9 January 2010: 4 killed and three injured when 2 drone missiles are fired on a compound in village Ismail Khan in North Waziristan, territory of the Haqqani network. Mahmoud Mahdi Zeidan, bodyguard for Al-Qaeda leader Sayeed al-Masri, was reported killed in either the 8 or 9 January airstrike. Jamal Saeed Abdul Rahim who was allegedly involved in hijacking of Pan Am Flight 73 in 1986 was also reported killed in this strike.

13 January 2010: Missile strike in Pasalkot village in a compound formerly used as a religious school in North Waziristan killed 15 people, among them 3 militant commanders. The apparent target of the strike was Hakimullah Mehsud, who reportedly left the compound before the attack occurred.

15 January 2010: Missile strike in Zanini village near Mir Ali in North Waziristan kills 3 people.

15 January 2010: Second missile strike of the day kills 6 in Bichi village in North Waziristan.

17 January 2010: Missile strike in Shaktoi area of South Waziristan kills at least 20 people. The leader of the Pakistani Taliban, Hakimullah Mehsud sustained injuries in this attack. It was initially believed he died but it was later learned that he survived.

19 January 2010: Two missiles fired at a compound and vehicle in Booya village of Datakhel sub-division, 35 km west of Miranshah, in North Waziristan kills 9 people.

24 January 2010: A drone crashes over North Waziristan, allegedly after being shot down by local tribesmen.

29 January 2010: 15 killed when drones fire 3 missiles on a compound belonging to Haqqani network in Muhammad Khel town in North Waziristan.

2 February 2010: Up to 8 drones fired missiles at 4 different villages of North Waziristan killing at least 29 people.

14 February 2010: 5 killed in a drone strike near Mir Ali in North Waziristan.

15 February 2010: Abdul Haq al-Turkistani, leader of the Turkistani Islamic Party, is killed by a drone missile strike in North Waziristan.

17 February 2010: Three militants killed by a drone missile strike near Tapi, Miramshah, North Waziristan. One of those killed was reportedly Sheikh Mansoor, a commander in the Lashkar al Zil.

18 February 2010: 4 killed in a drone strike in Northwest Waziristan including Mohammed Haqqani, the brother of Afghan Taliban commander Siraj who leads the Haqqani network. The missiles hit a vehicle belonging to Siraj that Mohammed was riding in, but Siraj was not in the vehicle at the time. Mohammed and Siraj were reportedly attending the funeral of Sheikh Mansoor, who had been killed by a drone strike the day before.

24 February 2010: Missiles fired by a drone killed at least 13 militants at a compound and at a vehicle in the Dargah Mandi area

of North Waziristan. Among the dead include Rana Afzal, the man behind the FIA HQ bombing in Lahore. Qari Mohammed Zafar, the head of Lashkar-e-Jhangvi and the person responsible for the 2002 and 2006 bombing of the U.S. consulate in Karachi was killed in this drone strike.

8 March 2010: Three missiles fired by drones killed five militants and wounded three in Miranshah. Hussein al-Yemeni (also called Sadam Hussein Al Hussami), an Al-Qaeda terrorist who planned the Camp Chapman attack, died in this strike.

10 March 2010: Missiles fired from drones struck a compound and three vehicles in the village of Mizar Madakhel in North Waziristan. The attack killed at least 12 and as many as 21 militants. Five drones reportedly attacked in two waves. First, four missiles struck and demolished the compound. After local militants cordoned off the area and began recovering bodies, a second volley of missiles struck. Hafiz Gul Bahadar, a local Taliban leader and chief of the North Waziristan Shura, survived the strike.

16 March 2010: Eight to ten militants were killed in a US drone strike in North Waziristan's Datakhel area. The militants were reportedly Al-Qaeda fighters, mainly Afghan, but included two officials from Syria and Egypt.

17 March 2010: Two drone strikes killed 9 militants. In the first attack, the drones fired five missiles at two vehicles, killing six militants. Late, drones fired 2 missiles at a compound in Datta Khel, killing 3 militants.

21 March 2010: Drone fires two missiles in the Datta Khel area of North Waziristan killing at least eight people and injuring several others.

23 March 2010: Drones fired two missiles on a militant vehicle parked outside a compound in the suburbs of Miranshah in North Waziristan. At least six militants were killed and three others were wounded.

27 March 2010: Drone strike in Mir Ali in North Waziristan kills 4 militants.

30 March 2010: Drone fired three missiles, killing 5–6 civilians and injure two, among the death are two women and one child.

12 April 2010: Missiles fired by a drone kill 13 people in North Waziristan, village elders said all thirteen killed were civilians.

14 April 2010: Drone strike targeting a vehicle killed up to 4 people and injuring 4 others in Anbarshaga area of North Waziristan. All of the dead and injured were Arab militants.

16 April 2010: Drones fired at least 7 missiles which hit two vehicles and a house in the Toolkhel area near Miramshah in North Waziristan killing 6 people and injuring 5 others.

24 April 2010: Drones kill 7 militants in North Waziristan in the village of Marsi Khel near Miramshah.

26 April 2010: Three missiles from drones strike a compound in the Khushali Toorkhel area, about 25 km east of Miranshah, North Waziristan, killing four or five.

3 May 2010: 4 militants are killed in a drone strike in North Waziristan.

9 May 2010: 10 militants are killed in a drone strike in North Waziristan.

11 May 2010: At least 24 militants are killed in two separate drone strikes in which the US fired up to 18 missiles. The first strike occurred when missiles struck cars, homes and tents in the Doga area of North Waziristan killing up to 14 militants. Hours later another pair of missiles hit a compound in the Gorwek area of North Waziristan killing another 10 suspected insurgents, including the brother of a reputed Taliban commander, Maulvi Kalam.

15 May 2010: At least 15 killed in Khyber Agency in the first drone strike in this area.

21 May 2010: Drones fired two missiles on a compound used by Afghan Warlord Hafiz Gul Bahadur and killed 10 people in Mohammad Khel, North Waziristan. Saeed al-Masri, the current 3rd in command of Al-Qaeda was killed in this strike along with his wife and 3 children. Other dead in this strike include two foreign militants, one of whom was reportedly Filipino. Five women and two children were reported injured.

28 May 2010: Drone strike killed 11 militants and wounded three others in the Nazai Narai area of South Waziristan.

9 June 2010: Drone strike killed 3 people in North Waziristan.

10 June 2010: Drones fired 6 missiles on a housing compound near Miranshah at the Afghan-Pakistan border, killing 15 alleged militants.

19 June 2010: Drone fired a missile striking a house in Haider Khel village near North Waziristan's Mir Ali town killing 16 militants. Al-Qaeda leader Abu Ahmed Tarkash was among the dead.

26 June 2010: A drone missile strike killed 7 militants in Pakistan's tribal region near the Afghan border. The missile, fired by an unmanned drone, destroyed a house near Mir Ali in North Waziristan. One of the dead men was a foreigner.

29 June 2010: Drone fired two missiles hitting a house near in Wana, South Waziristan killing at least 8 militants, including Hamza al-Jufi an Egyptian member of Al-Qaeda.

15 July 2010: A drone strike in North Waziristan killed 14 suspected militants in a region under the control of Hafiz Gul Bahadar.

24 July 2010: Drones fired at least five missiles at a militant compound in Dwasarak village, about 40 miles west of Wana, in South Waziristan killing 16 militants.

25 July 2010: Drones fired two missiles and hit a double-cabin pickup carrying militants in Shaktoi village in South Waziristan.

Taliban sources said 14 militants were killed and two others were injured in the attack. The militants belonged to the Hakimullah Mehsud-led Tehrik-i-Taliban Pakistan (TTP).

25 July 2010: Drones launched their second strike of the day when two missiles hit a house where some militants were having dinner in Landikhel village of Srarogha Tehsil in South Waziristan. Four militants that belonged to Tehrik-i-Taliban Pakistan (TTP), were killed and five others sustained injuries.

25 July 2010: Drones launched their unprecedented third strike on the same day when they fired two missiles at a house in Taipi village near Miranshah, the main town in North Waziristan, killing 7 suspected militants.

14 August 2010: Drone fired three missiles at a compound in Mir Ali, North Waziristan, killing at least 13 militants including Taliban commander, Amir Moaviya.

21 August 2010: A drone strike near Miranshah, North Waziristan, kills 6 militants.

23 August 2010: Missiles fired from drones in North Waziristan kill 10 alleged militants and ten civilians. Four women and three children are among the dead.

27 August 2010: Missiles fired from drones in the Kurram Agency hit 2 vehicle killing 5 suspected militants, the first such reported drone strike in the Kurram Agency.

3 September 2010: 2 separate drone strikes kill 12–15 suspected militants in North Waziristan. The first strike was near Miramshah, killing six militants. The second strike was near Data Khel, targeting the home of Gul Adam, and killed nine militants. SAMAA TV reported that a local Taliban commander named Inayatullah was reportedly killed in the strike.

4 September 2010: Drones struck two vehicles in Datta Khel village in North Waziristan district and killed four suspected militants.

6 September 2010: A drone strike in North Waziristan kills 5 suspected militants.

8 September 2010: Drones launch four separate attacks in a space of 24 hours. According to anonymous Pakistani intelligence officials: In the first attack, a house owned by Maulvi Azizullah, a member of the Haqqani network, in Dande Darpa Khel near Miranshah was struck killing at least 6 militants. In the second attack, drones fired missiles striking a car traveling a few miles from the border, killing four people associated with the Haqqani network. In the third attack, another house near the Miranshah area was struck killing another 4 militants. A few hours later US drones launched their fourth attack striking a compound outside Miranshah killing at least 6 militants and wounding 5 others. All told 24 militants have been killed in these 4 strikes. The strikes targeted the Islamic Jihad Group, which was planning terrorist attacks in Europe. An Islamic Jihad commander, Qureshi, who was training German operatives, was killed in the missile attacks.

11 September 2010: A drone strike on the house of Hafiz Gul Bahadur in North Waziristan kills 5 suspected militants.

13 September 2010: A drone fires two missiles at a house in Shawal, North Waziristan, reportedly killing 13 militants.

14 September 2010: A drone strike kills 12 militants in Dargah Mandi near Miranshah, North Waziristan. The numerous strikes in September are reportedly part of a campaign against the Haqqqni Network. The drone strikes in Pakistan against the network are meant to support concurrent special operations raids against the network's fighters in Afghanistan. Saifullah Haqqani, a military commander in Afghanistan and a cousin of Siraj Haqqani, was reportedly killed in this day's strikes.

15 September 2010: In an ongoing unprecedented drone offensive, a drone strike kills 4 militants in North Waziristan, including

Saifullah Haqqani, first cousin of Haqqani Network leader Sirajuddin Haqqani.

16 September 2010: Drones fired missiles at a house in Datakhel area, killing six militants.

19 September 2010: A drone fires two missiles at a vehicle in Dehgan village, in the Datta Khel area, North Waziristan, killing four militants.

20 September 2010: Drones launch two strikes killing a total of 12 militants in North Waziristan, the first volley hit a vehicle in the Datakhel region killing 5, the second hit a house in Miranshah killing 7.

21 September 2010: A drone strike kills 16 militants in the South-North Waziristan border region, including Taliban commander Mullah Shamsullah.

25 September 2010: A drone fired three missiles hitting a vehicle killing 4 militants in Datta Khel village of North Waziristan. Among the dead was Sheikh Fateh Al Misri, Al-Qaeda's new 3rd in command. Al Misri was planning a major terrorist attack in London, Paris or Berlin by recruiting British Muslims who would then go on a shooting rampage throughout these cities similar to what transpired in Mumbai in November 2008. The plan was thought to be its final stages and the stepped up drone campaign in September was done to disrupt and eliminate the key planners of this terrorist attack.

26 September 2010: Drones launch two strikes against militants killing 7. In the first strike, drone fired three missiles at a house in Lwara Mandi village in Datta Khel, killing 3 militants. Minutes later, a drone fired two missiles at a vehicle in the same area, killing 4 militants.

27 September 2010: A drone strike in Miranshah, North Waziristan, kills 6 militants.

28 September 2010: Drone fired a missile at a compound Zeba village, west of Wana, South Waziristan killing 4 militants.

2 October 2010: Drones launch two separate strikes killing 17 militants. In the first attack drones fired two missiles at a house in Datta Khel killing 9 militants including 4 foreigners. The dead were members of the Badar Mansur group, which is closely affiliated with Al-Qaeda. Four hours later another strike occurred in the same area on a convoy of vehicles and a house killing another 8 militants.

4 October 2010: Drones strike a building near Mir Ali, North Waziristan, reportedly killing 8 suspected militants including 20-year-old German citizen Bünyamin E. and three other German nationals. In May 2011, the German government announced that it would curb terrorist intelligence flow to the U.S. to make sure that it would not be used in targeted killings of German citizen.

6 October 2010: Two drone strikes, one near Mir Ali and one near Miranshah, North Waziristan, kill a total of 11 militants.

7 October 2010: A drone strike on a compound in North Waziristan kills at least four militants.

8 October 2010: Drone strikes by Miranshah, North Waziristan, kill a total of six militants.

10 October 2010: A drone fires four missiles at a compound and two vehicles, killing seven militants in the Shewa district of North Waziristan.

13 October 2010: Drone attacks kill 11 militants in the Datta Khel area of North Waziristan.

15 October 2010: Two drone strikes kill 13 suspected militants. The first drone strike killed six suspected militants in North Waziristan's Machi Khel area. Officials said two missiles hit an alleged militant vehicle. Later this day the second drone strike killed 7 suspected militants in the Mir Ali area of North Waziristan.

18 October 2010: A drone strike in the Datta Khel area of North Waziristan kills 6 militants. The strike may have also killed the 10-year-old son of Naeem Ullah, who lived next door.

27 October 2010: Two drone strikes 12 hours apart killed 7 militants. The first strike was on a house of militant Nasimullah Khan which killed 4 militants. The second strike was on a vehicle in Datta Khel kill which killed 3 militants.

28 October 2010: A drone strike in the Datta Khel area kills 7 militants.

1 November 2010: Drones fired four missiles at a house in the Mir Ali District of North Wazaristan, killing five or six suspected militants.

3 November 2010: Drones launch three separate attacks killing 13 militants. In the first attack, drones fired two missiles at a vehicle in the Qutab Khel area of Miranshah killing 5 Uzbek militants. In the second attack, missiles struck a house and a vehicle in Khaso Khel village, near Mir Ali, killing 4 militants. In the third attack, four missiles were fired hitting a vehicle in Pai Khel village in Datta Khel town, killing 4 militants.

7 November 2010: Two drone strikes kill a total 13 or 14 militants in the Miranshah area of North Waziristan. In the first attack, drones struck a house and a vehicle in the town of Ghulam Khan, north of Miranshah killing 9 militants. The second attack occurred an hour later in which drones stuck several vehicles in the neighboring town of Datta Khel, killing 4 militants.

11 November 2010: A drone strike kills 6 suspected militants in North Waziristan. The militants were reportedly Haqqani Network fighters returning from operations in Khost Province, Afghanistan.

13 November 2010: A drone strike kills five people in the village of Ahmad Khel in the Mir Ali area in North Waziristan.

16 November 2010: Four drone-fired missiles hit a house and

vehicle in Bangi Dar village of North Waziristan, killing 15 to 20 people, including 5–9 civilians.

19 November 2010: One drone strike kills 3 suspected militants in the region of North Waziristan.

21 November 2010: A drone strike near Miranshah, North Waziristan, kills 6 suspected militants.

22 November 2010: A drone strike fired missiles at a car and a motorcycle in North Waziristan killing 5 alleged militants.

26 November 2010: A drone strike fired missiles at a vehicle in North Waziristan killing 4 alleged militants.

28 November 2010: Drone missiles strike a vehicle in Hasan Khel village, around 30 kilometers east of Miranshah. Initial reports indicated the strike killed 3 or 4 militants. Local officials, however, later reported that the suspected militants had survived the strike by fleeing the targeted vehicle after the first missile missed.

6 December 2010: A drone strike in Khushali village, North Waziristan, kills 5 people. The strike may have also killed two noncombatants.

9 December 2010: At least four unknown people are killed by a drone strike on a vehicle in Mir Ali, North Waziristan according to anonymous Pakistani intelligence officials who suspect that they are militants.

14 December 2010: At least four suspected militants were killed by a US drone strike on a vehicle in North Waziristan.

15 December 2010: Drone strike targeting a vehicle kills 7 suspected militants in Spin Drand area of Khyber according to anonymous Pakistani intelligence officials.

17 December 2010: At least 60 suspected militants were killed in 3 drones strikes what is the highest death toll this year. According to security officials all the dead are suspected militants – a claim that

cannot be independently confirmed. The first strike occurred at a compound in Speen Drang where pro-Taliban militants from the Lashkar-e-Islam group were holding a meeting killing over 32. The second strike occurred in Nakai, Khyber hitting a compound killing around 15. The last strike occurred at yet another compound in Sangana, Khyber killing 6. According to unnamed official sources 39 of the killed belonged to Lashkar-e-Islam while 15 were Tehreek-i-Taliban (TTP) Pakistan. Extremist commander Ibn Amin was also killed in these strikes. He was a Taliban commander for the Swat valley.

27 December 2010: Two drone strikes near Mir Ali area of North Waziristan kill a total of 18 unknown people who were allegedly militants according to anonymous Pakistani intelligence officials.

28 December 2010: Two drone strikes in Pakistan's tribal region Tuesday kill 17 people. The drones fired two missiles on a suspected militant hideout in the area of Ghulam Khan. Later, a suspected drone circled around the blast site and fired two more missiles. Six people were killed. The second attack was on a vehicle in the same area, killing four more people.

31 December 2010: Drone missile strike kills 8 people near the town of Ghulam Khan in the North Waziristan tribal agency according to Pakistani security officials who suspect that they are militants.

The Human Rights Commission of Pakistan claimed that at over 900 people were killed in drone attacks in Pakistan's tribal areas in 2010.

1 January 2011: Drones launched 3 separate strikes killing 18 people. In the first strike, drones struck a vehicle and a suspected militant compound in Mandi Khel, near Mir Ali, North Waziristan killing 9 people who are believed to be militants according to anonymous Pakistani intelligence officials. In the second strike, drones killed 5 alleged Taliban insurgents. In the last strike, a vehicle was struck in Boya village, in Datta Khel, North Waziristan killing 4 people.

12 January 2011: Drones fired 4 missiles at a compound in Haiderkhel village near the town of Mir Ali in North Waziristan killing 6 people.

18 January 2011: A drone strike kills at least five militants in North Waziristan according to anonymous Pakistani security officials.

23 January 2011: According to anonymous Pakistani security officials, three drone strikes killed around 13 suspected militants in North Waziristan. In the first strike, two missiles hit a vehicle and a house in Doga Mada Khel village, killing four people. Hours later, another drone fired two more missiles, killing two people riding a motorcycle in the same village. In the third strike, a militant compound was struck at Mando Khel, 60 km south of Miram Shah near Razmak, North Waziristan killing 6 people. The same day around 2,000 tribesmen held a protest in Mir Ali, demanding an end to the drone strikes, saying they killed innocent civilians.

21 February 2011: Anonymous Pakistani intelligence officials announced that three drone-fired missiles demolished a house in the village of Kaza Panga, Azam Warsak district, South Waziristan killing seven suspected militants, including several Arabs and Turkmen. One of those killed was reported by Pakistani officials to be an Iraqi Al-Qaeda finance coordinator named Abu Zaid al-Iraqi. Later that day, four missiles struck a house being used as a base by Taliban in the village of Spalga near Miranshah in North Waziristan, killing eight suspected militants.

24 February 2011: Two separate strikes by drones kill 6 in North Waziristan.

8 March 2011: Drone strike in Landidog village in South Waziristan kills 5 militants according to Pakistani officials.

11 March 2011: 5 suspected militants killed by drones in Ghorsaka area near Miranshah in North Waziristan.

13 March 2011: 2 drone missiles kill at least 6 people believed to be militants in Azam Warsak area of South Waziristan.

14 March 2011: Drones killed 6 alleged militants near Miranshah in North Waziristan. Later in the day, another drone missile hit a vehicle near the Afghan border in Malik Jashdar in North Waziristan, killing three suspected militants.

16 March 2011: Unnamed Pakistani intelligence officials told AFP that a drone strike in Dattakhel in North Waziristan kills 5 militants. They also said that they do not know the identities of those killed in the strike.

17 March 2011: Forty-eight are killed and 50 wounded when several missiles fired from American drone aircraft hit a location in Datta Khel airstrike in North Waziristan. Those killed were mostly civilians involved in a jirga or dispute resolution council discussing a claim to a local chromite mine. Also killed were 12 Taliban helping adjudicate the meeting. Sherabat Khan Wazir, a top commander of Hafiz Gul Bahadur's Taliban faction, was killed in the strike, and in response Bahadur threatened to end the peace deal struck with the Pakistani government almost four years earlier. Ashfaq Parvez Kayani said that the attack was a "complete violation of human rights" and that there were children under the death. Pakistani officials said the strike will intensify protests throughout Pakistan over the release of CIA contractor Raymond Davis. The Punjab Assembly unanimously passed a resolution condemning the strike and demanded that the national government take a clearer stance on the issue. Parliamentarian Marvi Memon demanded to declare war on the United States. She suggested to order defence forces to launch a counterattack and said that it was the responsibility of the Pakistani government to protect its citizens.

13 April 2011: Two drones fired seven missiles in South Waziristan and killed six people. Reports conflicted on the intended target. One report indicated that the attacks targeted members of a pro-army group led by Maulvi Nazir although the deceased were said to

be ordinary tribesmen unaffiliated with Nazir. The six dead were all Afghans and members of the Haqqani network. Pakistan strongly condemned the attack and lodged a strong protest with US Ambassador Cameron Munter. The Foreign Ministry in Islamabad stated: "We have repeatedly said that such attacks are counterproductive and only contribute to strengthen the hands of the terrorists." Prime Minister Yousaf Raza Gillani said that Pakistan was also seeking the intervention of friendly countries to get the U.S. to stop the drone attacks.

21 April 2011: At least 25 people, including 4 women and 5 children, were killed and about 10 other wounded in drone attacks in the Mir Ali area of North Waziristan. The target was a compound of houses belonging to the Hafiz Gul Bahadur group, a pro-army group in the tribal area. The women and children were in nearby houses. Days before the strike US Joint Chiefs of Staff Chairman Admiral Mike Mullen clearly stated that North Waziristan is the hot bed for terrorists and accused Pakistan of not doing enough to combat militants. The Pakistani army rejected this as "negative propaganda" and Chief of Army Staff general Ashfaq Parvez Kayani said: "In the war against terrorism, our officers and soldiers have made great sacrifices and have achieved tremendous success. The terrorists' backbone has been broken and Inshallah (God willing) we will soon prevail." The day after the attack Pakistan stopped the U.S. from using Shamsi Air Base in Pakistan's Balochistan Province to fly drones. A senior military official told NBC News, "Yes, I can confirm that Shamsi Air Base is no more under the use of Americans and the 150 Americans previously stationed there are now gone." The base had been used for some time by the U.S to launch unmanned Predator drones against terrorist targets.

6 May 2011: 12–15 people killed and several injured at Dua Toi in the Datta Khel area 30 miles west of Miram Shah, North Waziristan in the first drone attack since the killing of Osama Bin Laden. An unnamed Pakistani official said the missiles hit a car and a compound belonging to Hafiz Gul Bahadar, and that four of those

killed were "foreigners". British and Pakistani journalists report that, in addition to 12 militants, the strike killed six civilians.

10 May 2011: 4 suspected militants killed in a drone attack near Angoor Adda village in South Waziristan. Two missiles hit a vehicle in village, wounding four others in addition to those killed. An unnamed Pakistani official said three of those killed were "Arabs". The area hit is under the control of Mullah Nazir.

12 May 2011: 5–8 suspected militants killed when a drone fired two missiles into a vehicle in Pakistan's tribal district of North Waziristan. Pakistani officials stated that some of those killed were "foreigners".

13 May 2011: 5 killed when at least 4 missiles strike a vehicle in Doga Madakhel village of North Waziristan.

16 May 2011: 2 strikes in Mir Ali in North Waziristan kill 10 suspected militants.

20 May 2011: 2 missiles fired by drones kill 6 people in North Waziristan.

23 May 2011: Drone strike on a vehicle on the outskirts of Mir Ali in North Waziristan kills 7 suspected militants.

3 June 2011: Drone strike in Ghwakhwa area of South Waziristan kills 9 militants. Top ranking Al-Qaeda militant Ilyas Kashmiri is reported killed.

6 June 2011: Three drone strikes kill 16–21 people. Unnamed Pakistani intelligence officials claimed that they were suspected militants. Other witnesses said that some were "Arabs" and seven were civilians.

8 June 2011: Five missiles strike a militant compound in Zoi (or Zoynarai) village in Shawal region of North Waziristan, near the border with South Waziristan, killing 15–23 suspected militants. Senior unnamed Pakistani officials as well as local officials

confirmed the strike. In response to a series of strikes against their group a spokesman for Taliban leader Maulvi Nazir announced that his group would send more people into Afghanistan to fight U.S. forces as they had no capability to shoot down drones over South Waziristan.

15 June 2011: Two strikes by drones in South Waziristan and one in North Waziristan kill 15 suspected militants according to Pakistani intelligence officials. The strike near Wana in South Waziristan reportedly killed 10 fighters from Mullah Nazir's army. In the other strike, near Miranshah in North Waziristan, 5–6 civilians were killed in a car. Later residents blocked roads with the coffins of the dead to protest the killing of civilians.

20 June 2011: Three strikes kill 15–17 the Kurram tribal area. Those killed were mostly alleged millitants but 2–7 civilians were also among the dead.

27 June 2011: Missile strikes from two drones killed at least 21 suspected militants in Pakistan's South Waziristan on Monday, Pakistani officials said. The first strike against a moving vehicle in Ghalmandi Panga village reportedly killed eight suspected militants. The second strike a few hours later reportedly hit a militant training center in Mantoi, killing 13 suspected militants according to an intelligence official who declined to be identified.

5 July 2011: Four killed and 5 injured in a strike on a militant hideout near Mir Ali in North Waziristan. According to two local TV station in Pakistan based on unnamed official sources, Saif Ullah, an Australian and Al-Qaeda supporter, was killed in the strike. However, there is no official confirmation for his death.

11 July 2011: Drone strikes near Gorvak village in North Waziristan kill 12 suspected militants according to Pakistani Intelligence officials. Over the next 24 hours several more attacks lead to the death of 45–61 suspected militants. The strikes sparked panic

among people in the area and the death toll is the second highest since the beginning of the airstrikes.

12 July 2011: 23 suspected militants were killed in South Waziristan, followed by a drone strike on a vehicle in North Waziristan, resulting in the deaths of 7 suspected militants, bringing the total death toll to 30.

21 July 2011: 4 people were reportedly killed in a drone strike in Khushali Toori Khel area of North Waziristan.

1 August 2011: 4–6 alleged militants are killed and at least seven other people are injured when two vehicles are hit by two drone-launched missiles near Azam Warsak, 15 kilometers west of Wana, South Waziristan. According to the Long War Journal, that area is controlled by Taliban leader Maulvi Nazir.

10 August 2011: Two drone-launched missiles hit a house 3 km east of Miranshah, North Waziristan, killing 21 militants, 14 of whom were members of the Haqqani Network. The rest of those killed were Arabs and Uzbeks, according to unnamed Pakistani intelligence officials who were not authorized to speak to the media.

15 August 2011: According to unnamed Pakistani officials 4 suspected militants were killed near Miranshah after 2 missiles fired by Drones. The identity of those killed is unclear.

19 August 2011: Four suspected militants killed in suspected drone attack in Sheen Warsik in South Waziristan according to Pakistani officials.

22 August 2011: According to unnamed Pakistani officials a suspected drone strike in North Waziristan killed 4 suspected militants. including Al-Qaeda's second in command Atiyah Abd al-Rahman.

4 September 2011: 7 suspected militants killed in a drone strike in North Wazirstan.

11 September 2011: Abu Hafs al Shari, Al-Qaeda's operational chief and the replacement for Atiyah Abdel Rahman, was killed along with 3 other militants by a drone strike on a vehicle and compound in Hisokhel in the Mir Ali area of North Waziristan.

12 September 2011: Two militants killed in a drone strike on their vehicle in the Esokhel area of North Waziristan. One of the dead was reported to be Hafeezulla, a commander in the Haqqani network. In another strike the same day three people were killed in an attack on a house near Mir Ali.

23 September 2011: 6 Haqqani network insurgents, including 4 Central Asians, were killed in a drone strike on a house in North Waziristan.

27 September 2011: 3 people are killed in a drone strike on a house in Azam Warzak, South Waziristan. Unnamed security officials who were not authorized to talk with reporters said they were militants while other sources said the militants escaped. The village is in the territory of Taliban leader Mullah Nazir and reportedly, according to the Long War Journal, serves as a transit point for insurgent fighters into and out of Afghanistan.

30 September 2011: 3 suspected militants killed in a drone strike Baghar Cheena area of South Waziristan.

13 October 2011: Two separate drone strikes killed a total of seven suspected militants in Waziristan. The first strike in Dande Darpa Khel village in North Waziristan killed four including Jan Baz Zadran, a logistics commander for the Haqqani network. The second strike killed three suspected militants in the town of Angoor Adda in South Waziristan who were launching rockets into Afghanistan. The widow of Abu Miqdad al Masri, a member of Al-Qaeda's Shura Majlis, or executive council, later stated that he, along with their two sons Al Miqdad Rafie Mustafa and Khalid Rafie Mustafa, were killed in a drone strike on or around this date.

26 October 2011: A drone strike in South Waziristan killed 13–22

militants, including Taj Gul Mehsud, a close aid to the Tehrik-i-Taliban Pakistan (TTP).

27 October 2011: A drone strike targeted Maulvi Nazir's faction of the Taliban in the Warsak area of South Waziristan. Four, including Nazir's younger brother, were killed.

27 October 2011: In a separate attack, a drone fired missiles into an alleged militant hideout near the North Waziristan town of Mir Ali, killing six men.

30 October 2011: Suspected drones fired six missiles at a vehicle in the Datta Khel area of North Waziristan, killing six alleged militants.

31 October 2011: Three people including two boys, Tariq Aziz and his 12-year-old cousin Waheed Khan were killed in a drone strike in the Miranshah area North Waziristan. Prior to his killing, 16-year-old Tariq Aziz had helped the Bureau of Investigative Journalism document civilian casualties caused by drone strikes. Human rights lawyer Clive Stafford Smith said: "I met this lad Tariq last week, and he was no more a terrorist than my mother."

3 November 2011: Three men, suspected as being Haqqani network militants, killed by drones in North Waziristan.

15 November 2011: 6 or 7 suspected militants were killed when a drone fired two missiles on a suspected militant compound in Miranshah Bazaar, part of the town of Miranshah, North Waziristan.

16 November 2011: 16 people, at least two of whom were Tehrik-i-Taliban Pakistan (TTP), militants, were killed after about six missiles from drones targeted a compound in the Babar Ghar area of Sararogha Tehsil, South Waziristan.

17 November 2011: 6 suspected militants killed in a strike near Razmak in North Waziristan.

10 January 2012: Drone strike near Miranshah killed four militants including three Arabs according to Pakistani intelligence officials. An US official who spoke on the condition of anonymity told Reuters they believe the attack have killed Aslam Awan, also known as Abdullah Khorasani, who has been described as a senior operations organiser for Al-Qaeda. Pakistani officials could not confirm that Awan was killed.

11 January 2012: According to unnamed Pakistani intelligence officials a drone fired two missiles at two vehicles driving towards the Afghan border in the Dogga area of North Waziristan killing between 6 to 8 people. Other Pakistani intelligence officials who spoke on condition of anonymity said that intercepted militant radio communications indicated that the leader of the Pakistani Taliban, Hakimullah Mehsud may have been killed in this drone strike. The Taliban denied that. Later reports indicated that Aslam Awan, a deputy to the leader of Al-Qaeda's external operations network, was killed in the strike.

23 January 2012: According to senior security official speaking to Agence France-Presse on condition of anonymity: A drone strike kills four militants, reportedly from Turkmenistan, in a vehicle in Degan near Miramshah, North Waziristan.

8 February 2012: According to unnamed Pakistani security officials, two US Drone strikes within 24 hours killed around 14 militants and their family members. In the first strike, drones fired a pair of missiles at a compound in the town of Tappi near Miranshah killing 10 Haqqani Network and Central Asian fighters. In the second strike, the drone fired a pair of missiles at a compound in Miranshah, killing Badr Mansoor, who was the Al-Qaeda chief for Pakistan along with his wife and 2 children. Al-Qaeda later confirmed Mansoor's death.

16 February 2012: Two separate drone strikes killed at least 21 suspected militants. In the first attack, US drones fired missiles at a compound in the town of Spalga near Miranshah, killing at least 5

suspected militants and wounded several others. In the second attack, a drone struck a convoy of vehicles near Mir Ali, about 25 kilometers east of Miranshah, killing at least 15 "Uzbek militants", according to unknown officials. There is no way of getting independent confirmation of the figures as reporters are prevented by the authorities from travelling to the region.

25 February 2012: According to Pakistani officials, a drone crashed in the Machikhel area about 20 miles east of Miranshah, North Waziristan. According to the officials, Taliban militants recovered equipment from the crashed drone.

9 March 2012: According to Pakistani officials, drone missiles killed 12–13 suspected militants in Makeen in the Mandao district of South Waziristan. According to The Long War Journal, the Makeen area is under the control of Hakeemullah Mehsud, the leader of the Movement of the Taliban in Pakistan. Later reports indicated that Samir H., a German jihadist, was killed in this strike.

13 March 2012: Two separate drone attacks occurred in the Waziristan region. The first, in the Drey Nishtar area of South Waziristan along the Afghan border, targeted fighters under Maulvi Nazir who were traveling in a vehicle and killed 8 suspected militants, including local commanders Amir Hamza, Shamsullah and Qari Haleemullah. The second attack happened in the Sara Khawra/Shawal area straddling the border between North and South Waziristan. 7 suspected militants in a vehicle died in that attack.

29 March 2012: According to unnamed Pakistani officials, drones fired a missile at a house in Miranshah, North Waziristan killing 4 militants and wounding 2 others. The strike occurred in the money changers market in the Miranshah commercial district.

29 April 2012: Drones fired missiles at an abandoned girls school in Miranshah, North Waziristan killing 4 suspected militants and wounding 3 others. A local resident, Haji Niamat Khan, said more

than two dozen militants were living in the school when it was attacked. It may be that Abu Usman Adil, emir of the Islamic Movement of Uzbekistan, was killed in this strike as the group announced in August that he had died in an April drone strike.

4 May 2012: Four to eight drone-launched missiles hit a compound in the village of Darr-e-Nishtar in the Shawal Valley in North Waziristan, killing eight to ten suspected militants and wounding one.

23 May 2012: A drone strike has killed at least four suspected militants in the North Waziristan tribal area, unnamed Pakistani security officials say, in an area known to be a stronghold of Al-Qaeda and the Taliban.

24 May 2012: A drone strike has killed at least eight people in a volatile tribal area of north-west Pakistan, officials say.

26 May 2012: According to unnamed officials, four to eight drone-launched missiles hit a compound in the village of Darr-e-Nishtar in the Shawal Valley in North Waziristan, killing at least four people. Pakistani officials said those killed were suspected militants, but this has not been independently verified.

28 May 2012: A drone strike has killed at least six people in north-west Pakistan, officials say, the latest in a barrage of strikes on a restive tribal region.

29 May 2012: Twelve people were killed and five others injured in two separate drone attacks in Mir Ali and Dattakhel areas of the North Waziristan tribal region.

2 June 2012: Pakistani security official speaking on condition of anonymity said, a drone strike targeting a vehicle in Pakistan's northwestern tribal belt killed at least four suspected militants.

3 June 2012: Ten suspected militants are killed when a drone fires four missiles at a gathering in the village of Mana Raghza

mourning the death of an insurgent killed in a drone strike the previous day.

4 June 2012: Sixteen people were killed and two injured when drones attacked a house and a vehicle suspected of carrying militants in Mir Ali in North Waziristan. Unnamed US and Pakistani officials stated that Al-Qaeda second in command Abu Yahya al-Libi was killed in the strike. Unnamed American officials said Abu Yahya al-Libi was the sole casualty of the strike however Pakistani officials said 16 people were killed in the strike.

13–14 June 2012: Two drone strikes within 24-hours in North Waziristan. The first killed four suspected militants in a vehicle in the village of Isha near Miramshah. The second strike killed three suspected militants in a building in Miramshah.

26 June 2012: A drone strike killed 5 and wounded 3 in a compound in the Shawal Valley of North Waziristan.

1 July 2012: According to unnamed Pakistani officials who spoke on condition of anonymity, drone-launched missiles strike a compound in the Shawal Valley of North Waziristan, killed eight militants from the Turkistan Islamic Party and loyalists of Hafiz Gul Bahadar.

6 July 2012: Drones fired six missiles at a compound near Miranshah killing up to 19 suspected militants. Pakistani officials stated that most of the killed were foreigners.

23 July 2012: Eight drone-fired missiles strike a compound in the village of Dre Nishtar in the Shawal Valley of North Waziristan, killing 12 suspected militants. According to the Long War Journal reportedly loyal to Hafiz Gul Bahadar including a local Taliban commander.

29 July 2012: According to an unnamed security official, six drone-fired missiles hit a compound and vehicle in Khushhali Turikhel near Mir Ali, North Waziristan, killing six to seven Uzbek militants.

18 August 2012: Unnamed Pakistani officials told that two drone fired missiles hit a compound and vehicle in Shuwedar in the Shawal Valley in North Waziristan, killing six suspected militants. The attack came as people were celebrating the festival of Eid-ul-Fitr.

19 August 2012: According to Pakistani intelligence officials speaking on condition of anonymity, five drones fire missiles at two vehicles in the Mana area of the Shawal Valley in North Waziristan, killing four to seven suspected militants. A short time later, additional missiles targeted recovery efforts at the destroyed vehicles, killing two more suspected militants.

21 August 2012: A drone strike near Miramshah, North Waziristan may have killed top Haqqani Network leader Badruddin Haqqani, according to Afghan intelligence reports. The Haqqani network denied that Badruddin was killed.

24 August 2012: Drones fired at least six missiles into a mud-walled compounds and at least two vehicles killing 18 people. An intelligence officials said on condition of anonymity that the leader of the East Turkestan Islamic Movement, Emeti Yakuf, also known by his local name as Abdul Jabbar, two Tehrik-i-Taliban Pakistan (TTP) commanders and three other militant commanders were among the dead.

1 September 2012: Four drone-fired missiles hit a compound and vehicle in Degan, North Waziristan, reportedly killing six suspected militants.

22 September 2012: Drone-fired missiles hit a vehicle traveling in the Datta Khel area of in North Waziristan, killing three suspected militants.

24 September 2012: Drone-fired missiles kill five or six suspected "foreign" militants in the Mir Ali area of North Waziristan. Two of those killed were reportedly Abu Kasha al Iraqi and Fateh al Turki. Abu Kasha reportedly acted as a liaison between Al-Qaeda's Shura

Majlis (executive council) and the Movement of the Taliban in Pakistan and the Uzbek Islamic Jihad Group. Al Turki was a previously unidentified, mid-level, Al-Qaeda leader. Taliban sources confirmed their deaths.

1 October 2012: Four drone-fired missiles hit a vehicle in the village of Khaderkhai in the Mir Ali area of North Waziristan, killing three suspected militants, including senior Al-Qaeda member Hassan Ghul.

10 October 2012: A suspected drone attack killed three to five suspected militants in a compound in the Mir Ali area of North Waziristan.

12 October 2012: A drone attack on Thursday killed 16–18 alleged insurgents – reportedly consisting of mostly Afghan Taliban – at a compound in the Buland Khel area of Arakzai in the Federally Administered Tribal Areas (FATA) near the border with Afghanistan, officials said. This is only the second known drone strike in Arakzai to date.

24 October 2012: Three drone-fired missiles hit a compound and vehicle in the village of Tappi near Miramshah, North Waziristan, reportedly killing four militants, a civilian, and three cows.

29 November 2012: A drone attack targeted a vehicle in the Shin Warsak village of Birmal tehsil. The Express Tribune reported two suspected militants died as a result, but the AFP reported no casualties.

2 January 2013: A drone strike killed 10 militants, including Mullah Nazir, in South Waziristan near the Afghan border.

22 March 2013: A drone airstrike has killed four people in Pakistan's North Waziristan tribal area, which borders Afghanistan, security officials say.

29 May 2013: Two security officials said that Waliur Rehman

Mehsud was among five people killed when a drone struck a house outside Miranshah, North Waziristan.

7 June 2013: At least seven people were killed when an drone fired three missiles at a house in northwestern Pakistan, according to an intelligence official, hours after the country's new prime minister announced his cabinet.

3 July 2013: A drone strike killed at least 16 people in Pakistan's restive border region early on Wednesday, Pakistani security officials said, in the biggest such attack this year, and the second since Prime Minister Nawaz Sharif took office. Most of those killed were fighters for the Haqqani network, according to three Taliban commanders and security officials. Two missiles hit a house near the main market in Miranshah, the provincial capital of the tribal region of North Waziristan. The region is considered a Taliban stronghold.

13 July 2013: At least two people were killed Saturday in an drone strike in a northwestern tribal region of Pakistan, according to intelligence officials.

28 July 2013: At least six militants were killed and four others injured after the latest drone strike in Pakistan's restive tribal belt on Sunday, Pakistani intelligence officials and militant commanders said.

31 August 2013: A drone targeted a vehicle in North Waziristan tribal agency, killing four suspected militants said to be of Turkmen origin.

5 September 2013: A drone strike on a house in the Ghulam Khan district of North Waziristan killed Mullah Sangeen Zadran, deputy to Sirajuddin Haqqani of the Haqqani Network, and Zubir al Muzi, an Al-Qaeda explosives expert from Egypt, as well as three others.

30 September 2013: A drone targeted a compound killed three, the attack took place in the Boya area of North Waziristan region.

30 October 2013: Three suspected militants were killed and three more people injured in a drone strike on a compound on Zafar Town area near Miramshah, North Waziristan.

1 November 2013: A drone targeted a vehicle in the Dande Darpa Khel area of North Waziristan. The attack killed five militants including Hakimullah Mehsud, chief of the Tehrik-i-Taliban Pakistan (TTP), as well as the leader's two key aides and fellow militant commanders, Abdullah Bahar Mehsud and Tariq Mehsud. Two others were injured in the strike.

21 November 2013: A drone targeted a religious seminary in Hangu District, Tal area of Khyber Pakhtunkhwa. Six were killed, including Maulvi Hameedullah and Maulvi Ahmad Jan, two senior aides to Sirajuddin Haqqani. It is believed the pair were attending a condolence meeting for Naseeruddin Haqqani who was killed on 11 November.

29 November 2013: Three suspected militants were killed and several other injured in a drone strike on a compound in Angar Kalli area near Miramshah Tehsil in North Waziristan Agency.

26 December 2013: A drone strike fired two missiles on a compound in Qutab Khel village, Miramshah, North-Waziristan, killing four and injuring one.

14 May 2014: A drone fired three missiles on a compound near Pak-Afghan Border, killing 10 and injuring 14 others.

12 June 2014: Two separate and successive drone strikes in Dargah Mandi village and Dande Darpa Khel area in North Waziristan killed at least 16 while injuring several others.

18 June 2014: A drone strike killed at least 6 in the Miramshah tehsil of North Waziristan.

10 July 2014: A drone strike killed at least 6 in the Madakhel village of Dattakhel tehsil in North Waziristan.

16 July 2014: At least 18 people were killed in a drone strike in Dattakhel area of North Waziristan.

19 July 2014: At least 8 people were killed in a drone strike in Doga Madakhel village of Dattakhel tehsil in North Waziristan.

6 Aug 2014: At least 7 people were killed in a drone strike in Dattakhel area of North Waziristan.

24 Sept 2014: At least 8 people including Uzbek Militants were reportedly killed in a drone strike Dattakhel tehsil of North Waziristan.

5 Oct 2014: At least 5 suspected militants were killed in a drone strike in Shawal area of South Waziristan tribal region.

6 Oct 2014: At least 8 suspected militants were killed and several other injured in a drone strike in Shawal district of North Waziristan.

7 Oct 2014: At least 3 suspected militants were killed in a drone strike in North Waziristan region.

30 Oct 2014: A US drone strike killed at least 4, injuring several others in Birmal Tehsil of South Waziristan.

11 Nov 2014: A US drone strike in Doa Toi area of Datakhel tehsil in North Waziristan Agency killed 4 suspected militants.

21 Nov 2014: Reportedly Five suspected militants including two commanders of 'Qaedat al-Jihad in the sub-continent', a newly established branch of Al-Qaeda were killed in a Drone strike in Datakhel region of North Waziristan Agency.

6 December 2014: A drone strike killed a key Al-Qaeda leader Umar Farooq along with four others in Datakhel region of North Waziristan Agency.

26 December 2014: Two separate drone strikes in the Kund and

Mangroti area of Shawal in North Waziristan Agency killed at least 7 suspected militants.

4 January 2015: A reportedly high value unidentified Uzbek commander of Taliban's Gul Bahadur group was killed along with 8 others by a US drone strike in Shawal area of North Waziristan Agency.

15 January 2015: A drone strike reportedly killed 7 suspected militants in Wacha Dara area of Liddah Tehsil of South Waziristan Agency

19 January 2015: A drone strike killed 6 while injuring 4 others in the ShahiKhel area of North Waziristan's Shawwal tehsil.

28 January 2015: A drone strike killed 7 while injuring another militant in the Shawal area of North Waziristan.

18 March 2015: A drone strike killed a TTP commander Khawrey Mehsud along with 3 others in Shabak area of Kurram Agency.

12 April 2015: A drone strike killed 4 suspected militants in North Waziristan.

16 May 2015: A drone strike Killed 7 to 13 people in the Mana area of North Waziristan Agency.

18 May 2015: A drone strike killed 6 suspected militants in Zoye Narye Area of North Waziristan.

2 June 2015: Four suspected militants were killed in a drone strike targeting a vehicle in the Shawal area of North Waziristan.

6 June 2015: At least nine suspected militants were killed in a strike in Shawal's Zoya Saidgai area, considered to be a hideout of the Afghan Taliban.

# SELECTED BIBLIOGRAPHY

- *Bededicte Grima.* (Author) Secrets from the field. ISBN 0195471644
- *Brigdier Haroon Rashid, SI(M)* (Author) History of the Pathans Vil 1, 2, 3, 4.
- *Sohail Masood Alvi.* (Author) FATA. Beginning of a New Area
- *Ishan H. Nadiem* (Author) Portrait of North West Frontier Province. ISBN 969351825-X
- *M. Athar Tahir.* (Author) Frontier Facets.
- *Major Aamir Mushtaq Cheema* (Author). North Waziristan Militua 18-95-2012 Tochi Scouts ISBN 9789699834004
- *Zubair Ahmed Kasuri* (Editor in Chief) Paradise Lost
- *Andrew M. Roe* (Author) Waging War in Waziristan. ISBN-13: 978-0700616992
- *Graham F. Reed* (Author) Walks in Waziristan. ISBN 1452026165
- *Brian Robson* (Author) Crisis on the Frontier. ISBN-13: 978-1862274037
- *Shuja Nawaz* (Author) Crossed Swords: Pakistan. ISBN-13: 978-0195476972

- *Naval Postgraduate School* (Author) An Examination of the Collateral Psychological and Political Damage of Drone Warfare in the Fata Region of Pakistan. ISBN-13: 978-1505367966
- *Safia Haleem* (Author) Pakistan - Culture Smart. ISBN-13: 978-1857336771
- *Moeed Yusuf* (Editor) Pakistan's Counterterrorism Challenge. ISBN-13: 978-1626160453
- *Shahzad Bashir* (Author) Under the Drones. ISBN-13: 978-0674065611
- *Abubakar Siddique* (Author) The Pashtun Question. ISBN-13: 978-1849042925
- *Aisha Ahmed* (Author) *Roger Boase* (Author) Pashtun Tales. ISBN-13: 978-0863566370
- *Leo Karrer* (Author) Pashtun traditions versus Western perceptions. Open editions books.
- *James Spain* (Author) The Pathan Borderland.
- *Bernt Glatzer* (Author) The Pashtun Tribal System
- *Juliaan van Acker,* The treason of the EU. ISBN 9789492161055
- *Wikipedia*

# AUTHOR'S PROFILE

John Tamerus is police commissioner. He holds the title of Head of Foreign Affairs of the Dutch National Police. In addition, he is a development officer of a company that deals withFair Trade in Third World countries. He is also the manager of a homeless shelter and an author of several books.

He earned his master's degree in Tactical Policing and Criminal Investigation in 2004 in the Netherlands Police Academy and wrote several books. As researcher and writer, he has a deep respect for people working worldwide on the front line in jobs such as the police force, the healthcare sector and development work. Their stories are evidence for him that individuals can make a difference in the world.

For John there was always a reason to travel. Far away, to the most special places in the world. In the last thirty years he has spent a lot of time in Pakistan and Afghanistan. There he has met the Pashtun people and become acquainted with their culture, traditions and beliefs. He became friends with a unique and special man, Dr. Mohammed Ashraf Khan. His personal story became the guide for this book. He is a Pashtun who continues to risk his life among the

Taliban and drones to realize the dream of his father. He bravely goes against the stream.

This story is a wake up call to society and policymakers. A wake up call to invest in recovery and positive initiatives in this region of the world with the same strategy and effort as the fight against terrorism.

This is a call to invest not only two trillion dollars in a war against terrorism, but the courage to invest in a worldwide force that will contribute to the restoration of peace and development of Pakistan and Afghanistan. There are numerous boys and girls who are victims of war in this area. There are refugees. There are internally displaced people. Recruit them, like jihadists are recruited, but rather to train them to rebuild their own country. Invest in them like we have invested in the war against terrorism. Young unemployed and uneducated people will become members of an immense recovery corps in the tribal areas between Pakistan and Afghanistan and also in countries like Iraq, Syria or Libya. They will rebuild and recover the destroyed countries. Give them uniforms and tools. Make them recovery professionals and the heroes of the future instead of potential dropouts or even terrorists. Dare to make different choices. Dare to invest in leaders with visions like Dr. Mohammed Ashraf Khan. Dare to invest our tax money in people like him and in countries like Pakistan. Dare to go after the opportunity. Dare to make the difference.

As a true idealist, John has decided that the author's fee of this book will completely go towards the purpose for which his friend Dr. Mohammed Ashraf Khan fights.

Printed in Germany
by Amazon Distribution
GmbH, Leipzig